A Life in Travel

Mike Stephens

Published by Mike Stephens, 2025.

A LIFE IN TRAVEL

First edition. February 3, 2025.

ISBN: 979-8230901549

Written by Mike Stephens.

In appreciation of my fellow travellers, especially Linda and Mark.

And in anticipation that Mia, Cole, Reggie, Ansel and Bodie may follow in my footsteps.

This book is not a travel guide. It is simply a rendition of my memories while I travelled the world. I wrote it because my three nieces all asked me to record the stories I used to tell them of my adventures, especially those I shared with their father. In large part, the book is written from memory aided by numerous photographs spanning the film and digital periods. I have also been able to call on some maps, especially of major cities and national parks in Africa. A few of the later holidays drew on notes taken at the time. I have tried to be accurate in my descriptions of places, but their beauty and significance are, of course, subjective matters. Sometimes accuracy has proved elusive, such as the size of the great pan in the centre of Etosha National Park, Namibia. The three authorities I consulted gave three different measures. It is true that the size of the pan can vary somewhat depending on climatic conditions but, even so, I was surprised by the wide disparity between the figures. Spellings can be another area where there is no full agreement. The beautiful savannah just north of the Serengeti is spelt Masai Mara or Maasai Mara – I prefer the latter since it sounds more musical and evocative. In Zimbabwe, I was taught to pronounce two local words for 'how are you' and 'thank you.' I have transcribed them as best I can but please forgive me if I offend actual Zimbabweans with my effort. I have been exceptionally fortunate to have spent many enjoyable hours with knowledgeable and informative guides, and I hope that I have passed on the information they provided accurately, but there may be an example where I misheard or misunderstood.

Finally, I must give generous thanks to Louise Nicholas who took the final manuscript from me and turned it into a format where it could be published. In particular, I am very grateful to Louise for uncovering the elusive umlaut among the myriad of diacritical marks within Word, and showing me how to apply it and other marks to actual letters. There are very few friends who can do that.

Chapter One: Beginnings and Juvenilia

I have travelled to many places around the world. It was not all expenses paid business travel, nor the luxurious sojourns of the privileged rich. I had no family incentives to roam the world for my parents had never been experienced travellers: indeed, my mam and dad barely left south Wales.

My father did have two trips to the continent as a young man and, in fact, they *were* all expenses paid affairs. The first visit was quite brief and limited in terms of location. The highlight occurred somewhere near Dunkirk where, in my dad's words, he found himself "holding up the whole of the fucking German army" to allow allied troops to escape from the beaches. He was badly wounded but somehow, among all the confusion and destruction, he was stretchered to a boat and returned home to a long convalescence. When he rejoined his unit – 2nd Battalion Welsh Guards – he was no longer an infantryman but a soldier training to be a tank commander as part of an armoured reconnaissance squadron driving Cromwell tanks.

Of course, this meant that on his second trip to Europe, his travels were much more extensive as you would expect when you have your own tank. The fighting in Normandy was much worse than he experienced at Dunkirk and, in the bitter struggles through the unyielding Bocage countryside, the death rate was often as bad as some of the bloody battles of the 1st World War. Hemmed in by the narrow sunken roads and the almost impenetrable hedges of the Bocage, tanks could be destroyed by one German soldier wielding a Panzerfaust. The battle for Caen provided more drawn-out death and destruction. But war, like travel, is rarely a uniform experience. In due course, the glorious liberation of Brussels occurred where my father's battalion was the first to liberate the city. A good time was had by all following that particular escapade! Operation Market Garden was the next big push towards Germany. Nijmegen was taken but the bridge at Arnhem remained beyond reach.

As you would expect when you travel, you tend to meet local people. In Nijmegen, my father encountered a man who urged him fervently to kill all the Boche he met on his way to Germany. More fighting happened in the Reichswald Forest and around Bonninghardt, but when the Rhine was crossed the war soon came to an end. My father had traversed large parts of France, Belgium, the Netherlands and, finally, northern Germany. He had seen many friends and comrades die or been terribly injured – not to mention civilians - while along the way killing a lot of Germans. No wonder he never travelled extensively after that. At the end of the war, the 2nd battalion was disbanded, my father was demobbed, and he came home to Tredegar and went back down the pits.

It was the winter of 1961 before my father returned to Europe – this time with me in tow as a ten-year-old. We went to Paris; why, I don't know, as dad had no wartime connection with that city. We went for one day – me in jeans and jacket and dad wearing his Welsh Guards blazer and tie, as if to remind the French who it was that fought so hard through Normandy. We took off from Rhoose Airport near Cardiff in a Cambrian Airways DC3, which was old enough to be a converted troop carrier from the war, and landed only a few minutes later in Bristol. I was sick somewhere over the Bristol Channel. From Bristol we flew to Le Bourget Airport, Paris. I was sick over the English Channel and, again, on approach to Le Bourget. From there, we took a taxi to the Arc de Triomphe. I was sick somewhere along the Avenue des Champs-Elysees, this time with no sick bag available which meant dad had to give the driver a very good tip. After that, our single day in Paris was all plain sailing if you discount the sheer terror of getting to the Arc de Triomphe without being run over by people who had clearly never had a single driving lesson let alone passed a driving test.

The Eiffel Tower was my favourite where we had something to eat on the first floor. Later, we ended up in the Bois de Boulogne where I managed to fill my small ruck sack with beautiful conkers. That was it, really; and we made our way back to Le Bourget and the flight home. I was not sick on the way back as I was asleep the whole way. At Rhoose, we were about to sail innocently past customs when we were pulled over. Dad had twice the permitted duty-free allowance for spirits and cigarettes. His argument that half of it was for him and the other half for me struck even me as a dumb move. He had to pay up. We were about to leave when a by now clearly disgruntled customs officer asked me what was in my ruck sack. "Conkers," I replied. I was rudely told to empty the contents onto the shiny aluminium counter. I did so, and in an instant dozens of French conker contraband were rolling all over the place. It took me ages to round up the last of them, during which time the customs officer had just buggered off.

That Paris trip, and two subsequent visits, was the first of what I think of as my juvenilia collection. I cherished those three visits to Paris with my father because I spent so little time with him on holiday. Another member of the juvenilia collection was a school trip to Germany, more of which shortly.

Dad and I returned to Paris in the spring of 1962, this time on an overnight stay. I climbed to the top of the Notre Dame cathedral while dad stayed in the square below having a drink in a small bar. I found out that it was not the physical effort that prevented him from coming with me, but that he was afraid of heights. We took a very pleasant break from pounding the streets and riding the Metro in the Jardin des Tuileries. We were enjoying a drink and a small snack when a middle-aged French couple came and sat next to us. The gentleman noticed the Welsh Guards crest on my dad's blazer and a conversation about the war in very basic English and French was soon in flow. I was scoffing my food while this mangling of French and English was happening. The lady surmised I was hungry and started emptying her shopping bag with the intention of finding something for me to eat. I heard her say a word that sounded much like "biscuit" whereupon a brown paper bag broke open as she placed it on the green metal table. Somehow, I got it in my mind that she was offering me some biscuits, so I took one and bit into it. Immediately there were squeals of mock horror and shouts of "non, non, non." I had just sampled a dog biscuit, which accounted for its strange shape and colour, but I must say that clearly the standards of culinary excellence tailored for the Parisian dog community were very high; it was delicious.

The school trip to Germany in July 1964 was altogether different from my experiences in Paris. For a start, I spoke a reasonable amount of the language having studied German for a few years. My adventures with my dad were largely unplanned; we went to places on a whim whereas the German expedition was just that – an expedition following highly organised and choreographed lines. We were away for almost two weeks and each location and date of arrival and departure were meticulously set out in our documentation. Dover, Ostend, Aachen, Freiberg, Titisee, Schaffhausen, and Cologne must have been delirious with anticipation at the arrival of such well-ordered thirteen-year-olds. The documentation provided for our happy group of fifteen boys informed us gravely that the Germans used the metric system. Clearly, we were going to a region that had not mastered the intricacies of the Imperial system. We tried not to judge the Germans too harshly for this deficiency. Distances between towns in Germany were given in both miles and kilometres and, lest we felt unable to deal with the financial complexities of the currency, we were told that the Deutsche Mark was divided into a hundred Pfennigs. One Pfennig in July 1964 was worth bugger all in pounds sterling!

All of this was no doubt necessary and useful but other aspects of the information struck me as somewhat tentative. We were advised to take three shirts in our ruck sacks, three or four pairs of socks, but only two sets of underwear. Even I knew that two sets for thirteen days were not enough. The whole stay in Germany was wonderful – all these young lads without any parental supervision and smart enough to avoid the most intrusive interventions of the two school-masters accompanying us. At the border with Germany, all the passports of the pupils were collected for inspection. We were then called forward to collect the passports individually and finalise immigration procedures. The officer called out "Yo-nez" twice before one of the masters told Jones to collect his passport. Indeed, I did not immediately recognise "Step-Hens" as my name.

A number of things stood out from the German trip. At the youth hostel in Titisee, we were offered butter milch by our hosts who genuinely believed they were placing a great delicacy before us. None of us could bear to take more than one sip. Beware of butter milch; it's bloody awful. In theory, the trip was intended to improve our German, but often that intention was undermined by the prevalence of Germans we encountered who spoke excellent English. For example, the question in German "Können Sie mir sagen, wo der Zoo ist?" was met with the answer "The Zoo? Yes, you walk about a hundred metres down this road, then you take the first right next to the cinema, and it's about another five hundred metres to the main entrance." Putting aside my frustration with language issues, I found that there was a great degree of tolerance when it came to thirteen-year-olds attempting to buy beer. Shopkeepers and restaurants simply sold it to us as if it were perfectly natural for a young teenager to order beer with his meal. The pound then was very strong against the Mark, so in Cologne I had more than enough money left to buy a very large toy crane for my little brother. It was a three-foot-long yellow Leviathan whose jib could be raised and lowered so that it seemed like the neck of a monstrous sea serpent. We had an excellent time playing with it on the train journey back to Ostend. Finally, we found out – how I no longer recall – that the five Pfennig coin was an exact replica in size for the UK sixpence. Back home you could get an awful lot of chocolate bars from dispensing machines for a Mark's worth of five Pfennig pieces. In Cologne, I changed five Marks for five Pfennig coins and I was quids in, so to speak.

My best friend, Allen Callaghan, came with me for my third visit to Paris in August 1967. Allen and I thought ourselves quite the grown-ups at the age of sixteen, and we confidently posed for pictures in our smart shirts, jackets and ties and with cigarettes in hand. We stayed a few days and, since it was Allen's first visit, we covered as many of the classic tourist spots as possible. Most of the time my father came with us but there were also occasions when he was content to seek out a nearby bar, have a few drinks, and wait for Allen and me to find him again. Dad returned once more to Paris, this time with my brother, Mark, in 1971. I went back three more times, twice with my wife and once with a girlfriend. I still have a great affection for the city, though it is now twenty-five years since I last walked along its stylish boulevards and enjoyed its fine wines and food.

The final journey in the juvenilia collection happened in 1970 when I was nineteen-years-old, and involved living and working in the Republic of Ireland. I include it here because of the typically rash teenage decisions I made before and after that sojourn. At 'A' level, I had been studying English, French and German in the hope of becoming a linguist. I passed English, but would have made an awful translator of French and German whose exams I failed. It was my fault; I was too interested in chasing girls than revising. University was out of the question but the careers bureau suggested an HND course in Tourism at Ealing Technical College, London. I attended for interview only a few days before the course started and was accepted. Some long-ago Monday in September 1969, I took the train to London with one suitcase, a few extra pounds from my dad, and nowhere to stay. Only a raw kid with boundless optimism, or naivety, would have done that. I look back now on that event and contrast it with every September when freshers arrive at my university. What I see is a fleet of Volvos, Fords and Toyotas filled to the gunnels with an array of stuff and driven by parents delivering their children to university. As it turned out, I found lodgings the day I arrived in Ealing, but I bet few parents would let their children do what I did. It was a rash decision to go to London without first having somewhere to stay, but to me it was no big deal.

The HND was quite interesting. I studied French, economics, business studies, tourism, accountancy and some other, rather oddball, courses. There was a learn to type course, the only bit of which I remember was the tutor exclaiming "fingers on the home keys." Then there was an attempt to turn us into wine and food experts, which was too superficial but I did enjoy sampling the wines. I was less keen on the raw steak concoction. Finally, there was speech and deportment. This consisted of being taught by what I took to be an out-of-work actor with a penchant for repeating 'Leatherhead Rep' for some reason. He would get one of us to leave the room and he'd tell that person that when they returned, they had to act as if they were a drainpipe. The rest of us had to work out what was going on. We failed abysmally! The tutor took particular delight in giving us various phrases that we had to say four or five times, but each time with a different meaning or nuance. The one phrase I could never forget was 'up your arse with a wire brush.' The day trips to holiday camps, airports, shipping lines, and such like were the most enjoyable but not necessarily that informative. I did two terms of this and, thus armed, I was sent out on a five-month placement to Dublin.

It seems I had become the blue-eyed boy of the course director, a certain Boris something-or-other from Belgium; I was certainly among the best students. My reward for this was the plum placement with Bord Fáilte, the Irish Tourist Board. The less favoured students ended up at a travel agency in Skegness, or at Butlins. I found lodgings in Harold's Cross at the home of a widow, Mrs Farrelly, with two children. There were also two medical students lodging with me. The work at the offices of Bord Fáilte, near the city centre, was very varied. Every few weeks, I transferred to another unit so that I built up experience of the agency's various functions. For a short period, I became a hotel inspector, aka a person of terror to hotel proprietors since I had the power to downgrade their star listings. I was also very fortunate to go on a variety of business trips throughout many parts of Ireland. Cork, Shannon, Limerick, the Ring of Kerry, the Curragh racecourse, and Wexford were all great places to visit. I even went horse riding with a group of Italian travel agents in the country to uncover its various delights. The Bord had a smaller office in Belfast to which I was sent for two weeks.

Belfast both fascinated and horrified me. The slums of the Shankill and Falls Roads made my own previous backstreet in Newport look like a gem. Prejudice, distilled and refined down the decades, even took a physical form with kerb stones painted in different colours to reflect an area's allegiances and obscene insults painted on walls denigrating the Pope or Paisley. I wandered around both the Shankill and Falls Roads several times, taking pictures occasionally. I struggled to understand why people living there fought each other so vehemently. But I was naïve about Irish politics and an atheist to boot. Religion meant bugger all to me. As far as I was concerned if I lived in such squalor, I'd join forces with others similarly placed to fight for improvement – not maim one another.

On my return to Dublin, one of my fellow lodgers gave me a British five-pound note and begged me on my next weekend at home to return with a fiver's worth of johnnies. Somewhile later, back in Barry to see my parents and my girlfriend, I sauntered into a high street chemist hoping not to be served by a woman. No such luck. I stood before her plucking up courage and then handed a five-pound note over the counter with the rather curt demand "Five-pounds' worth of Durex please." She looked at me oddly and now completely flustered, I blurted out "I'm only here for the weekend." It was only when I got off the ferry in Dun Laoghaire that I realized it was a criminal offence to import prophylactics. The rest of the summer passed pleasantly enough, and I especially liked the many lunch-hours I spent in St Stephen's Green. People at work were very kind to me as were the Irish I met beyond Dublin. The only thing that made me feel ever so slightly uneasy was the almost universal attachment to Catholicism, some of which struck me as being an autonomic response, devoid of reason.

In the Autumn of 1970, I was back at Ealing Tec' enjoying the student lifestyle and exploring the ins and outs of London. I did well academically and had an excellent report from Bord Fáilte, but increasingly I found the subject matter of the course to be irksome and the idea of being some sort of businessman in the tourist industry held few charms for me. Matters came to head in the spring of 1971 when Boris the Belgian informed me gleefully that he had negotiated a top-ranked and prestigious placement in Tunisia. "I'm sending you to Tunisia next month," he told me. I turned down the offer immediately because Tunisia seemed rather too exotic – I did not then have the confidence to undertake such a venture. I was by no means a sophisticated and accomplished traveller at that time, but the main reason for my refusal was that I did not see my future in the travel business. Boris the Belgian grew angry and I realized it had not been so much an offer as an order - Boris was used to getting his own way as director of studies. Matters got heated but ended with "well you can fuck your course and Tunisia. I'm leaving." And with that, I left the course and returned home to Barry – my second rash decision associated with the whole HND affair. I was now twenty-years-of-age with one 'A' level to my name, an incomplete and inglorious HND experience behind me, no job and not much by way of any prospects. In many respects, I was still a juvenile but it was now that I started out on a new journey – one that ultimately would turn me into an adult.

I was on the dole for a while on my return but, eventually, I got a seasonal job with Cambrian Airways at Rhoose Airport. It involved working out of a customs bond where duty-free cigarettes, alcohol, and other on-plane purchases such as watches and sunglasses were kept. These items along with soft drinks, food and non-duty-free goods were transported to the planes – the empty stocks were taken off and new items put into the aluminium cases. Basically, I stocked up the planes with the items passengers might want to buy during the flight. Being one of the first people to enter the planes through the rear door, I sometimes clandestinely took off expensive watches one of the female flight attendants had purchased but didn't want to pay duty on. I met them later to hand over the goods and to receive any favours going. All this travel going on around me and me going nowhere – going nowhere even more meaningfully when the job ended and I was back on the dole.

I took then the fateful decision to go back to school, so to speak, in order that I had something constructive and useful to do during the many months of enforced idleness. In the autumn of 1971, I signed up to do 'A' levels in economics and sociology at Rumney College in north Cardiff. It meant a train ride and a bus ride every Tuesday and Thursday to attend classes between six and nine p.m.

The courses lasted six months, not the two years as had been the case when I was in school. The dropout rate was ferocious and very few of us who started actually took the exams. I did, however, and got A and B grades. I subsequently gained much higher educational qualifications but these allowed me to start at Cardiff University in September 1972. Those two grades were the ones of which I was most proud because I had to work very hard to achieve them–the subsequent degree and doctorate came comparatively easily. The future I wanted depended completely on getting those two good grades, and I did it. I had grown up and was no longer a juvenile.

Chapter Two: The Skiing Years

The skiing holidays did not come immediately upon going to university but quite a few years later. However, in my second term at university, I met Linda who had moved into the three-storied student house in Cardiff where I lived with my mates. This was the woman to whom I would later be married for twenty-five years, and she opened new horizons for me and encouraged me to do things I might never have done otherwise. Skiing was one of those; I did not want to go skiing, had never wanted to go skiing, but under Linda's gentle persuasion, I went skiing.

In fact, the first holiday Linda and I had together was not a skiing one but a short trip to Paris over Easter 1973. We were so short of money we had no hot food for three days. Even so, the trip was memorable – to be young, to be in love, and to be in Paris: what more can you want? After we both graduated, I went to Oxford University as a postgraduate and Linda to work as a hospital pharmacist in London; our relationship continued through weekend visits. Eventually, Linda got a job in Oxford and we moved in together. We married in July 1977 and took our honeymoon in Rome, a place I was to visit many times after that first marvellous introduction. A year later, I too found full-time work as a lecturer in Leicester, and it was then that the idea of going skiing was first broached. In the winter of 1980, we took lessons on a dry ski slope in Nottingham and set off for a week on real snow in April 1980. Andorra was our choice. It was cheap and cheerful with duty free drinks in bars and hotels, and inexpensive lift passes and equipment hire. Moreover, most of the ski instructors were English, or else came from Australia and New Zealand, so there were no language difficulties between instructors and pupils. Finally, the slopes were rarely steep and narrow. You'd struggle to find in Soldeu anything like the number of black runs that the Alpine resorts typically had. It was the perfect destination for British beginners and intermediate skiers seeking a good time on the cheap.

We stayed in the small village of Encamp, a bus ride from Soldeu, where the French and Spanish influences seemed to exist in equal measure. Andorra is administrated by both French and Spanish authorities and both languages are commonly spoken. Our hotel, La Mola, was owned by a Spanish-speaker who was a most jovial host and typically referred to guests as 'caballeros' when he served them at the bar after a heavy day's skiing. He also served delicious flans and other delights to tide us over to dinner time. The only disadvantage to the hotel was that the walls were so thin that even the smallest noise made in a room could be heard in many other rooms nearby. In fact, we were not so much informed about this as we checked in as warned. No one warned us, however, about the habit of the bar staff to pour spirits by hand rather than use optic measures, so that a gin and tonic would have three-times more gin in it than in the UK.

Although Linda and I had been on a dry slope that used a drag line to haul us back to the top, neither of us had ever used a chair lift. The people in the ski hire shop firmly told us to carry our skis as complete beginners rather than wear them. Someone at the top of the two-seater chair lift would help us off, they said. This help consisted of large, burly men grabbing an outside arm, while we tried to hold and control skis and sticks with the other, and pulling us sideways out of our seat so that the chair could continue without hitting us painfully in the back of our legs. Such rough treatment did nothing to improve the state of our ski-wear – in those days the best that C&A had to offer. The chair lift was not the only danger at the resort; there were also button lifts. The button is at the end of a long pole that, in turn, is connected at its top to a supported wire that takes you uphill. You place the button between your legs so that it is nestling under your bottom and grasp the pole. When you trip the lever to start the ascent, the lift is meant to begin smoothly. But there were rogue button lifts that went off like small explosions. One of them pulled Linda's ski boots out of their bindings. Linda had the good sense to let go of the pole, but we saw one individual hanging on for dear life being dragged uphill along the ground for some distance before he loosened his hold. Then, he had to slide back down the slope to retrieve his skis.

We went to Andorra six times between 1980 and 1985 and emerged at the end of weeks of tuition as competent intermediaries – good enough to spread our wings and head to where the big boys go skiing in the Portes du Soleil. There, we spent two glorious weeks skiing in and out of the various resorts in France and Switzerland that comprised the Portes. Everything was more expensive than Andorra, Switzerland ruinously so. The mainly French skiers could be very impatient and even angry if you blocked their way as they tried to slam down the steep slopes only to encounter Linda and I going at a more circumspect speed. But gradually, we adjusted and became more confident. Linda, in particular, thrived and soon had such control when carving parallel turns that I nicknamed her 'The Edge Queen' – you could see the maker's logo on the base of her skis as she turned.

We were now addicted to the sport, and ridiculously expensive lift passes in the bigger and better resorts did not put us off. We bought our own skis and boots and lugged them all over the Alps. We returned to Chatel in the Portes du Soleil in 1988 and, in subsequent years, we were tearing it up in Cervinia, Val d'Isère, Meribel, Sauze d'Oulx, Mayrhofen, Bormio, Vancouver/Whistler, and Saalbach-Hinterglemm.

In Cervinia with its stunning views of the Matterhorn, I relished the long runs into the valley where I could perform wide, sweeping turns at high speed. In Westendorf, on a holiday I won for writing a travel article for some journal, there were blue, verging on red, slopes where I could practice short, sharp, tight turns without my speed becoming unmanageable. One beautiful but bitterly cold early morning in Bormio, I got off the telecabin at Cima Bianca and entered a red run, called Bimbi al sole, to find that the snow was still frozen solid: it was as if I were skiing over cobbles. This was not a place to fall – too steep and with painful hard lumps of frozen snow – yet neither was it a place to hang around until the piste had thawed. I got back to the restaurant below the red run rather more shaken than stirred. In some resorts that hosted World Cup ski events, I was able to ski on the actual courses that the professionals took, and I marvelled at how quickly they descended when sometimes I was metaphorically hanging onto the slope for dear life and wondering if it could possibly become any steeper. It wasn't just the skiing that was so satisfying, so was the food and the ambiance of the places where we ate. There is a magical quality about tearing down half a mountain, and doing it in style, only to come to a skid stop right outside a wood cabin complete with log fire and a mouthwatering menu. It's better still when you sit in the sun on the terrace and admire the jagged mountains that rise high above you into azure skies. There, I could discuss with Linda the day's skiing, admire the expert skiers that swept so stylishly by us and, most importantly, take great satisfaction in viewing those who were nowhere near as good as Linda and myself. Indeed, by the time of our eighth holiday, we no longer made stupid errors that led to falls, and we gained more and more confidence and poise as each year passed. We became advanced skiers able to tackle most pistes and able to carve parallel turns most of the time.

Occasionally, we skied with some Italian friends whom we had first met in Kenya. We would meet in Passo Tonale to ski the Presena glacier, or more often in Santa Caterina. Here, the highlight of the day was not so much the group of us skiing the varied terrain of the resort, as the delicious lunches we had in hotels hidden away from the gaze of most tourists. At lunch, we were often joined by non-skiing relatives of our four friends so that there might be ten or more of us around a table surrounded by constant joyous conversation. Linda and I loved it, but it was a hard test of the quality of our Italian. Lunch was so sumptuous we often did not ski afterwards!

There were few things on a skiing holiday that bothered me. I used to hate falling over, but as I became a proficient skier, I went years without a tumble. Even huge dumps of snow and dreadful conditions on one day could be tolerated for the fantastic skiing there would be the very next day. However, young children could sometimes be a nuisance. Children who live in Alpine regions are often taught to ski at a very young age by their parents and, in addition, it was not uncommon to see groups of very young children receiving tuition from professional instructors. Young children were not allowed on chairlifts unless accompanied by an adult. This led to a series of events that would raise eyebrows if in the UK you tried to offload your child to a passing cyclist – and a perfect stranger to boot - simply to get the child from one place to another. But this is what happens on the slopes around Europe. At the bottom of the chairlift in a special lane reserved for instructors and children, the ski instructor would place each of the children in her small group with an adult skier. Often adult skiers appeared to have no choice in their selection, which did not matter to local or experienced skiers but which for beginners (aka the British) was a nightmare. As the accompanying and supervisory adult, you had to get the child onto the chair next to you, and not let them slip off so that the chair hit them. Then, you had to pull down the safety bar and not let them fall out of the chair to their death. At the end, if the route out was flat, you had to put up the safety bar and guide the child off the chair and out of the way without falling over yourself and possibly crushing the little tot. If the run off was steep, it was even worse for you had to literally pick the child up, tuck them under your arm, and ski down the slope – again without falling over. Only then could you hand back your charge to the instructor who came up with the last of her group. On one occasion, as I got on a four-man chair lift, I found to my horror that I had been allocated *two* children. There must have been a special offer on them that day, a sort of buy one, get one free. Of course, these children, like our own, were taught not to talk to strange men, so that even when I was able to enquire in Italian if they were able to get off the chair on their own, they often said nothing – so under my arm they went!

Still, after a few years none of this bothered me any longer. But one thing I always found an ordeal was that mechanism of torture – the T-bar. They were most common in Switzerland and consisted of a long pole suspended from a wire at the bottom of which was a bar, like an upside down 'T'. The bar was placed behind your bottom, one skier on one side of the 'T,' another skier on the other side with the pole between the two of you. Even when I ascended a slope as the only passenger on the T-bar, they were far more difficult to control than button drag lifts. However, occasionally, I'd be selected to look after another of those infernal children, which meant the bar for the child was somewhere around their waist, while for me it was barely above my knee. Good luck controlling that lot! It did not help that the children expected you to be an expert, and shot you a dirty look if you had nearly turfed them into the snow. There were occasions when, if I saw a T-bar ahead, I would try to find another route with a chair lift.

The last skiing holiday Linda and I had together was in January 1999 in Whistler-Blackcomb, Canada. I remember it not for the immense number of pistes but for it becoming very clear that our marriage was coming to an end. This is very difficult to write but I must cover it, however briefly, if only to explain why the remainder of my own skiing career no longer included Linda. Linda left me in the summer of 1999. I have always admired her courage in taking that decision: I would have just soldiered on making the best of things, but Linda wanted something far more fulfilling. She told me that increasingly she felt unheard and unseen, and that problems at work were not helping matters. I take a large measure of the blame for not communicating with her as I should have done; for not supporting her as I should have done. The upshot was a divorce a little while later but we remained friends and in regular contact. I was glad of that, but to this day I regret losing such a remarkable and beautiful woman. In terms of the story-telling in this book, this is not the end of Linda's involvement for there are several long-haul journeys that I have yet to describe that were interspersed throughout the Alpine trips.

Life goes on, and in due course so did my skiing travels. I returned to Bormio in January 2000, partly for the skiing but also because it was an Italian resort and I felt at home skiing in that country. Sauze d'Oulx followed the next January, and then Mayrhofen in 2002 and back to Italy again at Madesimo in 2003. I spoke some German so staying in Mayrhofen was entertaining enough, but in the Italian resorts I really enjoyed myself. Sometimes, I would be mistaken for an Italian and asked for directions, which pleased me no end; other times people asked about my accent when I spoke Italian and enquired whether I were Swiss or Romanian. I knew what food to order, what range of Italian drinks to enjoy, and I never had a cappuccino after eleven in the morning since that would irredeemably mark me down as a tourist. In short, in Italy, I was not on a skiing holiday but indulging in all the delights of what Italians call una settimana bianca – a white week.

I returned to Madesimo in January 2004 not on my own but with my footballing friend, Richard, who was an absolute beginner. I took him up some 'baby' run on a chair and the first thing he did was to fall over immediately as he got off the lift. Then, on the gentlest of slopes, I tried to show him beginner snowplough turns. He fell into a ditch. After that, he enrolled in ski school where eventually I was able to help him, albeit indirectly. Richard did ski school each morning but in the afternoons, he skied with me when I got him to do two things: to practise his morning exercises under my tuition, and to gravitate to slightly more challenging slopes and slightly more difficult turns. Accordingly, the next morning in school, Richard impressed the instructor with how quickly he was progressing and how well he coped on steeper terrain. Often, the afternoon previously he had been out on those steeper slopes with me. And that's largely how our week progressed in skiing terms. In drinking terms, after our meals at the Hotel Ferré, we soon became regulars at the nearby Bar Centrale where we quietly but resolutely worked our way through the owner's wine stocks.

I had made all the arrangements for this trip to Madesimo, as I did when the two of us returned the following year with Richard's girlfriend, Sarah. Before too long another couple joined us on a subsequent holiday, then some other friends, so that at times there were as many as six of us taking to the slopes together. We always went to Italy, and everyone was content to let me do the bookings and so on. In resort, I normally ordered the meals and drinks we had during the day and, rather than collect money individually to settle the bills, we agreed on making equal contributions to a kitty. I was in charge of the kitty. Naturally, I teased my fellow travellers that control of the kitty money meant a very cheap holiday for me. One year, they got their own back by purchasing a small pink purse in the shape of a heart, such as a five-year-old girl would love, and insisting that the kitty money be kept therein. Worse, I had to reveal the purse in all its twee horror whenever I paid for drinks at the bar. I found that my fellow travellers became eager to make kitty contributions just so they could watch me trying to stuff all the notes inside this perfectly formed monstrosity. Fortunately, I suffered no permanent psychological damage from the memory of the pink purse. Indeed, quite the opposite, since I have many happy recollections of wonderful days in several resorts over the years. I especially remember the run in Sauze d'Oulx to Jouvenceaux that a group of us took in 2009. It is a very long, swirling piste but this was the first time in my three visits to Sauze that it was open all the way to the bottom of the run, such had been the intensity of the snow fall just prior to our arrival in resort. At one point, we briefly abandoned the piste and skied through the trees that lined much of the route. All hell broke loose as inexperienced skiers flailed around in desperate attempts to miss trees and to manage sudden, unexpected bumps. Greeting us at the very edge of the snow cover when we had skied the whole piste was a small bar – a blessed place of rest and source of dry white wine.

Another memorable event took place in Livigno with my good friend Iain who was a courageous intermediate skier. Livigno is a charming resort, with relatively easy-going skiing to match the town's easy-going nature. However, the piste map and signage were not perfect as Iain and I soon found out. We set off towards a blue, relatively easy run, as shown on the map and by a blue sign at the start of the piste. As we passed the blue sign, the terrain began to slope away from us, gently at first and then more steeply. Suddenly, we were hundreds of yards from the crest of the hill above us – too far to walk back up – and then looming out of the mist was a menacing black sign. Black denotes the most difficult pistes. Iain had now ground to a halt and both of us surveyed the route before us. It looked like a battlefield after the artillery had pounded it for some hours; piles of loosely heaped snow, some firmer but slippery moguls which pockmarked the piste like a series of vengeful hillocks, and in between these obstacles were treacherous gullies where it was even more difficult to control one's speed. Slowly, Iain picked his way down the mountain as I stayed nearby to offer encouragement. It was a severe test of his skills and stamina, and it took us an age to get off this brute of a run. However, we did so and at the end of the piste was a restaurant where Iain and I managed to grab the last available table. We had an excellent meal and then left along the gentlest of paths back towards Livigno. It was on that path that I caught an edge and nearly fell over. None of the group I skied with had ever seen me fall over and that was as close as Iain got to witnessing it. When Iain and I reminisce about that bastard of a piste, he understandably brings up the caught edge and near fall. And why not? It took courage and determination by Iain to get down. I did not much like it either!

Iain was also with me and several other friends when we went to Bardonecchia, Italy. The most memorable incident was a quiz we entered, organised one evening by two of the representatives of the company we were travelling with. It was held in a typical wood panelled bar within the resort, and attended by a bunch of lads like ourselves and several families. We answered the questions easily – on our table between us were seven or eight university degrees of one kind or another. There was also a task each quiz team had to complete – to be judged by the two reps – using a small number of items handed to each team, one of which was kitchen foil. We had to make some household item or implement. Iain found some Alka-Selzer tablets he carried for his indigestion and began crushing them to a fine white powder. Someone else made a silver pipe from the foil, and a third supplied a credit card. We had made a crack pipe and paraphernalia. We sat there giggling like little boys, but as word spread of what we had made, one family got up and stormed out.

The first of the two reps came over to berate us as "disgusting." The second assured us that within the night we would become legends in Bardonnechia. We won the quiz!

Although most of my skiing was now undertaken with friends, there were still some occasions when I would ski alone. My second visit to Westendorf in Austria in January 2011 also highlights what can happen when the snow is poor, or the weather too vile to venture into the mountains. Moreover, it provides an opportunity to introduce one of the most important ingredients in any kind of holiday – Mike's Bar. On almost all occasions when I have stayed for one week or longer in the same accommodation, I have sought out a bar that best suits my needs. In the tropics, it might be a bar overlooking an idyllic beach, while in the cosmopolitan cities of the world, it might be a bar that offers ambiance, comfort, and good service. On a skiing holiday that bar might overlook some of the resort's slopes, or be close to one's hotel where you can meet all sorts of other people and enjoy the apres-ski atmosphere. In Westendorf, Mike's Bar was *Feinsinn* restaurant-bar run by Sonja and Marcel and, since the weather was poor for most of my stay in resort, I spent more time than normal there.

On my first day in Westendorf, I decided to ski across to Brixen taking mostly quite demanding red routes. Normally, I would have coped well on such pistes but the snow was patchy and icy in places and unforgiving. I fell losing an edge on a steep turn and went fully a hundred metres down the slope, first on my side, then on my back, and finally on my other side. At one point, I actually overtook a skier. When I stopped, three skiers came to see if I were okay – I was – and one of them found my watch a few feet away that had been torn from my wrist in the fall. I was rather shaken up and not at all used to falling over, certainly not such a lengthy fall, so I went back to Westendorf and straight into Mike's Bar. There, I made a small but crucial addition to my German vocabulary as Sonja informed me that it was cheaper to buy wine in the quantity of 'ein Viertel,' a quarter of a litre, rather than by the single glass. I sat inside for a while, tenderly inspecting some of my bruises, and then I crossed the road to my hotel and got ready for dinner.

The next day boasted dreadful visibility, bad enough that it was impossible to see the piste markers at the edges of the runs. I was soon back at Mike's Bar having a cappuccino and, later, I bought some stamps and postcards at the post office: all rip-roaring excitement. The following day, with the weather still poor and the snow disappearing from more parts of the pistes, I visited the local church and graveyard. I noticed that there was a sign in the graveyard banning skiers from doing slaloms around the graves! I did have some skiing for the next few days when I went over to Hopfgarten but the pistes were in poor shape and it was not particularly enjoyable. Early returns to *Feinsinn* and a Viertel were in order on each of those days. The final two days of the holiday brought rain, most unusual weather for that time of year, and few people ventured onto the pistes. I walked along part of the valley and saw where cows were kept in solid wooden sheds, and I met quite a few locals walking their dogs. Back to Mike's Bar and soon, mercifully, back home.

Another solo visit was to Arabba in the Dolomiti Mountains in January 2008. I had been drawn to the area to ski the Sellaronda, the extremely long set of interconnected pistes, around forty kilometres, that take you in a complete circle around the central massif of the Sella. You can complete the circuit, which takes most of the day, in clockwise or anti-clockwise direction. I started from Arabba and eventually ended there, six hours later. But it is worth it, not just for the sheer variety of pistes, but also for the breathtaking views of the Sella massif. As I pirouetted around the carbonate sedimentary rocks that make the area so characteristically beautiful, the Sella massif changed colour depending on where I was on the circuit, the time of day, and the position of the sun. I could look up and see the massif in subtle shades of red and brown, and the next time I looked, they were distinctly orange and pink. It is simply a marvellous experience, so much so that I took the usual kitty culprits there in 2012. I took my friends around the Sellaronda, the Hidden Valley, and the Marmolada glacier, but it was not as captivating for me as on my previous visit. My experience in Westendorf the year before, coupled with more bad weather in Arabba, had doubtless taken some of the edge off my skiing. Also, the dynamics of this particular group were not as carefree as previous ones. In short, a lot of the joy had gone out of my skiing. I never went skiing again after Arabba in 2012; I was sixty-one and it was time to stop, but I'm very glad that my last outing was in Italy.

That's enough of la settimana bianca. Time now to retrace my steps and focus on long-haul travels.

Chapter Three: Policing and the Mentally Ill

Yes, I know, a weird title for a chapter on long-haul travel but accurate nevertheless. My first long distance adventure, other than a ski trip to Whistler, occurred in Madison, Wisconsin. I had a sabbatical from my usual university work, and I had been invited as a visiting scholar by the Law School of the University of Wisconsin-Madison to spend the summer of 1982 studying aspects of the criminal justice and mental health systems in Madison, which at that time was well-known for a largely progressive attitude in its treatment of those with mental health problems. This progressive attitude also applied to some aspects of the Madison Police Department (MPD), especially in the way its motorised patrol officers responded to mental health emergencies.

Madison's university could not have been more different to my own. Its estate covers 933 acres and is largely located along Lake Mendota, has a budget of over US$4bn, and teaches 34,000 undergraduates and 14,000 postgraduates – it even has its own armed police force. All these statistics dwarf those applicable to my university whose small security force amounts to a few dozen middle-aged personnel and some ex-coppers who had taken early retirement from the police. Madison is the capital city of the state of Wisconsin and in the centre of the city is the monumental Capitol Building, which also has its own armed police force. The city itself is policed by the MPD but there are also officers from the Highway Patrol and the state police, not to mention private security firms whose guards can also be armed. One way or another, the city has a plethora of armed police on its streets. When I first went there, the city was quite liberal in terms of welfare issues and, it was said, this attracted outsiders drawn by the hope of receiving decent benefits and services. Accordingly, the MPD frequently had to deal not only with homeless people committing public order offences, but also many more with mental health issues, often being played out as mental health crises in and around the city centre. Many of the people the police encountered had been decanted from state mental hospitals as part of the deinstitutionalization movement that started in the 1970s. The closure of many mental hospitals was meant to be accompanied by treatment in the community, but in many places community care proved to be wholly inadequate. Dealing with these people decanted from hospitals put a great deal of pressure on MPD patrol officers, many of whom judged their time-consuming responses as not being 'proper' policing. To such officers, proper policing was fighting crime, arresting criminals, and putting them behind bars, not this social work-like soft approach. To relieve this pressure and to improve and alter the perceptions of patrol officers, the MPD had evolved a partnership with the Dane County Mental Health Centre (DCMHC), located in downtown Madison. It was a relationship based on new training elements for officers and greater operational cooperation between those officers and DCMHC mental health professionals. I was there to study this relationship.

When I arrived in Madison that summer of 1982, I had nowhere to stay, but after two nights at the Memorial Union – one of the university's two student unions – I found a student flat close to the Capitol Building and not too far from the Law School. Actually, it was Susan who got me the flat. She was a postgraduate assistant to the law professor sponsoring my visit to the Law School. The flat was a rundown affair with tatty curtains and worn floors but it had the advantage that Susan herself lived there on the top floor with her then boyfriend. She clarified many of the questions I had, and was so helpful in many ways. One night, I was awoken by furious banging on my door; it was Susan telling me that there was a tornado warning for Madison, and I was to go down into the basement with the other residents for safety. All I could think of was that the basement was full of gas pipes and electricity lines, so I decided to stay put. I opened a window in my flat, pulled up a chair, and sat there hoping to catch sight of the tornado. The people in the basement thought I was mad: I recognised later that they were right! Susan and I became exceptionally good friends and we are still in regular contact nearly forty-five years later. Of course, I couldn't rely on Susan to find Mike's Bar so, after unpacking my stuff and buying various sprays to clean the flat's filthy shower cubicle, I set off to discover the enchanted sanctum. I found it along one of the boulevards that spread out from the Capitol Building. I cannot remember its name but when I left Madison the proprietor gave me a couple of pint glasses as souvenirs. On them was an advert for Berghoff beer and opposite the name 'Madison's Public House,' aka Mike's Bar.

It soon became clear to me that I was going to like living in Madison. The weather in summer was usually hot and sunny and I enjoyed walking around the campus admiring the architecture of the various university buildings. The Memorial Union was an interesting place to have lunch, in a huge heavily wood-panelled hall with large Gothic script written on the walls. It struck me as a replica of a Germanic hall from many years ago. The union building bordered a large lake and there were lots of places by the shore for students to eat and drink and to hold musical events. The chief of the MPD was very cooperative in allowing me to interview officers, to interrogate criminal files, and to accompany officers on car patrols – so-called ride-alongs. Moreover, the heads of the various departments at the DCMHC were equally as cooperative, and I had no problems setting up interviews with professional staff and with their clients with various mental health issues. In the UK, it would have taken me months and months simply to get the attention of the police, yet with a much more open culture at the MPD and DCMHC, I was up and running in a very short period. I even had my own office and phone in the Law School with a fantastic leather-covered swivel chair. I enjoyed access to the senior common room, which was replete with many newspapers and magazines, and an array of complimentary coffees. And to cap it all, Susan had got me an invitation to play football, or soccer as the Americans called it, for a local team – the Madison Chargers - one of whose players even lent me a bike so that I could get around more easily. Yes, I really liked Madison!

One of the first things I did was to investigate the work that the DCMHC carried out in the community. Most of the big, old-fashioned mental hospitals had been closed in Wisconsin and elsewhere, and many long-term patients had been discharged into communities ill-equipped to handle them. DCMHC helped such individuals to lead as independent a life as was possible given the fact that many of these former long-stay patients lacked many of the coping skills to live in what to them was often a strange and intimidating environment. The centre could provide help to find lodgings, offer practical advice on money management, and supervise the taking of their medicines. Its psychiatric nurses visited their clients where they lived and took them to the local laundrette to show them how to wash their clothes, while at other times they would accompany them to the nearest supermarket and teach them how to select and pay for their goods. As much as possible in the quest to allow these people to enjoy reasonably independent and dignified lives was done in situ in downtown Madison and its suburbs. This approach, time-consuming and heavily dependent on the relationships between nurses and clients, worked well but was not foolproof.

Some mentally ill individuals did not always sign up to the help that the DCMHC provided, preferring to live a rougher existence, while others would sometimes stop taking their medicines and their behaviour would become more erratic. These individuals would become the subject of complaints from shopkeepers who did not want them loitering in front of their premises and disturbing their customers. The MPD came under increasing pressure to deal with these individuals by moving them elsewhere and, sometimes, by seeking hospital admission. The most troublesome individuals from the police point of view were those who exhibited extremely troubled and disturbed behaviour in a public area – behaviour that might also include breaking the law. These 'street crazies' as they were known in some quarters had either to be arrested and jailed, or an emergency hospital admission had to be found, both of which were time-consuming but neither of which did anything to improve the mental state of those caught in the police web. Both jail and mental hospital were simply holding pens for a short while until the person's release, possibly to repeat the whole process once again. Moreover, the police resented that they were having to deal with these difficulties without much help from other city agencies. It was into this situation that the DCMHC introduced a new scheme to handle such situations – the Crisis Intervention Service (CIS).

When MPD patrol officers were called to deal with so-called 'street crazies,' they could in turn call CIS for immediate help. CIS professionals could attend the scene by car, often armed with the medical records and history of the troubled individual and, in effect, take the issue out of the hands of the police who could then swiftly return to their law enforcement duties. CIS personnel would decide what happened next but that would always be based on the therapeutic needs of the individual and would not involve jail. The appointment by the MPD of a 'Social Services Co-ordinator' helped to iron out any problems in the relationship between CIS and patrol officers. Roughly every six years when I had further sabbaticals, I returned to Madison. Sometimes, I stayed in downtown hotels and, other times, I was the guest in the home of a MPD police officer with whom I had become firm friends. I wrote various papers and book chapters based on my research, and I saw the DCMHC evolve and having to cope with increasingly difficult financial and political circumstances, but much of its good work in the community and with the MPD survived.

The police and mental health professionals I met frequently impressed me, but my greatest pleasure came from spending time with many of the damaged individuals who so endearingly strove to be happy and independent. Away from my official business in Madison, I also enjoyed many other great moments, one of which was also rather frightening. I had been on several ride-alongs with different officers only to be told how busy it had been the night or day before, so much so that I was beginning to think that the police dispatcher didn't want me going to real incidents of any note. Often, I sat upfront with the driver, resting my left arm on the upturned stock of a shotgun fixed into the floor of the car and only able to be released when the correct code was put into the locking mechanism. I was told the first shell loaded into the gun was designed to smash car engines while the others were 'normal.' I saw parts of Madison I would not have seen otherwise and drank poor coffee when, very occasionally, we got out of the patrol car for a quick break, but I saw little action. Until one night, Joe, my driver, was dispatched to a Cuban Community Centre where there had been reports of gunshots being heard. As we arrived, I could see in the dark street several people making a commotion and four other patrol cars parked outside the centre with their blue lights still flashing. This was more like it, I thought. My excitement was dashed, however, when Joe told me it was too dangerous for me to enter the centre. I was to wait in the car. As Joe got out, he turned to me and gave me the code numbers to unlock the shotgun, "just in case all hell breaks out and they start shooting at you," and off he went. I waited for what seemed like ages wondering what was happening. I knew relationships between the MPD and the Cubans were not good. Castro had expelled a group of citizens years earlier and they had ended up in various American cities, including Madison. Castro had been wonderfully sly, however, selecting a great many criminals and prisoners among those he expelled.

Suddenly, Joe returned and said it was okay now for me to enter the community centre. As we walked inside the building, some of the other patrol cars were leaving. Whatever was going on, we were clearly at the mopping up stage. I followed Joe into the centre and down to the bar where Joe needed to speak to another officer. The atmosphere was thick with two ingredients: tobacco smoke and hatred. Every Cuban in that place took me to be a plain clothes police officer, wearing my gun in an out of sight shoulder holster unlike Joe whose gun was in plain view. And they hated me. Their eyes followed me along the room as I rather hurriedly tried to catch up with Joe. I felt a lot safer in the company of two armed officers, and I was relieved when shortly afterwards all of us – patrol officers and pretend detective Stephens – left the place.

I had another incident of mistaken identity, but this time a much happier one. On my first training session with the Madison Chargers, I wore a black and white striped shirt, which to me recalled Newcastle FC, but to my new American playmates denoted a National Football League referee. Thus, during the practice game, opposing players would instinctively pull out of a tackle or back off whenever I had the ball. They soon got used to the NFL shirt, but they remained tactically very naïve in how to play the game. Remember, soccer was new in 1982 in the USA and not played much outside colleges and universities. The Chargers' goalkeeper hardly left his goal-line, even when an opposing player was through on goal with only him to beat. He waited patiently, one might say politely, as the opposition regained their defensive positions, before he kicked the ball up field – no attempt to feed the ball quickly to mount a sweeping counter-attack. The rest often stayed too far away from the men they were marking, offering lots of time to pick a pass. At the end of the session, I was asked by the captain to give the team my impressions. I mentioned what I have already described, plus several other matters. I thought perhaps I had said too much, but I needn't have worried because I was now generally seen as a tactical genius, someone whose undoubted on-field skills allied to such innovative knowledge made for a most valuable member of the team. And so began a fruitful and enjoyable summer season with the Chargers. I would cycle out to wherever we were playing and help my mates give the opposition a good kicking. At half time, a few of those capacious trucks that many Americans like to drive would pull up nearby and disgorge barbeques, folding tables, and chairs and all the other accoutrements for a feast. At full time, we walked off to pick up bottles of chilled beer and sink our teeth into enormous steaks that various girlfriends had cooked. Later, my bike was put in the back of a truck and I was driven home.

On a later study visit to Madison in the 1990s, I was staying at the home of Steve Cardarella, a sergeant in the MPD. Each day I caught a couple of buses to get to and from downtown Madison, so it was not a surprise that I was soon recognised by the drivers that ploughed those routes. On one occasion, as I was about to alight at my stop close to the Cardarella home, the driver turned to me, thrust a wallet into my hand and said: "I can trust you; you're British. I found this wallet on the bus earlier today. The owner lives just across the road in that housing project. Please drop it off for him. Thanks." Somewhat surprised, I found myself on the pavement looking towards the white, middle-class estate where Steve lived, while behind me was the housing project, largely populated by blacks and Hispanics, into which I had to venture to return the wallet. I found the man's ID and address and noted that the wallet contained quite a bit of money. I set off, asking directions as I went. Luckily, it was not far and in no time, I had rung the bell and returned the lost item. When I got back to Steve's house and told him and his wife what had happened, they were both horrified that I had actually set foot inside an area populated, they told me, by down-and-outs and troublemakers. I was met with similar gasps of disbelief whenever I mentioned to a white person that I travelled regularly on the buses. "But they're full of crazy black kids," one of them told me, as indeed they were – they could be loud and boisterous, just like many kids on buses in the UK, but otherwise harmless. At the heart of such incidences was the ever-present shadow of all the unresolved conflicts in America that centred on race.

Nowhere was this more recognisable than when, during a couple of my visits to Madison, I was able to gain entry to local jails and a Supermax prison in the state. For all the good that I had witnessed being achieved by the DCMHC and the MPD – often involving black people – this decency seemed like a veneer covering needless cruelty when I witnessed what happened in prison. Both the local Madison jail and the state's Supermax were disproportionally populated by black inmates. I lost count of the number of times prison warders told me that "black people are dangerous, prone to violence." I found the Supermax regime morally repugnant. Prisoners are housed one per cell but in complete isolation and with few or no personal belongings. Meals are served through ports in the cell and furnishings are plain. Inmates rarely meet other prisoners, have few or no communal activities, and only leave their cells when secured in chains around hands, waist, and feet for a short period of exercise. Moreover, given the American justice system's ridiculous but brutal penchant to award sentences running into more than a hundred years without parole, most of the Supermax inmates would be there for life. No attempt whatsoever at rehabilitation, just a life-time of being forgotten and tucked away from public scrutiny.

In 1982, I was busy with my research but not so busy that I was unable to plan a holiday in Canada and New England for Linda and myself at the end of my study visit. The American Automobile Association kindly distributed complimentary state maps, lists of places to stay, and details of major attractions to members of the British AA. With the help of these publications and the use of my office phone, I was able to book car hire and accommodation in the New England states I intended to visit. It was easy to work out the distances each day between places and soon I had a sensible, detailed, and firm itinerary. Two days before I was due to leave Madison, fly to Toronto to meet Linda and commence our tour, three things happened. First, I went for a haircut at an old-fashioned barbers. Second, I drank too many Kamikaze cocktails on the lake-side terrace of the Memorial Union with some mates from the Chargers as part of a send-off gathering for me. Third, I fell off my bike on my way home and knocked my face about a little. The result was that as Linda came through the arrivals channel at Toronto Airport, she was shocked to see a battered and bruised husband with a Marine close-cropped haircut who looked as if he had just left the battlefield.

We stayed a few days in Toronto, dodging a very large group of American Shriners who were there for a convention. These Masonic spin-offs got everywhere in their loud shirts and hats and Linda and I were glad to be rid of them as we drove along the north coast of Lake Ontario, passed into the USA, and headed for Lake Placid. In Vermont and New Hampshire, we enjoyed quiet roads surrounded by a forest of trees whose leaves dazzled us with the boldness of their red, brown, and yellow hues. Boston and Cape Cod, where we went whale watching, were also on our itinerary. New York followed and then we drove back to Toronto via Niagara Falls. In New York, we stayed with an old friend, Joe, from my days at Nuffield College. Joe took us to the Bronx where we were met by slums and decay that surpassed even Harlem – as ever in America we saw the cruel divide between rich and poor.

Chapter Four: Kenya

Linda and I spent three weeks in Kenya in the summer of 1983. I had not been on many long flights in large planes but even I could see that the Kenya Airways 707 was an elderly conveyancer of people. It was a plane down on its luck, no longer a swish intercontinental star. Some of its décor was chipped and it had clearly been a plane passed on like hand-me-down clothes, judging from the various signs in the cabin written in Spanish. Still, it got us to Mombasa with no alarms. We touched down just as the sun was rising and, as I stepped onto the airport apron to walk to immigration and customs, I could clearly smell the perfumes of many flowering plants above the reek of aviation fuel. Even in the early morning, the heat was impressive but not yet oppressive. We cleared immigration swiftly but had to wait patiently to pass through customs. Most of the people waiting were not westerners but black Kenyans. The young lady in front of us was a Kenyan of Asian descent. The customs officer took delight in rifling through her suitcase, holding up her underwear for 'inspection' and generally being rather aggressive and unpleasant. For the first time in my life, I felt out of place – a white westerner surrounded by mainly black airport workers, officials, and passengers. I certainly was not looking forward to my forthcoming encounter with the aggressive customs officer. As we presented our luggage on the counter before him, he gave us a big smile, marked our bags with chalk to indicate they were fine to enter the country, and bade us a happy time in Kenya. And with that we were in. It was not the last time that I witnessed harassment of Kenyans by their own authorities, but as white tourists nothing like that happened to us.

Our hotel, the Bamburi Beach Hotel, was set alongside a palm-fringed, pristine, white sandy beach a few miles north of Mombasa. In 1983, there were far fewer tourists visiting the country than is the case today. Accordingly, the beach was a magnificent white ribbon between an opalescent sea and palm-covered land with only a few people walking carefree and barefoot through the sand. There were some small boats and skiffs dotted along the beach and used for inshore fishing, but there were no stalls, no entertainments, no impromptu bamboo bars all designed to separate tourists from their cash. About the only commercial endeavour, which operated from time to time according to the tides, was a parascending outfit of one guy in a motorboat and two on the beach to 'launch' the punters into the sky. One day, as Linda and I strolled along the beach in the late afternoon, we were surprised to meet a Maasai moran who was looking to sell to tourists. He was carrying several home-made spears, typical of the kind that young warriors would use to defend their cattle against predators. They were lovely artefacts and I asked him how much they cost, but he spoke no English. Instead, he pointed at my Madison University T-shirt as an exchange. I took off the T-shirt, handed it over, and resumed my walk along the beach brandishing my new spear. Incidentally, I was also able to take the spear into the cabin of the Kenya Airways 707 and stow it in the overhead locker on the flight home. Such respective bartering and ignoring of sharp pointed weapons in the cabin would not happen today.

The block where our room was located overlooked the beach and was connected to other blocks by walkways, which was where the vervet monkeys hung out. Many guests had breakfast in bed and, afterwards, would put the serving trays outside their doors for collection. No lump of sugar, no piece of uneaten croissant, and no unfinished drop of juice were left behind by the vervet marauders.

The Bamburi Beach Hotel was a paradise for monkeys as well as humans. The hotel enjoyed extensive grounds, the centre piece of which was a group of pools of various shapes and sizes joined together by a labyrinth of connecting channels. It was a delight to swim there and to lay on my back gazing up at the tall palm trees, the pink and red hibiscus, and the mimosa that surrounded the swimming pools. One day, Linda asked one of the waiters for some coconut water to drink and was surprised when he replied: "I'll bring the gardener to you immediately." The gardener in his green uniform duly turned up, listened to Linda's request, and promptly climbed a nearby palm tree to cut down a coconut, the top of which he then sliced off effortlessly with a machete. The waiter inserted a straw into the coconut and handed it to Linda. It was a performance of unassuming style and panache. Not all surprises were so well received. Another day, an elderly man with a hessian sack approached me as I was sunbathing and indicated if I wanted to see what was in it. Before I could say anything, he lifted out a puff adder and was about to hold it closer to my face before I leapt out of the way. I retreated to a rondavel with its thatched roof of dried grass that served as a bar next to one of the pools, and ordered a cold beer. It was only then that I realized that the snake in question must have had its fangs removed or undergone some other horror to make it safe to handle.

Life in the hotel was relaxed and full of Jambo's with long sonorous stress on the 'a' when saying hello to staff, or else asking how they were – Habari – and, of course, Asante Sana for thank you. Linda and I often played frisbee in the shallow waters and, occasionally, ventured a little further out to the coral reef. Here, we snorkelled and marvelled at the different corals and the brightly coloured fish that darted around us. Where the reef ended, it was like a cliff crashing into the darkness as the colour of the sea changed from turquoise, to green, to blue and, finally, to black. Often, we saw small catamarans with bright red triangular sails just off the reef. On some evenings, a group of Maasai morans, freed temporarily from guarding their tribe's assets, danced for the hotel guests with their beguiling chants and high jumps, and stunned the audience with their long, tightly-braided hair and bright red robes. Sometimes, Giriama women arrived from their village and danced in their traditional white costumes, with bare midriffs and white plumed headdresses. The next time I saw Giriama women, there were five of them walking one behind the other along the edge of the road. They were not wearing their stylish traditional dress but everyday clothes and, instead of their elegant headdresses, they carried heavy plastic containers full of water – typical of the unsung, relentless but essential work that many women outside the towns and cities had to do each day.

We took several excursions from the hotel, for Linda and I could only sunbathe and mess around by the pool for a few days until we felt the need to explore elsewhere and forge new adventures. One day, we took a coach to Mombasa, a city that was different from settlements elsewhere in Kenya. In Mombasa, there was a greater mix of cultures, religions, and food as well as a bigger range of races, largely due to the city's historical importance as a trading centre. Ocean-going dhows had long sailed between the east African coast and Arabia, giving the city a distinctive Arabic population. There were also others settled in Mombasa who were originally from the Indian sub-continent as well as black Kenyans from the locality and further afield. Coaches arriving in Mombasa frequently used the Castle Hotel as a dropping off and picking up spot; a fact that was well known to local people. Accordingly, coaches would sometimes be welcomed by a sad group of beggars, some of whom had terrible deformities. Tourists carefully picked their way past them – some giving money and others unsure of what to do, but all of them wanting to be rid of an episode that did not fit in with their ideas of appropriate holiday experiences. I found the group of beggars to be somewhat overwhelming, especially those with deformed legs who determinedly dragged themselves towards me using their knuckles to propel jury-rigged wheeled carts. I handed out some money and I, too, was relieved to have found my way beyond their reach and able to explore the city.

In the harbour, there were a few passing dhows with their pointed bows, square sterns, and lateen sails. They looked too fragile to be able to sail all the way to the Persian Gulf, yet they had been doing so for centuries. I saw two sunken dhows close to the harbour wall – mere skeletons shimmering under the clear water. Later, Linda and I toured Fort Jesus, a late 16th century fort built by the Portuguese to cement its control over Indian Ocean trade routes. Afterwards, we spent some time in the magnificent fruit market packed to the gunnels with produce of so many colours, shapes, and sizes. Most of the goods on sale I could not name. It felt like being in a mystical sweet shop but unable to make any selections. Our day was rounded off by visits to several Hindu temples and, then, back to the Castle Hotel to await our coach, where we sat outside with a beer, avoiding the pleading eyes of those before us.

In order to go further afield and for convenience, I hired a car for a few days. We drove north along the coast where at one point the police were stopping and searching traffic. The black driver of a small truck directly in front of my car was witnessing two officers throwing building equipment from his truck onto the side of the road – searching for what I don't know – but it looked overzealous to me. Yet, when it came to my turn, I was waved on my way with a gentle smile. We briefly visited Watamu and Malindi on the Indian Ocean coast and then turned inland to visit the nearby Gedi Ruins. This Swahili town traced its origins back to the 12th century and consisted of the remains of stone-built houses, palaces, and mosques.

Parts of the ancient site had been overshadowed by centuries of tree growth.

Back at the Bamburi Beach Hotel, we saw an advert for fishing expeditions just outside the reef. A full day was expensive but a couple with whom we had struck up an acquaintance were keen to come with us and, as I still had the hire car, it would be simple enough to drive the few miles north to the inlet where the boat was moored. I booked the trip for the next day. Leaving the inlet, we were soon sailing through the shallow waters inside the reef; the sea was smooth and the sky crisply blue. The crew of three were very hospitable and the motorboat was well-maintained and equipped. We looked forward to a lovely day of fishing for exotic denizens of the Indian Ocean. However, that same ocean had a dirty trick in hand waiting for us. The day before, the crew subsequently told us, there had been a severe storm far out into the ocean and now, as we went beyond the reef, the remains of that storm hit us in the form of three-metre-high waves. We patrolled at a safe distance from the reef in parallel lines; first sailing south with the reef on our starboard side, and then turning through 180 degrees so that the reef was on our port side as we retraced our route. In each direction, the waves relentlessly bore down on us, so that as the craft rose on the crest of a wave, we were almost five metres in the air looking down into a very steep gulley. When we were at the bottom, another intimidating wave loomed above us. Turning around was worse, as the boat rose and fell even more quickly as if we were tied to some oceanic version of a bucking bronco. The crew were dutiful and baited the rods and threw out the lines, but I knew that the turbulent conditions would churn up sand and debris from the ocean floor, and make it extremely difficult for the fish to see the bait. I stood rigidly looking out to sea, holding onto a railing, and urging myself not to throw up. Three of us wanted to return to the estuary inlet immediately, but John wanted to stay out even though he was being sick. Eventually,

I told the captain to take us back. When we arrived, John insisted the crew take him out again and, thus, he dragged his wife with him. Linda and I watched them go; they would take a taxi back to the hotel when John finally gave up on this madness.

We interrupted our journey back to the hotel to visit an orphanage where the children and young people were not only educated, but also spent time making artefacts for visitors to purchase. The best of these were the woven baskets, frequently in two or three colour tones depending on the materials used. When the youngsters finished a basket, they wrote their name and age on a small piece of card and attached it to the item. I still have one of them in my home over forty years later.

The final place we visited by car was to a small national park south of Mombasa, the Shimba Hills Game Reserve. Today, I understand there are hotels in or near the reserve and a professional group of wardens patrolling the whole area. There are also accredited guides to take tourists on their safari drives. But in 1983, there was barely a proper park entrance structure and only one warden to collect entrance fees, and no guided tours. You drove yourself through the reserve, and you could get out and walk around wherever you wished, which is exactly what we did. On foot in hilly country in search of a waterfall, we had to struggle through high elephant grass. We saw nothing except elephant grass all around us until we came to a sudden break where the grass had been pressed flat and a channel about the width of an adult elephant snaked off into the distance. In the flattened channel were copious elephant droppings, some still steaming. We had just missed them, luckily for us, for such an unexpected encounter would have proved very dangerous. On our way back to the exit, we did briefly see a small herd of elephants along a tree line, behind which they quickly disappeared as soon as they heard or smelled us. We informed the warden at the exit what we'd seen and he told us we had been very lucky even to get a glimpse of the elephants.

When I booked the holiday to Kenya, I also included a three-day trip to Tsavo National Park, the largest in the country. The park is divided into Tsavo West and Tsavo East by a railway line from Mombasa into the interior. Tsavo East is slightly larger and the terrain is composed of flat and dry plains, while Tsavo West is wetter, with swamps in places, and contains Mzima Springs. It is also more mountainous. The journey by chauffeur-driven car from Bamburi Beach to Voi in Tsavo East was lengthy and, because of the poor state of the roads, uncomfortable. After several hours, our driver - Michael - stopped at what in the UK we might call a service station, but here the only apt description would be a rickety shack at the side of a dirt road. Nevertheless, they sold a wicked chilled Coca Cola. Three hundred metres away was a small lake, and Michael said it was okay to walk there if we wanted to stretch our legs. We had not gone that far when we realized that a flange of baboons on either side was taking an interest in us. They can be intimidating, especially the males, and I did not like the way that some of them were approaching us. Just as I thought about turning back, the baboons lost interest and returned to foraging for food. We continued to the lake and, suddenly, a breeding herd of red elephants appeared over the brow of a small hill and headed excitedly towards the water. They were the first elephants I had ever seen in the wild, and an instant lifelong love affair was born, but I did not understand why the elephants appeared red. I could have stayed there forever simply watching them drink but all too soon Michael arrived to beckon us back. He told us that the baboons are often very aggressive to local women, especially if the women are carrying food, but are more wary of males. He added that the baboons did not often see white people, so who knows what they thought, but they were generally more guarded. I asked him about the red colour of the herd and Michael replied that in this part of the park the soil itself was red, and when elephants had quenched their thirst, they would throw water over themselves and, then, trunk-fulls of red earth onto their skin to protect it from insects and parasites.

Eventually, we reached our destination, the Voi Safari Lodge, and enjoyed an excellent evening meal. At the reception desk, there was a chalk board where guests could indicate whether they would like to be woken if any animals of their choice appeared in the night at the lodge's waterhole. I wrote down my room number, elephant, and that I could be woken at any time, and then Linda and I went to bed. It must have been around three in the morning when we heard a knock on our door. An elderly, small gentleman – a kind of night watchman for the lodge – informed me that an elephant was at the waterhole. Linda and I immediately went to our balcony and there beyond the lodge's terrace was a massive bull elephant caught in the spotlight. This was Tembo, the Swahili word for elephant, in all his glory. He drank slowly but we could hear the water being expelled from his trunk into his mouth. The elderly gentleman appeared again on the terrace below us, this time wearing a dark green army great coat and he whispered to us if we'd like to join him on the terrace and have some tea. We eagerly said yes. We dressed and soon joined him. It was then I saw that the army coat almost touched the ground and that his slim frame was positively lost inside it. He explained that he wore it to protect against the cold. There was no irony in his voice as he brought tea to two guests wearing only light clothing and T-shirts, and not feeling cold at all. I gave him a US$5 note as a tip, which he much preferred to Kenyan Shillings. The three of us talked together for some while, but my eyes were never far removed from watching the lone bull. The animal was perfectly relaxed; it knew we were there but didn't care about us. This was his land, ours lay behind the terrace, and he knew that we would not cross it. It was his total disregard for us that I found so captivating. Eventually, when he had drunk enough water, he moved away in a slow, purposeful fashion and soon disappeared into the night beyond the lights. It was only then that I looked upwards and saw the beautiful mysteries of the Milky Way holding court majestically in an immense ribbon of sparkling stars set against a jet-black sky.

The following day, we saw many more elephants scattered throughout the seemingly endless plains. There were a few trees dotted around the land but much of the terrain was so bare and red-tinged that it looked as if a malicious god had taken a blow torch and scorched the place. Many of the elephants sported a distinctive red colour as they marched in their peculiarly swaying fashion in the endless search for food. When we moved to Tsavo West, there was more vegetation; the terrain was greener, with many more hills but there was no shortage of elephants. Indeed, at Mzima Springs, we encountered further large animals - hippopotamus. The spring was fed by a natural reservoir under nearby hills. Tourists were allowed to walk around the water's edge surrounded by lush forest growth and to watch the hippos fighting for space and seniority. We had such a good time on this short safari that, after we returned to Bamburi, we decided to go on another. Accordingly, with still more than a week to go at the beach, I went to a travel agency in Mombasa and booked another short safari to the Maasai Mara.

The overnight train from Mombasa to Nairobi was such a romantic journey. Admittedly, the diesel engine pulling the train did seem a bit clapped out, but the coaches and sleeping cabins, although old, were relics from a golden age of privilege when colonial officials and their memsahibs, along with white hunters and powerful entrepreneurs travelled in luxury. A few years later, when I saw the film *Out of Africa,* I thought back to that journey and felt that the dining car must have come directly from the set of that film. So it was that the train ambled out of Mombasa station full of promise. It oscillated for most of the journey along the single-track railway between slow and stationary, so that a journey of over 450 kilometres took more than eleven hours. Yet, none of this was a hardship, for Linda and I had a wonderful two-berth cabin where the seats were turned down and made up as beds by our steward as we were eating dinner in the dining car. The dining car itself was full of large, plush, blue-upholstered seats. The tables with white linen tablecloths and napkins and perfectly positioned plates and cutlery would not have been out of place at *The Ritz*. We were summoned to dinner by a steward walking along the corridor playing a stringed instrument resembling a lyre. The waiters wore smart white jackets and gloves, and soft lighting suffused the carriage. It was undoubtedly romantic.

At dawn, we awoke and enjoyed the breakfast our steward had brought us. Suddenly, outside the window appeared a herd of giraffe. We were travelling through Nairobi National Park and in the background, only a few miles away, was the outline of the city itself. However, the romance was swiftly throttled to death as the train chugged through the dreadful and extensive slums on the outskirts of Nairobi. We overlooked the shanties, closely crammed together, with their precarious tin roofs and splintered wooden walls. They stretched on and on, a landscape of poverty and for many of hopelessness. We were glad to get to the station and exit the train. The train had arrived late. Apparently, it habitually arrived late, but the driver and car to take us to the Mara had now gone, leaving us stranded in the middle of the explosively bustling city.

Eventually, a representative of the safari company found us and explained that the car could not wait for the train's late arrival. He informed us that the only way we could now get to our lodge in the Maasai Mara was to take a light aircraft from Nairobi's domestic airport. We took a taxi to Wilson Airport, booked a flight, and were soon off in a two-engine plane to the Mara Serena Lodge. The plane carried six passengers but I found myself sitting alongside the pilot. Flying relatively low over the bush, forests and rivers was stunning but the light plane was often buffeted by thermals. As we approached the lodge's runway, scraped out of the plain, I was not feeling well. I took a sick bag as a precaution. On what passed for a runway, a large herd of wildebeest was quietly grazing any grass that remained. The pilot approached them as if he were going to land and hope he did not hit any. At the last moment, he pulled up, and flew a few feet above their heads, which caused the wildebeest to scatter in all directions. He then banked violently and approached again on what was now a clear runway. It was at this point that I threw up into the bag only to discover it had no bottom; it was in effect an open-ended tube and my sick went straight through it and over the floor. When we came to a halt, the pilot shut off the starboard engine so that Linda and I could exit via the co-pilot's seat, slide down the wing onto the ground and collect our luggage from the small hold. And with that he took off again, leaving us on an otherwise deserted plain with a herd of wildebeest giving us the once-over.

After what seemed a long, not to mention an inhospitable time to be left in such isolation, we eventually saw a vehicle coming to take us to the lodge. The lodge itself was very comfortable with remarkable views over the surrounding terrain, but the best thing we discovered there were Paolo and Paola, Claudio and Patrizia, two Italian couples on a joint honeymoon. We were together on the same rugged vehicle that took us on our morning and afternoon safaris and, although none of us had much of a grasp of each other's language, we became great friends – a friendship that has lasted to this day. We visited several places in the vicinity, including Lake Naivasha where we dined al fresco next to the lake itself. This made a refreshing change from the heat and dust of the terrain where the wild animals lived. However, by far our most exciting safari was to the Mara River where we observed thousands of wildebeest and zebra crossing the river as part of their annual migration. Safely parked above one of the steep banks of the Mara, we could see how full and swift the river was running. To our left were amassed great numbers of beasts, all clearly reluctant to swim across the river. For them, it was potentially a river of death with many ways to die.

Some wildebeest were precariously perched on the very edge of the bank, barely able to withstand the pressure of the hundreds of others behind them. Suddenly, one, then two, then a whole stream of wildebeest had jumped from the cliff-like edge and had hit the fast-flowing water. Slightly further downstream, herds of zebra similarly inching towards the steep drop into the river were encouraged by the sight of the wildebeest, and they too started to slide down the precipice. The first of the deaths occurred here. Many animals, wildebeest in particular, would leap high into the air to land as far down the slope as possible. Some of them, however, would break a leg on landing. If they were lucky, a crocodile came to the bottom of the bank and claimed them. If not, they hobbled around until shock and exhaustion took them.

None of the animals could swim directly to the other bank for the strong current dragged them further downstream. Only the strongest eventually made the crossing. The second form of death awaited those who had not the strength to make dry land. They drowned, and their bodies piled up one on top of another in a bend of the river downstream from where they had started their fatal journey. It was like a corral of corpses. The oldest denizens of this place of death were already bloated and foul, and the vultures were picking their way through the entrails. At the waterline, crocodiles pulled at body parts and repeatedly rolled over to rip the meat free. Other crocodiles waited out in the river as panicking animals swam past them. Their huge jaws closed on the leg, neck or head of a beast and sealed their doom. Their death came by drowning as the crocodile pulled them underwater, abruptly cutting short their desperate calls. The final form of death happened on the far bank, which was also steep and densely crowded with zebra and wildebeest scrambling to reach safe land. The up-slope was not safe land for here, in the midst of the battle to reach the top no matter what it took, the weakest slipped back into the water and succumbed to crocodiles or drowning. Others broke legs on the way up the slope, or else were trampled. Crocodiles and drowning awaited them. Of course, the vast majority of this migrating army of animals made it safely across, but many mothers would still have to search endlessly to find their calves from which they had been separated. Did the calf survive or die? Who could tell amongst all that carnage and chaos?

Linda and I were supposed to return to Mombasa by train, but we got on so well with our new friends that we accompanied the Italians by plane. They were staying at a hotel close to ours and the day after we returned to the coast, I heard the distinctive voices of Paolo and Claudio calling out our names as they walked through the grounds of our hotel looking for us. They invited us to lunch at their hotel and two days later they left for home. However, in mid-December that same year, a sort of Red Cross parcel arrived from Italy, full of the treats that Italians enjoy at Christmas, such as panettone, Amaretti di Saronno, and good wine. We returned the favour, sending British types of tea and marmalade. We kept in touch and the friendship motivated Linda and I to start learning Italian. There followed many visits to Tuscany to see our friends.

Chapter Five: Thailand

Kenya was my first experience of a culture that was, in many ways, different from my own and I was keen to repeat the event. Thus, in 1986, Linda and I travelled to Thailand. There, we would find another culture that was new to us and, sometimes, even stranger because we could not understand the language or read Thai script. Our first port of call was Bangkok, the likes of which I had never witnessed before. If other major cities are said not to sleep, in Bangkok the citizens must be on speed. It is non-stop activity: pernicious, resentful traffic jams, crowded pavements and even more packed markets and shopping malls, tuk tuk drivers skimming in and out of traffic, motorbikes and mopeds annoying everyone stuck in a jam, wondrous and endless numbers of golden temples, simple street food stalls, heat and humidity and thunderous storms and deluges of rain that are often over in less than an hour; and through this sprawling metropolis runs the mighty Chao Phraya River full of barges, river buses and cross-river ferries and the famed long-tail boats that act as water taxis and tourist crafts, all of which make the Hudson River in New York look like a backwater.

We stayed at the Asia Bangkok Hotel. Like many three and four-star hotels in the Far East, our hotel offered large rooms, attentive service, and a level of luxury at surprisingly low prices. Eager to explore the city, we set off one morning through the marble-floored lobby only to be politely intercepted by a well-dressed member of the concierge department. He asked us if we'd like one of the hotel's chauffeur-driven cars to take us to our destination. He also gave us a small card with the hotel's name and address written on it in Thai, should we ever get lost during our stay and needed a taxi back to the hotel. The roads outside the hotel looked frantic, even slightly forbidding – and it seemed taxi drivers might not speak any English – so we took up his offer. It all went very well until our driver misunderstood something we had said to him. Instead of taking us back to the hotel, he pulled up outside some casino or club and the doors were abruptly opened by two bouncers. For a split second, I thought it was a robbery but it was soon sorted out and we left behind the disappointed enforcers.

The next day, we surmised that we had little to lose by hailing an ordinary taxi, much to the concierge's chagrin. Big mistake. The taxi we randomly flagged down was driven by an unnervingly eccentric individual. He constantly accelerated dangerously when the traffic allowed, and then would brake violently throwing Linda and I forward since there were no seat belts. I leaned forward and told him to stop it, but with little hope that he would understand. What I was not expecting, however, was the heavy, black revolver he pulled from his waistband and began to wave around his head. At the next traffic jam, when the taxi was stationary, I threw him some Thai baht and we both exited the taxi like lightning. After that, we saw no reason why we should not use tuk tuks to get around the city. Yes, they were noisy and had only three wheels and amounted to nothing more than a motorised rickshaw, not to mention how vulnerable they seemed among much heavier traffic. But they were the most glorious fun. They were so nimble and their drivers so skilled (or should that be daring) that they navigated almost any space with ease. The concierge wrote out the names of places we intended to visit in Thai, and we had no trouble using tuk tuks after that.

The Grand Palace, the official residence of the King of Thailand, is located along the banks of the Chao Phraya River, and is composed of many buildings set in fabulous gardens and courtyards. Many of its pavilions are protected by fierce-looking mystical figures, and fantastical multi-coloured guardians. The site is full of colour: steep-sloping red and green roofs, and pagodas that look as if they are covered in gold. Everywhere, there is the smell of incense as local people light their joss sticks and pray to the Buddha. Indeed, the most sacred temple in Thailand is within the walls of the Grand Palace: The Temple of the Emerald Buddha, which houses a figurine of the Buddha carved from a piece of green jade and decorated with diamonds and gold. It is revered throughout the kingdom, but also open to view by tourists. Two other well-known temples much visited by tourists are Wat Po and Wat Arun. The former houses the Temple of the Reclining Buddha, a truly awesome fifteen metres high and forty-six metres long and covered in gold leaf. The latter is known in English as the Temple of Dawn, and is famous for its stunning architecture and views over the Chao Phraya River. Both sites outdo the Temple of the Golden Buddha despite that temple's five-and-a-half-ton statue of the Buddha made from solid gold.

Linda and I enjoyed being on the river in Bangkok where we could visit floating markets and take water taxis. Although these markets were overwhelmingly for tourists, the floating boats and stalls were very impressive, packed closely together and offering myriad fruits, flowers, spices, and foodstuffs for sale. Best of all, however, was a tour of the Thonburi district on the western banks of the Chao Praya River sat in the bow of a powerful long-tail boat. Fitted with car engines and sometimes turbos, these boats could accelerate very quickly but were also ideal for making their way around the web of canals in the district. Here, among the canals or klongs as they were called locally, was a much quieter side to Bangkok. Along the maze of waterways were homes and small shops on wooden stilts to raise the premises above the waterline. I occasionally saw children swimming close to the shore in the main river, but here in the klongs it was common to see numerous boys and girls playing in the water. The klongs and their stilted houses presented a picture of Bangkok that was far removed from the overcrowded press of many other Bangkok locations. If I had ever lived in Bangkok, I would have chosen Thonburi.

In contrast, Patpong, which has been described as an entertainment district, is essentially a red-light area. It is full of rooftop bars, nightclubs, and girlie shows much frequented by tourists. If you are in Bangkok, it's worth a visit but you need to keep your wits about you. It is not uncommon for working girls to embrace you in the street and try to drag you into some smoky den where other girls are firing table tennis balls from their vaginas. Having none of the raucous and lewd activities of Patpong are the orchid farms that proliferate. They hand out orchids in Thailand like protesters hand out leaflets in the UK. You often are given them to take home on the plane with you.

Having survived the delights of Patpong and armed with yet more orchids thrust into our hands, we left Bangkok and travelled to Pattaya, about 104 kilometres south of Bangkok on the Gulf of Siam. We stayed at the four-star Asia Hotel set in tropical gardens with a swimming pool, and outdoor tennis courts, and close to the beach. But we did not escape the sex trade because two or three kilometres away was the notorious Walking Street in Pattaya City. After dark, the street is transformed into a spectacle of neon lights, lively pubs and nightclubs, and go-go bars. It was garish, kitsch, and in-your-face. When Linda and I visited the area, it was surprisingly quiet. This may have been because the weather in September is often very wet and there are not so many tourists. However, one of the sex workers in a bar where we were drinking told me it was quiet because a large contingent of the US Navy had just left port.

Later, we got chatting with a group of four middle-aged Australians who let slip that they had told their wives they were on a diving holiday when, in effect, they were sampling the female wares of Walking Street. I noticed that a young girl, perhaps six or seven, was constantly hanging around trying to sell cigarettes and matches to bar customers. Her small stock of goods was displayed on a tray. She looked pale and very tired – it was past midnight. One of the Australians we were speaking to called her over, bought the full contents of her tray, and told her to go home to bed. I watched the little girl walk away only to see her stop by a dark alleyway from which emerged an adult male who promptly filled her tray again, and sent her back out to work the streets. Later, one of the bar girls told me that when she was old enough, almost certainly that innocent would end up as a sex worker. It turned out that many of the bar girls-cum-sex workers weren't even Thai but came from desperately poor families in Cambodia and elsewhere.

There were, naturally, much happier memories from our time in Pattaya, notably a trip to a Thai boxing exhibition. The local Thai boxers were all fit, lithe, and skilful and the contests were exciting. However, at one point, urged on by the MC, a cocky, but possibly tipsy, Englishman was persuaded to try his luck in the ring. He must have been three or four stones heavier than his lightweight Thai opponent. The lightweight proceeded to kick his arse around the ring before the referee mercifully stopped the fight. As a Welshman, I had no problem with that contest.

On the beach near our hotel was a parascending outfit, which Linda and I both tried. I let her go first on the dubious proposition that I would take photographs of her in the air with my telephoto lens. Well, she survived, so I thought I would have a go! Strapped into my harness with the parachute trailing behind me and a long rope attached to the boat in front, I had only to run a few yards down the beach before the motorboat gained sufficient speed and lifted me skywards. I was told to pull on a certain cord among a great many others descending from the parachute's canopy when I came in to land so that I could slightly alter the trajectory, and miss the coconut trees – but only if I pulled the right cord, and pulled it hard enough, and early enough. Just in case I missed the beach and the trees but landed in the sea, I took with me a small waterproof camera and got some great shots from the air.

As was normally the case with Linda and me on holiday, we had to get away from the beach and explore elsewhere. We took a coach from Pattaya to Bangkok; the driver and even a few of the passengers insisted we sat right at the front of the coach, perhaps as some kind of courtesy. At Bangkok Airport we flew to Chang Mai in the north of the country. There, we stayed at the Suriwongse Hotel in one of the biggest hotel rooms I have ever seen with an immense hard wood floor, and a bed so large that you would need to communicate with your partner in semaphore. This part of Thailand is mountainous and contains thick tropical forests. It is also home to some of the minority people who live in Thailand such as the Meo, Lua, Karen, and Lisu hill tribes.

The city is surrounded by many villages, some of which specialise in making gold and black lacquerware bowls, decorative boxes, paper umbrellas, and ceramics. Many of these items can be found in the various street markets, while in the night bazaar you can shop for souvenirs and enjoy delicious examples of street food, such as satay, mango with sticky rice, and deep-fried meatballs. Undoubtedly, the most famous attraction – deservedly so – is Wat Phra That Doi Suthep, a venerated temple of staggering beauty perched on a mountain top. To reach the temple you must navigate a Naga Staircase with three-hundred-and-six steps. Two Nagas on either side of the staircase coil themselves all the way to the top and represent mythical, semi-divine beings that are half human and half cobra. They are, in effect, guardians for the protection of the temple. As Linda and I were about to ascend the Naga Staircase, it began to rain. Our protection arrived in the form of an elderly lady who approached us laden down with a raft of waxed paper umbrellas. We took one from her and she told us she would collect it and take payment when we returned.

At the top of the snake-adorned balustrade a magnificent temple greeted us and, at an elevation of over 900 metres, we were afforded good views of Chang Mai. Immediately before us was a chedi or gold-plated tower with spires and tiers. Inside the buildings of the temple complex were many statues of the Buddha in various styles. Sometimes we saw red-robed monks in contemplation. The pagodas, stupas, chedis, and statues all have a sheen to them and indicate the immense historical and cultural importance of the site. In one of the squares within the complex, we saw two young girls aged about eight wearing the traditional dress of the Meo hill tribe. One of them had a baby strapped to her back. Their delightful black and red costumes and braided bonnets were reflected poignantly in the large puddle of water in which they stood: poignantly, because they were dressed up to encourage tourists to give them money and because such a young child was forced to be a carer for a sibling while the mother worked elsewhere.

This sight was to be repeated the next day when Linda and I visited a Meo hill tribe village set further into the jungle beyond Chang Mai. We hired a four-wheel drive vehicle, driver, and interpreter, and set off along a narrow dirt road to the village, being attacked by monkeys on the way who threw small branches and fruits at the car. As we entered the village with its collection of small wooden-sided and grass-roofed dwellings, we saw only a flurry of free-roaming pigs, and a gaggle of young children, some with babies wrapped in sheets and anchored to their backs. Here, there was no sign of the intricate and colourful traditional dress; these children were clad in old stained clothes and had unkempt hair and dirty faces. They were perfectly at ease when we drew near to them, but one or two held out their hands for money. We asked where their mothers were and they told us that the adult women were working in the fields below the village where they cultivate various crops. An enquiry about their fathers brought forth only one child pointing in the direction of a rectangular building eighty metres away. In the gloom and smoke inside this larger building, we found some of the village's adult males. They were sat or lying down smoking opium. One of them half-raised himself from his stupor and said something to us. The interpreter told us he was asking if we wanted to smoke. There were so many opium fumes in the room that you didn't need to smoke it directly to get high. I asked the interpreter how this could happen but he seemed reluctant or unable to give a coherent answer. I surmised it was what happens to marginalised minorities when they are not treated fairly by the majority culture, even as their own culture is being minimised. It may be different and much better today, but in 1986 we were saddened by what we saw. We drove back to the Suriwongse somewhat deflated.

Before we returned to Pattaya, we went to an elephant sanctuary, where we saw them move logs around as they would have done when employed in the logging industry. The beguiling part was when the mahouts took their charges down to the river edge to wash them. It was a well-choreographed and well-recognised routine by both elephant and mahout. The elephants knew when to lay down, when to roll over, and when to get up and march off to their night quarters; just as the mahouts knew when to walk over the flanks of their animals to wash them rigorously with a brush, and when to lift their voluminous ears to do the same.

A few days later, we were boarding our return flight to London. Naturally, we carried a gift of orchids intended to encourage us to return. We did, but first we explored Thailand's near neighbours.

Chapter Six: Kuala Lumpur, Malaysia, and Singapore

This was a journey of roller coaster proportions: the breathtaking modernity of Singapore dominated by its Chinese population and culture, the much quieter and diverse Kuala Lumpur, the delightful beach experience at Kuantan, and the island of Penang where many cultural pleasures were also combined with a sojourn by the sea. It was also a holiday that came with an old folder full of receipts, maps, and those IATA airline tickets no one sees anymore – all printed regulations, and pages and pages of airline codes, each page extracted at each airport check-in until only the final, blurred red copy remained. Even a cursory examination of that folder, containing the surviving detritus from the journey, would reveal that Linda and I made a lot of purchases, and many bar bills to settle. A selection of the purchases included: a ticket for the Singapore Cable Car (last departure seven p.m.), an entrance ticket to Sentosa Island, an overseas phone call from the Kuantan Hyatt Hotel, the payment for made-to-measure clothes at Oriental Silk House, an invitation to attend the lighting of the flame at the Hyatt's 'Mini-Olympics,' an Avis car rental agreement, a receipt for a pewter ornament from Selangor Pewter Marketing in Kuala Lumpur, and Kuoni's final invoice for the holiday. The bills for food and drink, especially drink, were of a completely different order: two pages of closely typed charges for sundry refreshments at the Golden Sands Hotel in Penang, *three* pages of the very same at the Kuantan Hyatt Hotel with an ironic 'Thank you. Please visit us again' printed below the huge total due, and – rather stylishly – a bill for 150 Singaporean dollars for drinks in the Writers Bar in Raffles Hotel.

The holiday began in Kuala Lumpur, or KL, as everyone seems to call it. We stayed at the Regent Hotel but rarely ate there so good was the food sold at hawker stalls in the city. Linda and I especially enjoyed satay - pieces of chicken, lamb or beef marinated in a spicy sauce and charcoal grilled on a skewer and served with peanut gravy, called 'kuah,' onions, cucumber, and rice cake. For dessert, we tried and liked 'ice kacang,' a colourful mountain of shaved ice, splashed with 'gula melaka,' or palm sugar, sweet syrup, and filled with red beans and creamed corn.

KL's Chinatown was full of street vendors and small shops with colourful awnings; they sold all manner of items including rubber stamps, lion-headed masks, hats of varied shapes and sizes, and a fabulous array of colourful kites of many different designs. There were also stalls selling fruits and vegetables all enclosed within narrow streets through which people, animals and trishaws made their laboured way. Many of the tall houses were rather grand if also a little battered. Weeds and even stunted trees grew out of cracks in the masonry, and clothes were drying as they hung from horizontal poles fixed next to the upstairs windows. Some windows were adorned by tall, wooden shutters that were now dilapidated and weary. It all seemed like a type of shabby chic to me.

The diversity of KL, and of Malaysia itself, contrasted with the greater homogeneity of Singapore. Malaysia is a long peninsula with the Indian Ocean on its western edge and the South China Sea on its east. The interior is composed of dense jungle, hill stations, and rubber and palm tree plantations. Malays form the majority of the thirty-five million population and tend towards Islam, but there are also many Chinese who favour Buddhism and Taoism, and Indians who follow Hinduism. Singapore sits at the foot of the peninsula and is a small island of just under six million people. Ethnic Chinese comprise over three-quarters of the population, while indigenous Malays and ethnic Indians amount to fifteen per cent and seven per cent respectively. If KL seemed largely Malay to Linda and me, then Singapore struck us as mainly Chinese. It also struck us as a thriving tourist destination, in part, based on intense shopping experiences. Singapore is full of exceptional buildings but also an exceptionally high population density. The old and traditional can still be found, but the city is about modernity and capitalism wrapped within a political concern for security and obedience. It felt a lifetime away from KL.

The Regency Hotel in Singapore was excellent, as I had come to expect of hotels in the Far East, but again we mostly ate elsewhere. Our favourite hawker stalls were at Newton Circus and, since this was Singapore and not KL, you could metaphorically eat off the floor at Newton Circus so tough and well-enforced were the hygiene laws. Newton Circus was so well-known that Japanese tourists actually came to watch and photograph customers eating their food, although I never saw them eating there themselves. Away from the city, I found the harbour fascinating. I had never seen ships of such immensity nor so many riding at anchor. The world's commodities all seemed to converge on Singapore before being dispatched around the rest of the globe. I think Linda found the harbour less fascinating, but she took a great interest in the jewellery shops on Orchard Road. We found one where they sold cut but unset gems. Linda began rigorously to examine an array of dazzling sapphires and diamonds. While I sat at the counter idly watching Linda inspect the gemstones for cut, colour, clarity, and carat, the manager's assistant brought me drinks. When Linda had finished and selected her stones, which later she would have set into rings and earrings of her own design at a Nottingham jewellers, I paid the bill. I was always happy to do so, and bought a lot of jewellery for her over the years, and here in Singapore the gems were much cheaper than in the UK.

I was less happy, however, when I walked through the 'Nothing to Declare' zone at Heathrow customs with the little buggers wrapped up in my pocket.

The power of sapphires and diamonds was not enough to hold us in Singapore, so we said goodbye to the impressive Travellers Palms that grew throughout the city, and we flew from Changi Airport back to KL and, then, to Kuantan on the east coast of Malaysia overlooking the South China Sea. The Hyatt Hotel had grounds lovingly cared for by dedicated gardeners who tended the palm trees and the hibiscus plants with their peach-coloured flowers that grew on the balconies of the guest rooms. Orchids were placed in the bathrooms. Outside, broad-winged buzzards whirled and wheeled above, while in the hotel's gardens small iridescent birds sucked nectar from various flowers through their long, thin beaks. Sunbirds with their black heads and green and yellow bodies flitted to and fro, paying special attention to the jacaranda trees. The market in Kuantan was disappointing after the ones we had seen in Singapore and KL; it sold mainly household items, cheap shirts, and various fruits – especially rambutans that were piled up in large mounds. There was, however, a good handicraft centre selling batik, Chinese silk prints, woven baskets, and kites. Essentially, Kuantan was a quiet resort with only a few hotels along the beach. The Hyatt was, therefore, a great place in which to relax.

A more adventurous pace of life was afforded by our journey to Lake Chini to visit an Orang Asli village in the interior. The Orang Asli are the indigenous people of mainland Malaysia and its oldest inhabitants. Today, they comprise a tiny proportion of the country's population and their way of life is completely different. To a tourist, their activities and the nature of their village may be of great interest but, in reality, many of the Orang Asli must contend with encroachments on their ancestral lands, and limited access to proper housing, medical facilities, and education. To reach the village, we had to go by boat against the current along the broad brown-coloured River Pahang, which flows to the sea. Somewhere in the interior, we left the Pahang and entered a small tributary that was full of silt that coloured the water a shade of yellow. The Chini River was much narrower, overhung by tall trees with thick buttresses, and enclosed by thick vegetation. We saw troops of monkeys high in the dark green canopy leaping from branch to branch with a certain insouciance. Just above the water flittered myriad butterflies and dragonflies all of them completing a complex choreography. Eventually, we entered Lake Chini with its covering of water lilies and made our way across it to the far shore, where we found the Orang Asli kampong. The kampong was no more than three wooden huts with palm leaf roofs that provided shelter for extended families. Apart from hosting occasional tourist visits, the people there made their living from fishing in the lake and hunting in the jungle. In the tangled confines of the jungle, the hunters use long blowpipes with poison-tipped darts. Visitors to the kampong are invited to have a go using ordinary darts. Invariably, such attempts rarely hit the target set up in the village's enclosure, whereas the Orang Asli hit it every time.

Back at the Hyatt and once again comfortably embraced by the trappings of modern life, Linda and I enjoyed walking along the beach and watching the sampans fishing offshore. On the other side of a nearby headland was a simple beach bar where Linda and I would often have lunch. If we timed the tide badly, we had to wade back across the headland to our own beach. We watched the pretend Olympic opening ceremony put on by the hotel to mark the Olympic Games taking place in Seoul, and we even won medals in the 'Mini-Olympics' for our efforts in the tug of war competition, where I suspect the staff graciously let the guests win. Exhausted or elated, we could always refresh ourselves with a drink on the sampan that the hotel had converted to a bar in its grounds. What made our stay at the hotel even more delightful was Terry Shine. Terry was there with his wife; by trade he was a postman, by nature he was a saint. It's an old cliché about Germans, sun loungers and beach towels, but in the case of the Hyatt, true. Two early rising German tourists were bagging the best positions around the pool for themselves and their friends, leaving some others without a sun lounger at all. Terry single-handedly thwarted them. If the Germans thought they were up early, Terry's postman definition of early beat them to it comfortably. Linda and I, several elderly couples, and assorted odds and ends were the beneficiaries of Terry's dawn generosity! When drinks had run out in our respective hotel room minibars, Terry and I would walk to a small shop two kilometres or so from the Hyatt and return with our rucksacks full of fresh supplies. Sometimes, I saw Terry from our first-floor room as he was walking through the gardens, and I would throw down a can of beer to him from Mike's (balcony) Bar.

All too soon, it was time for us to leave Kuantan and fly west to Penang Island on the Straits of Malacca where we stayed at the Golden Sands Hotel on Batu Ferringhi beach. The capital of the island, George Town, was full of the usual mopeds and scooters that could occasionally feel threatening when on foot. I hired a car and never gave them another thought after that! We drove to the Snake Temple where dozens of snakes live inside. Some are venomous but all of them are well-fed and practically out of their tiny minds on incense burned within the temple. The moped drivers are a greater danger to visitors than these particular snakes. Wat Chayamangkalaram is a Buddhist temple housing one of the world's largest reclining Buddhas; the locals call it the Sleeping Buddha, but it actually represents the Buddha at his death. Behind the enormous statue are lots of niches containing the ashes of believers. Just as impressive is the Chinese Kek Lok Si Temple with its incredible stupa of several floors with a golden roof. The complex contains countless images of the Buddha, and many carvings, sculptures and murals in its halls, pagodas, and archways. It is arguably the most ornate and beautiful temple in the whole of Malaysia. Less than four kilometres from the temple is Penang Hill Station that can be reached by funicular railway. At the top of the hill was a small shop selling snacks and drinks, and boasting excellent views of the city and the sea beyond it.

More relaxing and certainly less tiring than walking around all these temples was Batu Ferringhi beach by our hotel. Its shallow clear waters hosted jet skiing, windsurfing, and parascending, while its white sands held impromptu volleyball games. Outside the Golden Sands Hotel, we often encountered a delightful elderly gentleman with his trishaw on which he took tourists around the island. His vehicle was adorned with numerous flags representing the many nationalities to which he catered. It was not the most comfortable ride for trishaws are more suitable for use by Malays; it was normally a tight squeeze to get two British bottoms onto the seat. There were also goats that trotted in front of the hotels along the beach. They might soon have been for the pot; who knows? More permanent were the shops near the hotel selling good quality but imitation Lacoste T-shirts. We restocked the minibar in our room not with the hotel's offerings, but those from Lim Kuan Joo, an English-speaking Chinese gentleman who ran a general grocery shop. Laundry was similarly cheaper outside the hotel, and Linda and I used 'Boey' who returned our clothes in immaculate condition. On the fringe of Batu Ferringhi beach were some 'jungle' walks where we were assured there was no danger of encountering snakes. Indeed, the only snakes we saw were in the possession of snake charmers who roamed the beach and, on one occasion, a group of teenagers who had one tied to a leash as if taking it for a walk.

The time I spent in Malaysia was so good, it seems impolite, even churlish, to abandon the Far East now simply in the service of chronological exactitude. Rather, I propose to follow the thread of the journey so far and stay in the Far East. I will deal with Cuba and Mexico and, finally, India at a later stage. Writing about India last in the series of holidays with Linda is appropriate for it was very nearly the last holiday we ever took, in the sense that we came within a reasonable chance of being killed there.

Chapter Seven: Hong Kong and its 'Environs'

In the approximate eighteen months between early 1995 and the summer of 1996, Linda and I were fortunate to visit Hong Kong on three occasions, while it was still a British colony. Each time, we combined Hong Kong with other countries in its environs, such as China, Thailand, Malaysia, and less convincingly in terms of geography, Sri Lanka.

Unusually for us, we enjoyed good luck on our 747 British Airways flight to China in that there were only about forty of us on board - not many tourists were venturing to Beijing in December 1994. Linda and I each had a whole row of seats on which to crash out, surfacing now and again to summon a reasonably good selection of French wines from the less than overburden attendants. Except for our last full day in Beijing, when it snowed, our week in China was greeted with clear and sunny skies, but temperatures occasionally getting as low as -10 Celsius. Beijing and the surrounding area are very flat but the city itself is one huge urban sprawl with very little of architectural interest among the modern buildings. The city has *four* massive ring roads along the side of which are wide routes entirely given to the use of cyclists. The population of Beijing then was eleven million and there were eight million bicycles. To cross an eight-lane highway - four of which are for bicycles - you advance a few yards, stop, let the cars go past you, advance a few yards, stop, let the cycles go past you, and hope.

Around Tiananmen Square where so many Chinese were killed by the army in 1989, there is now no trace of their deaths. The Chinese like to visit their major attractions as much as foreigners do and, even in the winter, Linda and I were easily outnumbered by local people. In the square, we occasionally collected a curious glance from locals. However, everywhere in the square, including the underpasses, there were uniformed soldiers who seemed uninterested in us and somewhat ill at ease with their own people. The rate of change in the country was phenomenal, and we were as likely to find shops selling sweet drinks squeezed from sugar cane with a primitive mangle-like machine as shops selling cellular telephones.

In the north of the square is an entrance to the Imperial Palace, or the Forbidden City. The grandeur of the buildings and the elegance and simplicity of their designs, especially the sloping roofs with their delicate arrangements of coloured tiles and decorations, were evident from the moment we entered the complex. Only the Emperor was allowed to wear or use yellow, which symbolised his position as the Son of Heaven, and accordingly there are a lot of yellow roof tiles in the Palace complex. As we left the palace, close to sunset, we saw the last rays of the sun striking the yellow tiles on the temple roofs so that they shone like gold.

In contrast to the immense wealth, privilege, and security that the Forbidden City symbolised for centuries, the streets of Beijing offered a more down-to-earth view. We saw grimy self-employed men selling baked sweet potatoes to passers-by from coal-fired converted oil drums, which were mounted on old, rusty bicycles and which served as a kind of brazier. We watched old men by the side of the road under the shelter of some trees set up impromptu cycle repair 'stops.' They laid out their few tools and offered to fix anyone's puncture or mechanical problems. Short, old ladies with weathered faces patrolled a small area of pavement, taking a small fee from each cyclist to look after their bike while they were in work or shopping - these cycle parks were all over the place. Old women are employed to wave red flags on long bamboo poles from the safety of the pavement in the faces of the hordes of cyclists to get them to stop when the traffic lights turn to red; but not everyone obeys. We saw lots of people in uniform, but a good many were civilians, we learned later, who for reasons of local fashion just happened to be wearing long, green, padded coats that looked like army-issue. We marvelled at just what a human being could transport using a two-wheeled bicycle and especially a three-wheeler with a kind of platform at the back. We took our hats off to the man whom we witnessed cycling along with a three-piece suite on the back of his trike, but later were completely lost in admiration for another who was transporting *two* three-piece suites. The name of one of the most popular bicycles was the 'Flying Pigeon.' What can you say to that?

Another day we visited the Temple of Heaven where the Emperor used to pray for a good harvest and, later, we travelled to the outskirts of Beijing to see the Summer Palace. This is a large complex with administrative, religious, and entertainment quarters, including a three-storey Peking Opera stage where shows were put on for the exclusive enjoyment of one of the Empresses, a certain Chi Xi. The site contains a very large man-made lake, which was completely frozen so that groups of Chinese families were out on it towing their children on makeshift sleds, and some men were boring holes in the ice to go fishing.

Undoubtedly, however, the highlight of our stay in Beijing was the trip 125 kilometres northeast of the capital, to one of the restored sections of the Great Wall at Badaling. Although we had seen it before in countless photographs and TV programmes, nothing prepared us for the breathtaking splendour of the Wall's sheer physical achievement in following the sharp contours of the steep and ragged mountain terrain. The entrance and the part of the

Wall close to it were rather crowded so we headed north for quite some time, the Wall itself always climbing steeply to follow the exact shape of the mountains, until we were more or less on our own and we had reached that part of the Great Wall where it reverts to a ruin once more. From this spot, we could see the Wall striding across several valleys, like some gigantic serpent unfurling its coils along the peaks of the hills. It was one of the most magnificent sights I have ever been privileged to see. That night, as we relaxed back in our hotel foyer, listening to classical singing and piano-playing, we both marvelled how any ancient civilisation could have built such a structure along one localised range of mountains, never mind over thousands of kilometres of mountains.

We spent an enjoyable but short time in Beijing and then flew to Xian, the walled city that was the start of the Silk Road in ancient times. A few miles outside Xian is the site of the Terracotta Army. The individual members of the army really are individuals, and differ in height, shape, function, hair styles and facial features, and are all life-size. Touring the three covered pits that are substantially excavated and open to the public was again one of those great joys and privileges. However, if we thought that Xian itself would be an anti-climax for the next two days, we were wrong. The city is even more hustle and bustle than Beijing with over three million people living within the walled part of the city - a few square kilometres in area. Our hotel was right opposite the hugely impressive Bell Tower whose bell used to be rung to sound the closing of the city's gates for the night. The walls themselves are incredible; very tall and thick and so wide at the top that you could easily have three lanes of traffic driving along it. We walked most of its length on payment of a few pence, and it afforded excellent views of the packed and narrow streets and parks, where old men met to gamble with cards. Occasionally, below us in small grassy areas, we saw a few people practising Tai Chi in their slow and dignified fashion. Close to the Drum Tower, another ancient monument used to signal the opening and closing of the gates, one can still find the descendants of Genghis Khan who conquered the area centuries ago. They are Muslim and live in the so-called Muslim Quarter. Here the streets are especially narrow and bedecked with shops selling all kinds of food and other products. All the meat is hung up in the open air, including in summer when the temperature is around thirty Celsius rather than the minus eight it was on the day we were there. We saw parts of animals and types of creatures few people from the UK would possibly want to eat; yet here, they were often considered delicacies. It was in this Quarter close to one of the city gates that I selected some 'chops' or stamps made from soapstone which were carved by a Muslim woman who had great dexterity and even more charm. I warmed myself over a small round brazier in the biting cold and watched this woman carve into the base of two chops our respective names in both English and Chinese. She turned the whole thing into an experience rather than a commercial transaction. It was all too easy to forget that this women and her fellow Muslims were persecuted and discriminated against in China. We left for much warmer climes in the shape of Hong Kong.

The one thing I knew about landing at Hong Kong's Kai Tak Airport was that it is an event in itself, provided you are sat on the *right-hand* side of the plane. Pilots had to be specially trained to land at Kai Tak. The initial approach was close to hills on Kowloon side, and then pilots had to locate a large red and black checkerboard on Checkerboard Hill. Planes were aimed directly at the board and would then turn sharply to the right and descend steeply to land on runway thirteen. That turn was known as 'The Kai Tak Heart Attack Approach.' On your left, there would now be rugged terrain, but on your right were tall buildings that appeared to be within touching distance of the tip of the right wing. Within a few seconds, the plane has lost height so that much of those tall buildings are now *above* the wing tip. In addition, you suddenly realize that there are people in these buildings; you are so close that you can see them through their windows, you can see them get up from the dinner table, you can wave at them. Finally, the plane feels as if it has dropped out of the sky completely, before it hits the runway and pulls up without shooting into the sea. Very impressive! Later, when we were in Kowloon looking for designer outlets, huge jets would flash past overhead barely clearing the tops of the buildings. Our hotel, the Excelsior, had both an excellent view of Hong Kong Harbour and the landing flight path of the planes. When we came back to the hotel at night or when we awoke first thing in the morning, we would enjoy both views, but the landings and the sight of planes flashing past the rows of buildings and getting steadily lower and lower, as if the runway were a walkway attached to the fifteenth floor of one of them, never ceased to fascinate.

Our first full day, sunny and very warm, was spent at Stanley Market and at Aberdeen Harbour where we hired a small sampan for ourselves and toured the harbour in which can still be found a few families living on old junks. The bus journey to get there was itself an enjoyable event, as the double decker scuttled along providing some spectacular views of the island. Indeed, one of our great delights was to travel on public transport, especially the old trams that trundled along the central and flat part of Hong Kong Island. It rained on and off for the remainder of our time in the city and the trams offered a dry but ever-changing vantage point simply to view the city and its people. We also took the cog railway up The Peak - in fact, we went twice, by night and by day - in order to view Hong Kong's skyscrapers and the huge Christmas messages on the buildings along the harbour front in Kowloon. The illuminations were spectacular and, at times, we could see some of the skyscrapers emerging out of the low clouds and mists. Trips on the Star Ferries across the harbour were another delight and offered fantastic views.

We visited the Jade Market where many local people buy all different pieces and kinds of jade, which is very important in Chinese culture. Linda got some jade and some pearls from there. We also saw the Bird Market, where locals make purchases of caged singing birds, or take their own birds along in their elaborate wicker cages with their tiny enamelled drinking and feeding jars to introduce them to other birds in the hope that this will improve their singing, or simply to allow other bird owners to admire their possessions. Owners were also there to buy plastic bags of live grasshoppers, which they fed individually to their captive birds with chopsticks.

We spent Christmas Eve at Planet Hollywood with Liz and Ian Aston, two great friends who had flown out to Hong Kong for a ten-day holiday to coincide with some of our visit. It was, as you might expect, a big party atmosphere and we were still covered in comical hats and long strands of multi-coloured streamers when we got back to the foyer of our friends' hotel, where a few people thought we were quite mad. Christmas Day lunch we ate off banana leaves at a restaurant close to our hotel, while in the evening we had an Indian meal at a place near the harbour-front with a wonderful view of all the buildings and illuminations. We had a brief, hectic, but very enjoyable time in Hong Kong and left with many purchases of new clothes.

The transfer to Thailand went off fine, but Bangkok now seemed to have more traffic than ever. However, when we got to Cha-am, about 160 kilometres south of the capital on the Gulf of Thailand, we had no need ever again to give any thought to such matters. The place was like an oasis where we could simply rest in the sun - unwaveringly thirty-three degrees Celsius during the day all the time we were there -and recover from the exertions of our tours in China and Hong Kong. Accordingly, save for walks along the wonderful beach, we never left the hotel grounds for the week we were there.

The Regent Hotel had a large choice of places to eat, three pools, and extensive and very lovely grounds, including a fishing lake and cycle paths. However, we became friendly with a group of local women who ran a small beach café, selling drinks and Thai massages. We started having a few drinks there - Linda had a massage - and soon they were giving us free fruits and ornate sea shells along with the Cokes and Singha beers that we bought. The proprietors operated an honesty policy; you helped yourself to beers from the fridge and settled up later according to the number of bottles on your table. It had transformed itself into a Mike's Bar. Next to it were a few places that cooked proper meals, so we started eating on the beach, especially at night, sat on rustic bamboo chairs at bamboo tables and served by delightfully friendly and attentive Thai people who could apparently work miracles with their primitive cooking equipment. Mind you, having such fresh fish and huge tiger prawns to work with certainly helped. A fleet of small fishing boats, whose moorings were right beside the beach outlets, delivered them fresh each day.

Other than such excursions, we did very little and loved every minute of it. On New Year's Eve there was a gala night put on by the hotel. The food was okay, but the effort put into the decorations, the fireworks display, and the concern by the staff that the guests should have a good time was most impressive. But at around US$90 for a bottle of champagne we contented ourselves with celebrating the New Year with something less expensive. However, when we left the gala evening, we were able to enjoy a small amount of very good brandy from our duty-free supplies as we sat on our balcony and listened to the South China Sea lapping away beneath us. Not a bad way to see in the New Year, I thought to myself at the time.

In August and September 1995, we returned to Hong Kong and combined it with a journey through Sri Lanka. Unfortunately, Linda was sick on the Cathay Pacific flight and still felt rather unwell as we waited patiently in a large queue to clear immigration. Suddenly, a lady and her daughter from Taipei, who realized Linda was unwell, called for an official and we were marched off to the immigration office where Linda could sit down. After a few minutes we were clear to enter. The lady told us that a few weeks earlier someone had died of a heart attack waiting in the humidity for a long while to clear immigration. Once again, we stayed at the Excelsior Hotel in a harbour view room to which was delivered a giant basket of fruit from Michelle, a former student of mine whom I'd arranged to meet.

Sunday morning was spent with Michelle at a dim sum restaurant where we had several delightful small dishes and jasmine flavoured Chinese tea. Then we went shopping at various places, including the Lanes and Mongkok, where we toured the market, sheltering from the occasional very sharp monsoon rain. At the Ocean Terminal Shopping Plaza in Episode, Linda bought a blue silk jacket at a ridiculously low price. We ate dinner at the top of the Hopewell Tower in 'Revolving 66,' which strangely is on the 62nd floor. Even so, it was a marvellous panorama of night-time Hong Kong and all three of us thoroughly enjoyed our pepper steaks.

The next day, Monday 28th August, was a bank holiday and thousands of Filipino women, who act as maids and nannies to rich inhabitants of Hong Kong, were out in force around the Bank of China enjoying a rare day off. They were gathered in small groups to chat, to have their hair done, and to have their nails attended to by other Filipino women. We took the 'tram' to the Peak where we had a light but excellent meal and watched the planes coming in to land. As usual we took the bus, or 'rodeo ride' as the bumpy road would better suggest, back to Central where we explored the Lanes, bought some film, and where I visited the FCC - Foreign Correspondents Club. In the evening, we met some friends, Katie and Ann-Marie, for drinks in the Dickens Bar at our hotel and then had dinner with them at the LRC - Ladies Recreational Club - in Mid-Levels where only women are allowed to be full members and where following a divorce, the woman decides whether her former partner can retain his associate membership of the club. We had no idea as we left the LRC that typhoon 'Kent' was on its way.

Next morning, we were greeted with typhoon warning level three and some doubts about our evening departure to Sri Lanka via Bangkok. We went off to the Bird Market and then lunched at La Cité in Pacific Plaza with views onto a huge pristinely clean marbled concourse during which typhoon warning level eight was hoisted at one o'clock. Accordingly, all the shops and offices began to close to give people time to get home before public transport stopped. We took the MTR (underground) back to Causeway Bay where even Giordano's had closed. It takes a typhoon to stop shopping in Hong Kong. Despite the worsening rain and wind, we were taken to the airport at five o'clock and were ready to take off at the correct time, though we had to don the most ridiculous plastic Macs to get from the terminal to the bus and from bus to plane. Then the Air Lanka pilot waited over an hour while conditions got even worse - all other flights were either delayed or cancelled - but our chap just decided to go. And go he did. We tore down the runway in the middle of this advancing typhoon and took off. It was rather bumpy for a while and then it was just like a normal flight, except for the Chinese passengers on board. They were 'mules' taking goods for sale in Bangkok and bringing back Thai goods for sale in China - all for an entrepreneur. Most of them had never flown before - the Chinese government restricted the number of external flights they could take – and, consequently, they did not know how to behave on board. They frequently switched seats, hauling their incredibly heavy and voluminous cabin luggage with them as they did so. They tried to get air blowing on their faces even though this make of plane had no individual nozzles above the seats. Moreover, they could not understand a single word said to them, so for food and drink all they could do was point. One man came across a tooth pick in his meal tray pack and thought it was a Western implement for eating his food. Accordingly, he used it to spear his bread role and to turn it around as he ate it. Finally, as the plane landed at Bangkok Airport, they were out of their seats and crowded around the exit doors even as the plane was still on the runway. The flight attendants just let them get on with it.

On our first full day in Colombo, we visited a government appointed craft shop, *Laksala*, which was something out of the 1950s - old wooden and glass displays and lots of bureaucracy. Even so, it was a charming place and one delightful assistant helped Linda to buy some cornflower blue sapphires. Back at the hotel, I met Mervyn our Sri Lankan guide on the tour of the island we were about to take. We got on so well that Mervyn was decided from the start to ensure that Linda and I were well-looked after on the tour. And that's exactly how it turned out.

The tour departed at seven o'clock the following morning, and started as it meant to go on with yet more early starts. In our ten-seat minibus were only our driver, Sunil, from time-to-time Mervyn, and Richard and Michele with whom we got on very well. There were another three buses in our party; one with four and the other two with six passengers. On the way to Anuradhapura in the north, we passed all sorts of plantations - coconut, rubber, pineapple, mango, tobacco - and saw all manner of birds, as well as many old-fashioned adverts for Rinso ('washes even whiter') and 'Lifebuoy for Health.' All the women were in saris and the men in sarongs and shirts, often with no shoes. And lots of activity - people working in the rice fields, dehusking coconuts, tending the working elephants with the steel chains and bells around their necks, bathing them in the river shallows and women doing their washing there. Along the dusty roads, the fruit stalls were almost overwhelmed with produce. We learnt how to tell which were the freshest pineapples. They are cut originally with long stalks and obviously look freshly cut; but each day the stallholder must cut a little more off the stalk to make the fruit still look freshly cut. So short stalks equal less fresh fruit. Amongst all the human activities were a few that seemed characteristic of a third world location; for example, we saw an impromptu 'car wash' spring up as a few young men simply pushed their vehicle into a shallow part of the river and proceeded to clean it vigorously. Along another part of the river where the water was even lower, men were taking sand from the partially exposed river bed and carrying it up the bank for sale to builders.

Anuradhapura was the first capital of the island and one of the most ancient sites associated with the emergence of Buddhism in Sri Lanka and it has many temples in the form of dagobas, monks' quarters and bathing pools. Close to one temple is a sacred Bo tree said to be several thousand years old. Each year the main dagobas are whitewashed from top to toe to prepare for the May celebrations - the Buddha was born, achieved enlightenment, and died during the full moon in May. There is also on site an old but highly effective system for water use and preservation in which the first 'tank' is used for drinking, the next connected tank for bathing, and the third for washing clothes.

After touring the ancient site at Anuradhapura, we drove to Sigiriya Village, arriving around six o'clock. Our part of the village was laid out as a series of 'huts' around a small paddy field - the place was comfortable and had character, and more importantly it also had Kandula a male twenty-five-year-old elephant who took guests for rides through the surrounding bush country. Linda and I fed him the next morning with a supply of bananas we took from the breakfast table. The paddy field also had snakes, one of which was seen just sticking its head out of a pool right by the entrance to one of the huts. We also saw another in front of reception, which was obviously venomous, judging by the decidedly gingerly fashion in which one of the drivers was trying to shift it away from his car.

Later, near the palace complex at Polonnaruwa, we saw bee-eaters, cormorants, Brahmin kites, yellow and white breasted kingfishers, a paradise flycatcher, parrots swooping over fields to take the seed heads of cut rice, and even a mongoose and a water monitor with its powerful and heavy tail. En route to Polonnaruwa, we saw so many Morris Minors in quite good condition that we thought this was the vehicle paradise where all such cars went on their 'retirement.' The ancient city itself was full of intricate carvings, especially of elephants, but the best part of the site by far were the carvings of the four Buddhas modelled out of a single piece of rock. The workmanship was serene.

Fed Kandula his bananas, and then we set off to climb Lion Rock, which is a huge, roughly circular, ochre-coloured edifice that rises almost vertically from the surrounding plain. The last half of the route is not for the faint-hearted. We walked along a metal gangway stuck to the side of the rock by a few rather old-looking and rusty bolts - at times the metal 'planks' beneath our feet swayed and creaked. Then, we had to climb a distinctly rickety spiral staircase to view the few remaining but beautiful fifth century frescoes. Finally, on the last pitch, we clung to a narrow and exceptionally steep gangway to get to the summit. It was worse coming down than going up, since on the way down we felt as if one slip would catapult us over the rail and into the void. But the views from the summit of Sigiriya Rock and from the smaller elephant rock of the surrounding countryside were fantastic.

As we left later that day for Kandy, we called at a small house of some local people close to Sigiriya Village, where a lady demonstrated how they wove palms for roof material, made rice and coconut oil for cooking, ground chillies - and all of this done with great patience and even more humour as she demonstrated the common-place to our first world, unbelieving eyes. We gave the children lollipops and pens and then the adults wanted some too, all accompanied by warm laughter and gentle manners. At the Hotel Suisse in Kandy, Lord Mountbatten's old Second World War HQ, the doors had elephant-shaped knockers and the waiters asked you if you preferred a small or medium gin in your gin and tonic. The Suisse is now an example of faded imperial grandeur and a death-trap of mosquitoes in the public areas, but it is very close to the scenic lake and a short walk from the town centre.

We set off the next day for the elephant orphanage at Pinnawala where there were sixty or more animals, some nine of which were born at the sanctuary. The first one we saw was a huge, low-slung tusker - Rajah - tethered to a palm tree and who had been shot and blinded, although the sight was said to be returning in one eye. The animal had taken to one mahout in particular who tended to him daily. The rest of the herd was arrayed before us along open ground in small 'family' groupings with a few mahouts in attendance. The highlight of the trip, however, came an hour or so later as the elephants, led by the matriarch with a mahout on her back, filed down a track to the river. As they approached us, we could hear their cries and could smell their musty odours. We saw the dust rising beneath their thick, sure feet as they plunged excitedly off the dirt track and into the blissful river where attentive mahouts washed each animal in turn. Here they bathed and submerged themselves, with trunk just emerging above the river like a periscope. Of course, they held us spell-bound, and it was not hard to gain the feeling that elephants really love to play around in water. For such large animals, they were incredibly sure-footed and confident even in the relatively fast flowing centre of the river, which they reached by walking across scattered shoals of gently protruding flat rocks. Here and there, mahouts could be seen giving commands to the older elephants to alter their position as they were scrubbed, or else the men - clad only in a loin cloth - took a breather simply perched on the shoulder of a luxuriating beast, which was enjoying the flow and touch of the waters. It was a scene that Linda and I will never forget.

We got up very early the next morning and walked along the lake into Kandy, but even at seven a.m. the roads were busy and there were loads of school children in their neat white and blue uniforms making their way to lessons. Many people wished us 'good morning' as we strolled along, including one man who called to us from a high balcony overlooking the lake. At nine o'clock, we began the journey and the climb up into the Hill Country to Nuwara Eliya, stopping en route at the Glenloch Tea Plantation at Katukitula. In the tea growing Hill Country, the landscape is a patchwork quilt of rows of metre-high tea bushes, some of which are 125 years old, typically grown across steep slopes along which low cloud and mists descend. It is cold by Sri Lankan standards, and often wet, and the locals wear thick clothing. Linda and I had romantic ideas of happy women picking tea in bright sunshine and wearing even more brightly coloured clothes, but the reality was much more sombre and it certainly looked like hard and uncomfortable work. The best tea is grown on the steepest and highest slopes, which are frequently cut by deep fissures and waterfalls. Each plantation was laid out in a very orderly fashion with steps cut into the hillsides so that the pickers can get to the bushes and with signs erected to show ownership, middle or high division, date of last pruning of the bushes, and so forth. The leaves can be picked every seven days, and since the pickers are all women, who must pick a minimum of twenty-five kilos per day, the plantation companies supply crèches and some rudimentary form of housing for families. The tea factories themselves can turn leaves into various qualities of tea ready for drinking within twenty-four hours of picking. We saw the seven stages that the leaves go through - which is done with basic 1920s-style machinery or by hand and we sampled some of the BOPF variety (Broken Orange Pekoe Fanings) as well as buying some to take home.

At the Hill Club in Nuwara Eliya, where we took lunch, Mervyn had arranged for Linda and I to have the North Suite, which happened to be the best set of rooms in the place, and Richard and Michele had one of the south-facing suites. The Club still operated in some ways as if it were the 1890s - there was still a reading/library room, a Ladies lounge, a billiards room (where a decent level of silence is obligatory), a Gentlemen's-only bar as well as a mixed bar, and a women's entrance (the latter now no longer in use), and everyone must dress up for the silver-service, candle-lit dinner after which one takes coffee (and cigars) in the reading room next to the log fire. On the heavily wood panelled walls were plaques denoting former club secretaries and chairmen, and portraits of the Queen and Churchill. Hot water bottles were delivered to our room just before we retired. Here, there was no automatic wake-up call on a slick telephone; a uniformed porter knocked on the door at the appointed time.

In the morning, we made the long and twisting descent through the tea-growing region from Nuwara Eliya to our ultimate destination, Yala Safari Beach Hotel. Most of the party went directly to the hotel after lunch, but a small number of us were driven in a large open top truck to Bundala Game Park where we saw a great many animals - pointed and open-billed storks, pelicans, cormorants, large grey heron, sandpipers, serpent eagle, ibis, Indian rollers, egrets, peacocks and hens, kingfishers, mongoose, deer, fox, hare, various species of monkeys, a positive profusion of crocodiles lying 'doggo' around the shallow banks of the lagoons, cattle, a craite snake (deadly venomous), wild boar, and literally last (when we had just about given up hope of ever seeing them in the wild), elephant. We saw five of the twenty-five or so resident in the park, and at one point as we drove slowly down a narrow track with thick thorny bushes hemming us in on either side, a juvenile elephant suddenly burst through the bush and charged the vehicle. As the driver swiftly rammed the truck into reverse, Linda and I at the front of the open-topped platform first saw the animal briefly gain on us while trumpeting loudly, and then in the next instant, we saw it obviously decide against its present course of action and turn tail and run away. It was all over in a few seconds, but what excitement! Our tour of the park ended right at the ocean side, where on a shallow cliff we looked down on the makeshift huts and the small skiffs of a small group of fisherman who used the southern tip of Yala as a base from which to work, before returning to their villages elsewhere on the island at the end of the fishing season.

Our excellent and very friendly guide, Mervyn Karunaratne, was not originally going to accompany the tour because he wished to attend the funeral of the two sons of a neighbour killed in their patrol vessel by the Tamil Tigers just before we arrived in Sri Lanka. As it turned out, he did have to guide the tour and his first act on leaving the hotel in Colombo was to stop for a brief while at a church so that he could make his own private prayers for those who had died. That civil war was still raging while we were in Sri Lanka, but where we went it never impinged on our experience; yet in other parts of the island people were being killed. Now, on the final leg of the tour, we visited Galle. En route, we passed a stunning procession of bands, ceremonial elephants, and people dressed in marvellous costumes to mark the Buddhist national holiday of the Full Moon. The other curious thing about the day - apart from the stilt fishermen who were really there to pick up tourist money rather than to fish - was the fact that the group never really said goodbye to one another. Before we knew it, after leaving Galle the various vehicles were heading off to different beach hotels or back to Colombo. Fortunately, Mervyn was in our vehicle and so we said goodbye to him and to our driver, Sunil, at the Bayroo Beach Hotel after what had been a magnificent tour of the island in the midst of very enjoyable company, not least the various Sri Lankans themselves whom we met briefly along the way.

We found to our delight that we had been allocated a superior room at the hotel, even though we had not requested nor paid for one. It had a very restful view of the hotel gardens and the beach, and we could often hear the waves of the Indian Ocean crashing upon the nearby reef as Linda and I sipped our drinks on the hotel room balcony. As ever, 'Mike's Bar' was always open for business on the balcony. Chipmunk-like creatures also came to the balcony to take nuts directly from our fingers, and it also served as a kind of studio for Linda who sometimes sat on the balcony and drew some of the surrounding scenes or else caught them in watercolours.

We had our fair share of water in other ways, for although it was generally very hot and sunny, there were occasional tropical downpours. Sometimes we would swim in the pool and watch everyone else scurrying for cover, or we would simply order another beer from whatever beach side bar we were frequenting and huddle a little closer under the palm covers until the rain storm had stopped - generally after only ten or so minutes. Once or twice at sunset, we were still swimming in the pool and, later, we would sometimes stroll in the gardens and study the night sky filled with bright stars.

While the beach immediately in front of the hotel had rather coarse sand, there was a lengthy stretch of reef, which at low tide offered wonderful views of the hotel and the coastline. Around one headland was a smaller hotel where some of the people from the tour were staying, and we occasionally visited them until they had to leave for home. Around the other headland was a magnificently long and striking beach made of fine white sand, along which were some more hotels and small rustic places to eat and drink. Our favourite small bar turned out to be the 'Sun Flower' where, during the course of our two weeks at the beach, we became 'regulars', and soon got into conversation with the charming people who ran it. They served decent beer in large bottles and supplied the Styrofoam holders to keep it cold. The Sun Flower became the daytime Mike's Bar and, sometimes, the place revealed its own land monitor that we would watch as it sniffed around the sand before locating and digging out small crabs to eat. The beach also had occasional beggars, usually disabled in some way and often piteous to behold, and a decent number of men and women who walked endlessly along the beach each day or else camped just by the hotel perimeters and who tried to sell tourists anything from shells, fruit, cigarettes, carvings, and clothes. But there was never once a sense that Linda and I were being 'pressurised' by any of them. They never pursued us, nor gave us an aggressive sales pitch. In fact, they were always unfailingly polite, always took 'no' for an answer, and were a delight to deal with when we were interested in buying anything from them. Indeed, on most days, I used to buy a few bananas from an old lady a little way from the hotel en route to the Sun Flower - so much so that even if I didn't want to buy anything, she always waved to me to go over and talk to her. One day, I took three bananas from her and gave her some coins and walked off, only to find her running after me and pressing more fruit upon me since I had 'overpaid' her it would appear. Our brief, but highly animated, conversations were always rather odd since she spoke no English and I spoke no Sinhalese beyond please and thank you. Yet, it was a little ritual to which I looked forward each day.

Our hotel was very comfortable, so much so that the island's ruling political elite in the form of its prime minister, Mrs Bandaranaike and her daughter and son and respective families were staying briefly at the hotel, as they do quite frequently, we were told. Security seemed distinctly low key to say the least, given that the Tamil Tigers had vowed to kill them. One day, I found the telephone and address book of Bandaranaike's private secretary on a table in the foyer, which contained all manner of information the Tigers would have been pleased to receive. I returned it sharpish to some official. When the now frail Mrs Bandaranaike was accompanied to the water's edge, she would dip her feet in the ocean while still fully clad in a magnificent sari. Close by there were only two unarmed local police officers on duty. They seemed to ignore tourists and to give some perfunctory attention to the local people, some of whom were not allowed to walk past the prime minister, and some of whom were. When the prime minister and the other VIPs were inside the grounds of the hotel, these two officers usually took cover under a shady tree close to the headland where they enjoyed a quiet smoke beneath the branches. Sometimes, we saw them paddling in the sea. Later, one of the waiters told us that posing as local tourists were some plain clothes police officers. While this party was in residence, there was a certain frisson around the place as all we westerners, seeing on the TV almost daily reports of Tamil Tigers being killed or else killing members of the army, wondered whether there would be some kind of attack at the hotel.

However, as far as I was concerned, the real star in and around the hotel was not any member of the Sri Lankan political elite, it was Menika, a thirty-year-old female elephant who came to the hotel gardens twice a week to beguile everyone who saw her. I always knew when she was on her way. Long before I saw her mahout with his pointed metal rod that he used to signal commands, I could hear the melodic sound of Menika's bell hanging from her neck, which struck rhythmically in time to her elegantly swaying but deliberate gait. This was a big star and she always held centre stage; when Menika arrived, people stopped swimming or reading or lazing around and they went over to her. To touch her, to ride on her back, to be sprayed with water from her trunk, to be picked up by that same trunk and carted around as if humans were made of straw, and simply to listen to the deep sonorous sounds that welled up from inside her – all were marvellous. Menika lifted Linda in her trunk and later did the same for me. Linda described it as being firmly but safely held with just enough pressure. When the mahout had collected some money and signalled to Menika that she should leave, she would amble along the beach, with the chime of her bell fast receding. It felt to me as if the best part of the day had come and gone.

The food at the hotel was decent enough but always a buffet style affair. Even so, the special orders that Linda requested of jumbo prawns were magnificent, while the afternoon teas by the pool were very relaxing. Most evenings there was some entertainment in the hotel, but we tried to avoid the 'Raindrops' combo whenever they flitted from table to table with their kitsch musical offerings. Although we didn't especially like the musical entertainment, we were often quietly amused by the descriptions of the food available, which included scotch borath, grepe juice, cheesse, harsh browns and, on a different topic, the availability on the TV of Kricket. Goodness knows how our attempts at Sinhalese would have turned out.

I often walked down a lane outside the hotel to a 'shop' that was little more than a shack where I could buy some nuts, bottles of water and Coke to mix with our own bottle of Barcardi kept at Mike's Bar. The prices were ridiculously cheap *and* there was money back on the Coke bottles. At the shop, I saw workmen buying single cigarettes, bullocks pulling carts, and at the same time a smart businessman using a mobile phone. When we ran out of Barcardi, I set off, in the heat of the day, to find the one 'off licence' in the whole district that sold alcohol, which I was told was in the next village two kilometres away. It was in the next village but it was five kilometres away. But what a walk, and how friendly the people were that I met on my way, though doubtless they thought I was mad to be walking rather than riding in a taxi. On the way back, I called at another of these shacks that are the Sri Lankan equivalent of the corner shop to buy a cool drink. I got talking to the owner about cricket and he told me that the Pakistani team were not popular in his country. Matters turned brighter when I mentioned that I had seen the great Sri Lankan cricketer, Aravinda de Silva, playing in England. No sooner were those words out of my mouth than he called in his cousins from the rear of his shop and also some passing workmen, and told them all that I had seen the great man himself playing for Kent over the English summer. On such a happy note, I left the Pearl of the Orient. A few months later, Linda and I returned to Hong Kong for the third and last time, sharing the city excursion with a holiday in Sabah, part of Malaysia situated on the island of Borneo.

In September 1996, we again stayed at the Excelsior Hotel. Our few days in Hong Kong involved the usual round of sightseeing, shopping, and dining out. We revisited a number of old favourites, such as the Peak with its stunning views of Hong Kong Island; Stanley Market where in the early morning, before the coach loads of tourists arrive, it is still possible to stroll through the narrow lanes and to search out good bargains in a relaxed manner; the Regent Hotel on Kowloon side from whose coffee shop one can marvel at the number and variety of boats passing through the harbour; and, of course, the Star Ferries themselves that ply every few minutes across the harbour managing to resist the strong current and to avoid all the passing traffic. In addition, we travelled by ferry to one of the islands, Lamma, where the pace of life and scenery along its small back-streets and green hills are completely different from the skyscrapers of Hong Kong Island and the crowded bustle of Kowloon.

At the Jade Market, Linda bought some gorgeous South Sea pearls - a long necklace and matching earrings - and the stall owner gave me a ton of change for the trams and ferries since it is soon used up. From there, we strolled through Reclamation Street where there is another market. All the signs were in Cantonese and there were lots of places selling cheap clothes, fruit, and open-air butcher shops. There were plenty of old ladies selling dried fish tied with pink string. 'Official hawker' No.73 was an old man selling bundles of incense, who was sat next to a crate of live (but not for long) chickens. A young man was cleaning scales from the fish he had for sale and some of the fish were still flicking around. Other larger fish had been partly opened up, but still had the swim bladder attached; perhaps because this is a local delicacy. In contrast to this open-air market with its meat hanging down from hooks and its rows of dried fish and shrimps, there was one air-conditioned supermarket along the street, which offered the same produce but chilled and shrink-wrapped. It was a dull place compared to the streets.

One evening, we went to the Ladies Recreation Club (LRC) for a meal with Katie and her friend Jeremy, who kindly supplied me with a jacket. The restaurant upstairs was very attractive with excellent food and service. Our hosts told us a little about life in Hong Kong and how employers, with no laws to worry about in terms of equal opportunities, can and do advertise for "an attractive, large-breasted, English-speaking secretary." Moreover, some night clubs provide all manner of fantastic offers to attract young women to their establishments. Some of the flats in Mid-Levels, Katie told us, cost £10,000 per month to rent, and the higher up and the better the view the more it costs. Since all property is based on the formula of *x* dollars per sq. ft, everyone knows their own square footage. We were the last out of the LRC well after midnight as they were turning out all the lights.

On our last day in Hong Kong, we went early to the Bird Market where we saw the loveliest and largest collection of small songbirds. We also witnessed one of the stallholders cutting the legs off live grasshoppers, which are fed to some of the bigger birds. There were macaws and African Greys on perches as well as robin-like blue and black birds. Chinese men often hold up their own birds in ornate wicker baskets next to another to entice them to sing. As we left the market, we saw a man catch a rat in a wire cage and then swing the cage forcefully to the ground to kill it.

After an uneventful flight from Hong Kong, we arrived at our hotel near Kota Kinabalu (or KK, as the locals call it) in the Sabah region of Borneo. By the pool, staff circulated among the guests offering small pieces of fruit or else handing out chilled cotton towels. Another waiter travelled around on a tricycle like a 'stop-me-and-buy-one' character. From his cool box and under the shade of his large umbrella, he dispensed all manner of cold drinks. In the background, Mt. Kinabalu loomed majestically but ominously whenever it emerged from the cloud cover that surrounds its peak for much of the day. The mountain literally towers over the rest of the countryside, and we were due to climb it in a few days' time. From our balcony, we could see four of the five islands in the Timku Abdul Rahman Marine Park.

We got up before dawn to catch the plane to Sandakan and the orangutan sanctuary and rehabilitation centre at Sepilok. Soon after take-off on the forty-minute flight, we passed by Mt. Kinabalu, which looked very high, very steep, and very rugged. I began to have some misgivings about our projected climb of this mountain. The rest of the landscape was virgin forest and meandering rivers, save for some quite appalling areas where all the trees and most of the vegetation had been stripped away and only smouldering fires and billowing smoke remained. Our short transfer to Sepilok from the airport ended in a mini traffic jam as Benjamin, a seven-year- old orangutan who is fond of tourists, simply walked into the road and held us all up. Straight afterwards, we saw a rhino horned hornbill, the national bird of Sabah.

First, we had some breakfast and viewed a video about the centre and its work before we set off into the jungle along a set of raised wooden walkways. After a short wait, the orangutans came out of the surrounding jungle and headed along ropes or along the floor to the feeding station where a park ranger fed them watermelon and milk. We watched entranced for thirty or more minutes at Branley and her adopted baby, which clung to her as the older ape ambled over the platform, and at Jimmy and Kong, who had each lost an arm, but who scrambled across the ropes with no apparent difficulties. When the food ran out, most of the orangutans returned to the jungle slowly disappearing one after the other as the ropes, which served as their thoroughfares, reached further into the jungle cover. However, a few animals accompanied us back to the administrative centre during the course of which they proceeded by turns to 'terrorise' some of the more faint-hearted; showed off in the trees by swinging from overhanging branches; completed forward rolls along the walkways; eyed up any object that took their interest and tried to pinch it; posed shamelessly for photographs; and, finally, one of them grabbed a woman by the wrist and insisted she walk along with him back to the centre. Branley and her baby were especially good at playing to the gallery and some of the local women would shriek in alarm whenever they came too close. For a while, the baby and the adopted mother were swinging together from an overhanging branch as we gazed on. It looked like the baby was going to get knocked off as sometimes they collided; but their grip is so strong there was no mishap. Their bodies were covered in ginger-coloured hair and they had such expressive eyes that it was difficult not to believe that we were being observed by creatures of some intelligence and sensitivity.

Back near KK at our hotel, we went to Sapi Island, the smallest in the marine park. Our journey from the hotel's marina took about fifteen minutes as we sped across a clear sea. The beach at Sapi had trees coming right down to the sands, which were white and soft to the touch. It was very hot and sunny, but the small 'shop' had a good supply of cold drinks, but no food unless you wanted to dine out on crackers. We lazed the day away next to the turquoise sea. As we left

Sapi in the late afternoon, beneath the jetty we saw shoals of small fish and two crocodile fish stalking them. We even saw one of the crocodile fish catch its prey and then it had to swim away quickly so that the other one couldn't steal it from him. So quickly did they go that they breached the water several times and seemed almost like flying fish. Two boats took the people from the hotel back home, and the two young lads in charge raced each other at full throttle all the way back.

Even hotter today, so the chilled face towels were a delightful relief when they arrived. At midday, we went to the mercifully air-conditioned gym and afterwards, feeling very virtuous at having had a strenuous workout, we enjoyed a beer in Mike's Bar. In the evening, we dined in the seafood restaurant, which is on a man-made island connected to the hotel grounds by a small causeway. Although the candlelight made it very difficult to read the menu, our choices of tiger prawns and Borneo red snapper were both excellent. At sunset, which was unbelievably marvellous and varied, a large swish yacht, called *Antipodean*, slipped anchor and headed off, we guessed, to the Philippines. Some guess! Next morning, she was back at anchor at the same spot after her lucky and undoubtedly rich owners had been out for a romantic dinner cruise around the islands.

The big day arrives. We left at six o'clock with Ahsing, our driver, for Mt. Kinabalu (4101 metres). Just before the Kinabalu Park HQ, we stopped at some roadside stalls to buy some finger bananas (light weight but high energy) for the climb. At the HQ we registered for the climb and were introduced to our guide, Julius. Our starting point was at 1,900 metres and our destination on the first day of the ascent was the hut at Laban Rata at just over 3,290 metres where we would stay overnight. This involved a route of six kilometres. Each kilometre point was greeted with great relief. There were also six 'shelters' en route to Laban Rata where one can sit in the shade, use a 'flush' toilet (if you can stand the flies in the corrugated tin hut), and top up one's water supply from tanks fed by pipes that run down the mountain and that collect their water from the granite massif above Laban Rata.

At first, we felt that we might have some difficulties with Julius whose English was not very extensive and made worse by a speech impediment that might have been caused by the huge gaps in his front teeth. But as time went on and we became more and more tired, even despairing of reaching our goal, and especially when Linda twisted her ankle, Julius proved himself to be a sensitive and kind man. Moreover, provided you listened to him carefully, he had a great deal of information to impart - about his village of 272 people five kilometres from the Park HQ to which he jogs in order to keep fit; about leading different groups of people up the mountain; about carrying an injured Japanese woman down the mountain on his back; about the plants and animals he pointed out to us on the climb; about the easier routes he picked out for us on the massif, avoiding some of the steep, rope-supported paths; and about his mother's excellent home-made, and very strong, rice wine.

At the foot of the mountain, the vegetation and terrain reminded us a little of Ingleton Falls, but higher up we became more aware of the tropical nature of our surroundings - tree ferns, bamboo, and tall palms. Just below Laban Rata, these gave way to small gnarled trees, some hundreds of years old, not unlike junipers with pale green-grey moss hanging from the branches - a legacy of the swirling mists. There were also rhododendrons with bright red leaves; and Stapf's Vaccinium which is a kind of wort, and of course, there were spectacular pitcher plants just a little way off the trail. Normally, it was very quiet and we saw few birds other than the mountain blackbird, which behaved just like our own version. At the shelters on the way up, we often saw ground squirrels, and even the odd vole. With the exception of these distractions and one spectacular necklace orchid with its white delicate colouring, we were for the most part caught within a green tunnel surrounded by verdant vegetation and an endless succession of steps hewn from tree roots or else made out of wooden slats. Occasionally, a veritable ladder of steep steps lay ahead and it was almost all we could do to focus on the next step in front of us.

It was very hot and even more humid, and when we rested at some of the higher shelters or when the clouds descended and we walked through mists, we also got chilled. Occasionally, we caught sight of the countryside below. Usually, one side of the path was a steep drop into a valley or ravine. Of the various groups going up the mountain, the super fit shot off into the distance never to be seen again until we reached the hut, or else mere mortals ended up intermingling with members of other groups. Thus, at different points on the climb, we would pass a familiar set of faces and later, as we rested, they would walk slowly by us, or perhaps join us for a time until one group or the other decided to set off again. At such meetings, chiefly at one of the shelters en route, there was much banter about why the hell were we all doing this, and how mad can we be to pay for this torture. Periodically, porters, destined for the rest hut and carrying up to forty kilograms of rice, would pass us and make us feel right wimps. But, wimps or no, the longer the climb went on - the higher we got, the more the air became thinner, the more frequent the times when we became chilled, the constant exertion and sweating, the greater the aching in our legs, the keener the sensation of the packs digging into our backs, the more insistent gasping for air - the more like torture this climb began to feel.

For me the last two kilometres were truly awful for although I didn't realize it at the time, I was becoming not only dehydrated but also had low blood sugar. A mild dose of altitude sickness meant that I had no appetite and it was all I could do to eat a small amount of chocolate that Linda pressed on me. When we reached the hut itself around two p.m., Julius - no doubt seeing the state I was in -

suggested that we didn't have to go on to the summit the next day. We said we would see how we felt when it was time to set off in the early morning. Later that evening, we dozed fitfully until two a.m. when it was time to have breakfast and to set out for the top.

I felt much better even at this ungodly hour of the day and enjoyed the toast and jam. We set off at three a.m. and, as soon as we drew away from the hut, we could see the beautifully clear sky awash with iridescent stars. At first, we walked up through low stunted vegetation climbing the same old steps and traversing steep columns of wooden staircases. After an hour of this snaking along the trail with torchlights flashing above and below us as little knots of people made their way along, we encountered the granite massif. Here it was much colder and we put on our fleeces and, later, our waterproofs to give greater protection against a slight but distinctly chilling wind. The route on the massif was generally less steep except for some portions where we grasped tethered ropes to haul ourselves up. Not everyone was so adept at using the ropes and sometimes there would be a small 'traffic jam' as climbers waited their turn to ascend an especially steep pitch. These hold-ups were not unwelcome as they provided an opportunity to rest and to gaze at the stars. When we were about halfway to the top and completely exposed on this huge slab of rock, the torches of the climbers twinkled all around us. Below us some of the slower groups could be seen, their lights moving methodically up the slope. Above, the lights of other climbers revealed a twinkling meandering route to the top, like a torch-lit procession. Because it was dark and cool and it was not so steep, and because we only had two kilometres to go, Linda, and especially myself, found the climb somewhat easier. Even so, in the grey light just before the dawn as we approached the top of the mountain towards six a.m., we were again very tired. But we had made it! We stood watching the dawn and then we looked down into Low's Gully with its sheer-sided one mile drop into the ravine below, which seemed in the half-light to be like a forbidding black hole. It was now windy and very cold so we took our photographs and retreated.

The descent went well at first. On the steep parts, it was quite easy to hold the rope and to walk forwards down the slope rather than descend in reverse. However, no sooner had I said to Linda, after we had completed the last of the really steep pitches, " be careful not to sprain your ankle," she promptly did so. A passing German policeman, bless him, got out some first aid stuff and bound Linda's ankle and we tied up her boot very tightly and in this way we managed to stop it swelling too much. Julius got her a stout stick from the hut when we arrived there, and carried her pack for her. I spent most of the next six kilometres acting as a kind of arm or shoulder support for Linda as she took each steep step with deliberate and painful concentration. She was soon very tired from favouring her left side, from getting blisters on her right hand where she held the stick, and from concentrating on each and every step in order not to do any further damage to her ankle.

Well, we did eventually get off the mountain and back to the hotel, armed with our certificates of a successful climb. But was it worth it, I hear you asking? The view of the massif itself and the sight of the dawn were fantastic, and we have seldom seen a more dreadful prospect than the chasm that was Low's Gully, which fell away below us as we stood on the summit. It was chilling in its unforgiving and menacing countenance. For people who were supposed to be on holiday, the climb turned out to be a form of masochism. Yet despite the privations and the pain, there was great humour on the way up; Linda was magnificent in helping me to get to the top and even more so in getting herself off the mountain; we encountered a lot of friendly concern and felt that we were sharing something important with the others on the climb (whom I must say were nearly all much younger than us); and at the end, we did stand on the roof of S.E. Asia and surveyed all the land below. Finally, as we sat in the pool-side loungers back at the hotel, Mt. Kinabalu despite being over eighty kilometres away would sometimes reveal all its glory from beneath the swirling clouds. On these occasions, we looked up at the summit and felt a growing pride that we had actually stood there. However, for the first day or two after our ascent, it was difficult to traverse the various steps in the hotel. Our awkward and stiff transition of these 'obstacles' was known as the 'Kinabalu Shuffle.'

Having partially recovered from the aches and pains of the climb, we set off to Manukan Island one morning. We walked along the beach and chose a good spot - two wooden sunbeds in the shade of some pine trees, and two washed up logs on the beach a short distance from the clear water where we sat for ages reading our books. With hardly a breath of wind and no waves, the snorkelling was unbelievably good, and we saw all around us schools of different tiny fish as well as parrot fish and sea slugs on the coral strewn floor. We fed some bread to the fish, which came right up and took it from our fingers. Even when all the bread had gone, there were still lots of zebra fish swimming in circles around us in hope that there might be more. The holiday as a whole was an eventful mixture of city sightseeing, lazy sunbathing, and painful exertion. But Mike's Bar, in session both at the HK and KK hotels, never once ran out of beer, and so in the end the trip could not have failed to be a success.

Chapter Eight: India, Cuba, and Mexico

In the last two months of 1991, Linda and I were in India; chiefly in the old Portuguese colony of Goa on the Arabian Sea, but also in Bangalore and Mysore in the southern state of Karnataka. Our hotel in Goa, the Ronil, was a relaxed establishment with low-rise, whitewashed accommodations, and only a few minutes' walk from Baga Beach. The hotel was built around a large rectangular swimming pool at the top of which was a low terrace where Linda and I often had breakfast. The grounds of the hotel had space for many sun loungers resting beneath tall, swaying palm trees. On some evenings, dance troupes entertained the guests with their colourful costumes and garish masks that depicted mythical creatures. At the rear of the hotel was an expanse of paddy fields where we saw women harvesting their rice crop. It was back-breaking work. There was also some dry scrub land where Linda and I saw small boys playing cricket with a rough-hewn bat and a bare tennis ball. At mid-off to this cricketing contest was a small Hindu shrine featuring images of two elephants.

To reach Baga Beach, we had to walk down a narrow lane to the long expanse of soft sand. In the lane were all kinds of hawkers and traders who were very persistent in approaching tourists and urging them to buy God knows what. Linda soon realized that tourists with the whitest skin – right off the plane - were an especial prey for these people; the ones with golden skin tans less so. Thus, as the holiday progressed and Linda and I caught some sun, we were bothered less and less. Perhaps, the hawkers thought that tourists who had been there for a week or more had by then bought all the knick-knacks they could possibly want. While reaching the beach proved to be a release from the attention of the traders, it did not prove to be a beach beyond compare. It was not exotic; there were no luxury sun loungers for exclusive use of hotel guests; there was no delivery of luscious fruits and enticing, iced cocktails; there were no motor boats for hire or to drag parascenders into the air; and, most damning of all, no Mike's Bar. It was a rather long, plain beach with beige sand, along which were occasional fishing smacks with outriggers to improve their stability. However, it was an interesting beach. It had things you did not normally see, if at all, on the white sand beaches of the Far East and the Caribbean. For instance, it had groups of young men and women dressed in ordinary clothes dancing in a circle – it was, perhaps, the harbinger of a Goan real-world Tinder club. Older females dressed in saris were chattering enthusiastically and paddling in the shallows. There were unattended cows that entertainingly wandered along the sands, dropping their dung as they went, and occasionally catching a sunbathing tourist unawares and frightening the life out of them as the beast's muzzle came too close for comfort. Best of all, the beach sported an old man wearing only a loincloth and carrying a large old fashioned medical syringe. He would politely approach sitting tourists, hold the instrument close to an ear, and enquire if they wanted their ears syringed. I could just about imagine that a few tourists might give him some rupees out of pity, but I could not envisage any of them actually letting the old man syringe their ears.

Felix was a young man who worked at the hotel with whom Linda and I became friendly. He invited us to his house one afternoon and pointed out the paddy fields nearby that his family also owned. At that time of year, he and his extended family were not growing rice in all their fields; some were still flooded but were being used to farm prawns. He told us that they did this at night using fires to attract the prawns closer to the surface and then threw weighted nets to catch them and drag them to the bank. Felix invited us to come and watch the following evening. The next day as dusk fell, Linda and I carefully picked our way along the pathways through the paddy fields next to the hotel, until we could see the flickering lights of several fires. Felix was there with a few others, all up to their thighs in the water, and throwing out nets at regular intervals. When I stood by the edge of the field, I saw a few snakes in the water. I asked Felix if they were venomous. He said no, but that they did sting painfully when they bit you.

A day after, we saw an even harder way to earn a living when we visited a small quarry where labourers cut stone for the building trade. They did this all day in the harsh sun and debilitating heat for twenty-five rupees per day, the equivalence of fifty pence. They loaded the heavy stones onto wooden carts pulled by bullocks and off they drove down the dirt road to a collection point. An outing with a group of birders later in the holiday revealed yet more ways in which many Indians labour for very little reward.

Linda and I got to know a small group of bird watchers and their tour leader, Paul, a professional ornithologist. They went off on daily excursions in their minibus much deeper into the rural countryside where there was far more jungle, steeper terrain, and clear streams – all offering a habitat for many different species of birds than could be seen at the coast. Paul offered to take us with them on the next excursion in exchange for simply chipping in to pay the petrol costs. On our way there, slowly traversing a narrow and bumpy dirt track, I caught sight of a haystack walking towards me! As we drew closer, I could see a pair of thin legs under this mound of straw; the farmer was moving this resource manually to a shed further along the road. After spending a few enjoyable hours peering into dense woodland to identify birds the like of which I had never seen before, we arrived at a slow-paced broad river with a narrow pencil of an island within it. Here, we found around a dozen or so long wooden boats with two-man crews. Usually, the younger of the two men dived to the riverbed, dragging a plastic bucket behind him. There, holding his breath far beyond what I could do, he filled the bucket with sand and then hauled himself and the heavy bucket to the surface where it was heaved onto the boat by the older man. This was happening continuously, and only stopped when one of the boats became filled to the gunnels and was rowed to shore. The sand was unloaded by the bucket-full ready to be taken away for use by the building trade. My god, it was hard work.

Paul spoke to one of the boat crews, which had just unloaded all their sand, and they agreed to take our little party out onto the river – and receive significantly more money for an hour's use of their craft than they would for a day's worth of labour hauling sand. We were taken in the boat close to the thin island in the river and we all sat there quietly wondering what was going to happen. As dusk fell, it happened. A blizzard of birds of various kinds came swooping down from the darkening skies and found safe places to roost on the island. There were so many, it felt as if they must be an inexhaustible supply. Inexhaustible or not, it was without doubt memorable.

Back at the hotel, Felix had a friend who was willing to hire his scooter to Linda and me for a few days. To drive a scooter in India when you are from the UK is an act of sheer bravado or insanity. Fortunately, the back roads in Goa are not the dangerous thoroughfares of Mumbai. I was warned about two things: police officers who might stop us because we had no helmets, and cows. We met no police, but there were numerous encounters with cows, although no collisions. With the scooter, Linda and I visited some of the other beaches in the neighbourhood such as Anjuna Beach and Vagator Beach, where we saw cricket being played on the sands. On the route to Tiracol, we had to use a ferry to cross an estuary. It was full not just with vehicles but with people who stood as close as possible to the end of the off-ramps without falling off the vessel.

Mapusa Market was one of our favourite destinations. As ever, such markets in India are awash with colour, clutter, fruits and agricultural produce, and a glorious array of people shopping for all manner of goods or else tending to their stalls and small shops. Here, we witnessed one man with ten trays of soft drink cans on his head expertly navigate the throng as he weaved his way along the narrow passageways. Most of the women selling from small stalls wore bright saris and, often, they had strings of tiny, decorative flowers woven into their long black hair, and held umbrellas to shield themselves from the sun. Above an outlet selling earthenware pots of every size and shape, Linda drew my attention to a very large advertisement for 'Palmolive – Deluxe Lather.' Just as we were leaving the market, we spotted a public notice sign: "It is hereby notified to all that no person should use any place except the public toilet within the Mapusa Municipal Market for answering natural calls." The cows that wandered through the market, eating unwanted produce that had spilt into the road, could not read.

The inevitable happened after we had been in Goa for a while – we made an impromptu journey to Bangalore and Mysore. I say impromptu but Air India's booking protocols in Goa made it anything but. We had to queue outside what was little more than a shack in Panaji, the capital of Goa. When it opened, I literally had to shove and push against the throng to get to the counter where, after a tangle of bureaucracy, I was finally issued with our tickets. Our stay in Bangalore was a brief overnight affair since we arrived there during the evening. The city had yet to become the IT capital of India or to alter its name, but in any event our primary destination was Mysore, which we reached by train on a narrow-gauge track. The train was not particularly crowded at that time in the early morning, but one man was doing good business cooking breakfasts for passengers. He did his cooking on a small paraffin-fired stove balanced on the steel buffers between two carriages. When he completed an order, he brought it to the passengers in the carriage wrapped in banana leaves.

Our base in the charming but bustling city of Mysore – the City of the Palaces - was the Hotel Metropole. It had colonnaded balconies running along its two stories. The outside balustrades were constructed in metal shaped to an open-patch design, whereas on the other side, outside each guest room, were two white wicker chairs and a small table. Palm trees were in close attendance and rose above the second story. The room allocated to Linda and me had the biggest bathroom I had ever seen. The main room had an antiquated television but no channels at all. If a guest wished to see a film, they had to visit reception and choose from a small selection of video cassettes. The receptionist would place it into the cassette player, which was linked to all the TV sets in the rooms, so that from that point onwards everyone could view the film selected by an unknown stranger. It was that or nothing. The same receptionist told us that the hotel used to be the Maharaja's guest house – presumably for those deemed insufficiently important to stay in the Maharaja's Palace. The Palace, also known as the Mysore Palace, was one of the most elaborately decorated and sculpted buildings I had ever seen; at night its façade was lit with thousands of points of light so that it looked like a fantastical creation in a Disney cartoon. We ate at the hotel in the evenings and enjoyed a delightful selection of various vegetarian meals that we, in the UK, would call curries but went by different names in Mysore. On our first visit to the hotel's restaurant with its high ceiling and elegant gallery, the waiter clearly felt we had ordered something that would prove to be too hot and spicy for us. He told us that he had seen previous guests from America and Britain find some of the dishes they ordered to be too hot. He was simply looking after us and we appreciated that. Then Linda said: "We're from Leicester and eat curries there all the time." Immediately, his concerns disappeared and we were able to order what we liked without any further attempt to tone down the selections.

The streets of Mysore were eternally crowded and busy with old buses belching dark diesel fumes, Hindustan Ambassador taxis and cars, all sorts of two-wheel vehicles, and the usual stray cow. Buses were so packed that often people were hanging onto the doors as drivers crunched their way through the gears. Lane discipline was poor, to say the least, and in India big has the right of way even if big is on the wrong side of the road on a blind bend. Thus, while cows were sacred and probably safe from being hit, lorries and buses had right of way, which meant cars, mopeds, cyclists, and pedestrians had to get out of the bloody road. Linda and I successfully dodged the lot of them to visit a number of locations, such as the Maharaja's Palace with its colonnaded Durbar Hall. We also travelled to the Chamundi Hills to see the Nandi Bull, a four-and-a-half metre tall and over seven-metre-long creature carved from a single slab of granite. Finally, we visited a wildlife sanctuary where a one-year-old, orphaned elephant with thick brown hair on the top of his head, took displeasure with me and headbutted me. Even so, that sanctuary was far better than the one we had visited near Goa where we saw one elephant in deep distress, being tethered by metal chains and left alone. The staff there also showed us a baby leopard; it was not so much shown as wrenched out of its small cage and swung across the floor towards us. It was less a sanctuary and more a badly run zoo.

All too soon, our short journey to Mysore came to an end. We expected to take a taxi to the train station to return to Bangalore and a plane from there to Goa. The hotel manager told us that today was a national strike in the state of Karnataka in protest about water rights being shared with the neighbouring state of Tamil Nadu. Farmers in Karnataka felt strongly that too much water was being allowed to flow south to Tamil Nadu, thus making it difficult for them to grow their own crops. A day of no transport movements had been declared, and there were no taxis. To be honest, I hadn't taken the situation too seriously believing that the trains would still be running. Linda and I set off on foot to the railway station only to find when we got there that a mob had already torn up a section of the track. Undaunted, we walked to the bus station where matters were worse – two buses were still burning out of control. We returned to our hotel and there we met an Italian couple, Alberto and Giovanna, who had also been staying at the Metropole and, like us, needed to get to Bangalore Airport. The manager offered us the opportunity to stay another night, but our attitude was that this dispute had nothing to do with us, and we wanted to be on our way. The manager informed us that he might be able to find a taxi driver willing to drive us the 146 kilometres from Mysore to Bangalore.

After an hour or so and several phone calls by the manager, a black Ambassador taxi drove into the hotel's grounds. This type of sturdy, lumpish car was first made in India in 1957 and was based on the British Morris Oxford. They became so ubiquitous throughout the subcontinent that they were dubbed 'King of Indian Roads.' The driver spoke decent English and told us there might be some problems along the route but that he was confident he could find a way around them. We agreed a fee with him and all four of us set off, with me in the front next to the driver. Incidentally, to this day, I am still embarrassed that I never asked him his name – so 'driver' he remains. In Mysore, there were signs of agitation in the streets and some people shouted insults or hurled stones as we sped past. Soon, however, we were in the countryside and all was quiet; we smugly believed we were going to get away with this plan. How wrong we were.

Eventually, we arrived at a small town on the road to Bangalore. There are no bypasses in such places so we had to drive through the heart of the settlement until we came to a small square. There, the taxi was immediately halted and surrounded by a group of two hundred or more people who had been congregating in the square. They pressed up against the bodywork of the Ambassador, banged on the roof and windows with their fists, and tried to open the boot. For a short while, the crowd pushed the car as if trying to tip it over but they soon ceased that activity much to our relief. At first, there had been an almost comic book aspect to such a whirl of activity, but it soon dawned on us how different this was to action in a merry-go-round cartoon. Our faces denoted anxiety and apprehension; theirs anger and outrage. The body language of the crowd was aggressive, while ours was defensive. I knew how deeply in trouble we were when a policeman came towards the taxi, looked inside, and walked away never to be seen again. The stalemate between crowd and us, or more accurately between crowd and sturdy car, continued for some time, but gradually reduced in intensity – perhaps in response to what our driver was shouting to those closest to the vehicle. We had no idea what was going to happen next but, fortunately, our driver took the initiative. Suddenly, he exited the car, locking the door behind him, and began speaking to what appeared to be the group's leaders. When he returned, he told us that it had been agreed we could go no further and that we should stay in the square. As we pondered the thought of sleeping overnight in the taxi, the driver then said that when the crowd all got fed up of hanging around the car, we would be off. He urged us to have some kind of plausible reason to get past any other blockade we might encounter. He said he'd had a lot of difficulty speaking to these people and we needed a backup plan.

Giovanna came up with the idea that one of us should pretend to be very ill – she was duly elected to that position. Linda and Alberto would be seen to be caring for her in the back seat. I was to be the supervising doctor. After what seemed like a long time due to the fear we felt, but was only about thirty minutes, the crowd had largely dispersed as our driver had foreseen. Slowly, he drove the taxi to the exit of the square as if it were a mechanical cat slyly creeping away. In no time at all, we exited the square and were travelling along a bumpy road so narrow that it was impossible to open the taxi doors without hitting the front porch of the houses that lined either side of the lane. Linda was busy applying cream to Giovanna's face to make it look very pale, and Alberto had some water ready to sprinkle over her to make it look as if she had a high temperature and was sweating profusely. The inhabitants of the houses we slowly passed while we undertook these theatricals glowered at us but took no action. Surely, soon we would be out into the free countryside and it would be plain sailing once again. In fact, we turned into another, smaller square at the end of which was a wooden bridge piled high with bullock carts and other paraphernalia. Again, we were immediately surrounded by an angry mob. This crowd made fewer physical assaults on the car but the anger on their faces was as plain as before. It was probably just as well we could not understand the abuse they shouted at us. Our driver turned to me and said: "They won't listen to me; you'll have to get out and speak to them."

Those were the last words I had wanted to hear and, fearfully, I wondered if they would literally be the last words I heard. I had no choice, so I got out of the car; the driver immediately locked the door. Linda told me much later that she thought she might never see me alive again. I was very afraid as I stood next to the car in front of this shouting and angry mob. I took an entirely useless scintilla of hope from the fact that I stood a good few inches taller than most of the people around me. I had not worked out how this could possibly help me, if at all, when a man pushed through the crowd and addressed me in perfect English. Would I please accompany him to speak to the man in charge? The crowd pulled back and quietened considerably; I had no difficulty following my guide to the bridge where I was passed on to a man of some presence, who was clearly giving orders to others. He was tall and athletic, and wrapped around his neck and extending down to his knees was a bright green scarf. In English, he asked me what I was doing travelling during a transportation strike. Fearfully, I told him I was a doctor and that I had in the taxi a young women with acute appendicitis who needed immediate surgery at the American Hospital in Bangalore. I didn't even know if such a hospital existed and I prayed the man in charge didn't know either. I shuddered to think what would happen if we were found out in this subterfuge. I was ordered back to the car and he followed. As we drew near, I could hear screaming and, closer still, I could see Giovanna pretending to scream in pain and being tended by Linda and Alberto. The man with the green scarf took one look, told me to get back in the taxi, and strode off to order the clearance of obstacles from the bridge. Within minutes, we had crossed the bridge and indeed were in relatively open countryside again soon afterwards.

Joy unconfined - until in a small village youths threw rocks at the car, and in another we had to weave around much larger rocks that had ben placed to try and block the path. In yet another village, one man run out and hurled himself against the side of the car. It hit him and he bounced off. I didn't think we had badly hurt him but no one was going to stop to find out. Even on the outskirts of Bangalore with our journey nearly over, we still had reasons to be afraid. We passed two cars on the other side of the road. They had been burnt out but there were bodies still inside them. Our driver told us that the cars had probably been stopped because they had Tamil Nadu number plates, and then petrol thrown over them. Tamil Nadu was the state with which Karnataka was in dispute, and people had died because of it.

We did, by the grace of some god I wouldn't even believe in, reach Bangalore Airport. We asked our driver what he would do now, and he replied that he would park up near the airport and stay overnight. The next day the strike was over and he could return to Mysore safely. We thanked him sincerely and profusely for what he had done for us, paid him the agreed fare, and gave him a very large tip in addition. Driver, Giovanna, Alberto, Linda, and I all said our goodbyes and we parted ways. Linda and I caught our plane to Mysore and arrived back at the hotel late in the evening where we sat in the grounds, had a beer, and tried to understand what we had gone through. The manager came to see us and told us he was so glad we had returned safely. He said that shortly after our plane had left Bangalore, the army had been called out, the airport closed, and some individuals shot dead in the streets. We recounted to him much of what we had experienced that day. Rather inappropriately, given our despondent mood, joyous shooting stars appeared overhead.

By the morning of the next day, word had got around many of the guests what had happened to Linda and me. There was even a ripple of applause as we sat down for breakfast, which embarrassed me. It had been my arrogance that led us into this dreadful affair – the idea that we, as westerners, should be allowed to travel when we wished. I should have stayed the extra day in Mysore. It taught me a lesson. However, I harboured no hatred of India or Indians. We had been in the wrong place at the wrong time and had failed to defuse the situation.

Cuba was our destination in the summer of 1992. We flew there with Cubana Airlines on an old Russian-built Ilyushin plane, which did not have the range to fly non-stop London to Havana. Rather, we had to refuel at Gander Airport in Newfoundland. From there, the plane hugged the Atlantic coast of America but never breaching its territorial waters since Cuba and the USA were not exactly on friendly terms. We loved Havana with its faded grandeur, crumbling buildings, and vibrant culture. We admired the classic American cars from the 1950s, as they defied their age and lack of new parts to patrol El Malecón, the combined seawall and esplanade running along the coast in Havana.

The Hotel Inglaterra was an interesting place; the oldest hotel in Cuba with a neoclassical facade and apparently declared a national monument in 1981, and centrally located. It was comfortable enough but was in need of modernisation. Its staff were polite and helpful and the hotel possessed a rooftop terrace with great views over the city. One evening, Linda and I visited the terrace to enjoy a cocktail before dinner. A waiter patiently explained to us that they had virtually no fresh fruit with which to make cocktails. We said we would be happy simply to have orange juice with the vodka cocktail. No orange juice, he replied and then added, no vodka either. They did have rum. I'd rather have a beer, I told him. He went off somewhere to check. No beer. We had two rums. As we sipped our drinks, the same waiter came to ask us if we would be eating in the downstairs dining room or here on the terrace. We were delighted at the prospect of dining in the open air with soft breezes and delightful décor. However, while the décor did not change, the soft breezes did. As the first course was served, a tropical thunderstorm hit. The thunder and lightning were most impressive but the rain was unwelcome. The waiter and his fellow worker hauled over two large umbrella stands and positioned them to keep most of the rain off us. Thereafter, our subsequent courses were served at our table by a succession of waiters holding plates in one hand and umbrellas in the other. Further water problems occurred the next day in our room when the shower refused to work. I rang reception and expected them to send a plumber. Twenty minutes later an elderly man knocked on our door carrying two pails of water, which he left in the bathroom. He came back with two more. Linda and I took it in turns to step into the shower cubicle to have the other throw lukewarm water over one another. It wasn't the perfect shower but certainly a memorable one.

There are many good bars in Havana but two them are famous because of Ernest Hemingway, the American author, who it is alleged drank there in the pre-Castro era. The two are El Floridita and La Bodeguita del Medio. The former styles itself as the cradle of the daiquiri, a boast that is etched into the red bar. When Linda and I were there, it was a very noisy and busy room full of red chairs and decorations. The latter has heavy wooden décor, framed photographs of film stars and other celebrities, and graffiti covering its walls. The mojito cocktails were all lined up along the counter waiting for punters like Linda and me to snap them up. Both bars are usually crowded, always expensive, overly touristy, and lacking any significant presence of local people. The two bars are undoubtedly successful but there is no historical evidence Hemingway ever drank a mojito in La Bodeguita – not one mention in his writings. If you want any kind of authenticity, you would be better off at La Floridita where the high living author did sink innumerable daiquiris.

We left Havana and were driven about 150 kilometres along the coast to the Paradisus Resort in Varadero. By now I am tired of describing how marvellous such resorts are, how attentive the staff, and how relaxing the ambiance. I will say only one thing about the hotel: they often ran out of fresh fruit. Linda and I might find a melon or pineapple for sale in some local shack nearby – the barman at the pool bar used to keep such fruit in his refrigerator for our exclusive use. Linda became friendly with the maid, Maria, who each day cleaned our room. One day, rather tentatively, she approached Linda for help. Many things in Cuba could only be obtained by its citizens through an official rationing scheme. If an ordinary Cuban wanted to buy a shirt, or a saucepan, or whatever, they had to exchange so many coupons from their ration book to obtain the item. They paid in pesos and ration coupons, whereas in completely separate shops, tourists paid for items in US dollars. I could have bought designer socks, for heaven's sake, in such places – places from which Cubans were barred. Maria was a mother with a small child who needed milk powder, nappies, and such like. She asked Linda if she would take the dollars she had earned from tips, and buy the baby goods in a shop she could not enter. Linda was happy to do so and, in one sense, Maria was fortunate because her job allowed her to pick up US dollars from guests.

To round off the account of our time in Cuba, I shall deal only with the day trips we took to other towns on the island; all of them by air. I shall not distract you with tales of the towns we visited with their quaint squares, cigar factories, pottery emporiums and so on. They do not matter: it is only the flights that matter. The first flight Linda and I took within the island was aboard a twelve-seat, Russian-built, Polish-converted crop sprayer. I believe it was an Antonov biplane built in 1947 and it had one bulky engine fitted in the nose of the craft so that its propeller spun in front of the faces of the two pilots. Catering to the passengers was a single steward and, at the rear of the plane, a very young soldier with a rifle. He was there to prevent any pilots from turning the plane north and making a dash to Florida and freedom about 650 kilometres away.

From my aisle seat, I could see into the cockpit and I was doing so when the co-pilot entered the cabin to get a coffee. He recognised my interest and invited me to sit in his seat, an offer I gratefully and quickly accepted. In the cockpit, it was even noisier than in the cabin. Many of the control surfaces of the various knobs, switches and handles were worn away to a shine. The seat I occupied had seen better days but the views to my right were wonderful. We flew quite low over the countryside and therefore could see fields, crops, cattle, buildings, and the occasional vehicle in good detail. The view dead ahead was not so good, however; it was even a little scary for the windscreen was covered in a thin spray of oil from the engine, which the pilot attempted to remove occasionally by switching on the wipers. On re-entering the cabin, I passed the co-pilot returning to his station, and I noted that the steward was preparing coffee towards the rear of the plane in what passed for a galley. However, to my surprise it was not the steward who served Linda and me; it was the young soldier who had propped his rifle against the plane's rear door and proceeded to help the steward with his duties. The landing followed soon after, on grass. On what might be termed the airport apron, but was in fact just more grass, there were two other similar airplanes to ours. The arrivals lounge, which also starred as the departure lounge, was a wood shack with a truly execrable toilet. But the most delightful thing I remember about it was the lady sat by the entrance selling fresh fruit.

Our second flight involved a much bigger aeroplane but just as old as our converted crop sprayer friend. It was a DC3 of World War Two vintage taking passengers from the Varadero area to Pinar del Rio and the Vinales Valley. There were about twenty of us climbing the steep rake within the plane and then being asked to move seats in order to 'balance' the craft. We landed at a military airport and were taken by coach to Pinar del Rio. On our return, the gate from which we had exited the military base was now closed so the coach could not drive to our DC3. Our guide decided we would walk to the plane, which was in sight a few hundred metres away. We set off through a small entrance for foot traffic and, shortly, encountered a uniformed soldier on guard duty. We envisaged we would simply walk past this callow youth with a polite nod here and there. But no; he really was on guard duty and no one was going near the Russian-built Mig fighter jets that were in his charge. First, he called something to us that we did not understand, so we walked on. Next, he held up his hand as a signal to stop; still we advanced. Then, he fired his rifle three times over our heads; not only did everyone stop but most of the party were also cowering on the floor. I had eyes only for one of the spent shells that had been ejected and was now very near to where I was standing – how I longed to pick it up and take it home as a souvenir. While I was considering the merits of such an action, we heard a whistle being blown, and to our left coming along a road was a bicycle. In front was a soldier, hunched over the handlebars – no doubt a private - peddling furiously and, behind, sat on the saddle was an officer. There followed a heated discussion in Spanish between our guide and the officer, while the soldier on guard collected the spent shells and resumed his position. Eventually, we were escorted to our plane by the officer. As we passed the Migs that the soldier had so assiduously guarded, I saw that none of them, not one, had any jet engines. They were useless hulks.

I did not know it then but after visiting Mexico, I appreciated Cuba even more. It was a place where there was rationing of ordinary goods, where doctors earned much the same as labourers, but it had an excellent health service and good levels of literacy. It also had the dictatorship of Castro, but no Americans who were not allowed by their own government to go there. Someday, the Americans will get back there but it will not become a panacea. Rid of authoritarian rule, certainly, but with greater inequality coming down the line, undoubtedly.

Linda and I flew to Cancún in September 1993 to enjoy the beach and to tour the Yucatán region of Mexico. The white sand in front of our hotel, the Intercontinental Villas Plaza, was composed of finely crushed seashells so that even when the sun and heat were at their strongest, the sand felt reasonably cool underfoot. Our room had views of the beach, the Caribbean Sea, and part of the lagoon behind the hotel. We often sipped tequila on the balcony (aka Mike's Bar) and watched flights of frigate birds and pelicans as they sailed serenely past. Mike's Bar was kept well-stocked by frequent raids on the local supermarket. On a few evenings, we witnessed spectacular thunderstorms – that balcony really was a focal point of so many pleasures. The resort is strung out on a long strip of land between sea and lagoon and is packed with hotels, restaurants, shopping malls, boutiques, and countless tourists – mainly American. To say it was a commercial setting would be to underplay the tone of the place. In the evenings, we rarely ate in the resort preferring instead to take a short bus ride to Cancún Town where many of the Mexican and Mayan employees of the hotels lived. It was less touristy than Cancún the resort, and we heard a lot more of the Mayan language being spoken. We were there one night for Mexican Independence Day when the town positively exploded in wild celebration. Linda and I did the usual things back in resort and we enjoyed the beach activities, but we were happy to leave Cancún behind for a time while we set off on a tour of the Yucatán Peninsula.

Our guide and driver, William, was a qualified archaeologist. With us was one other couple. We headed to the famous and dramatic ruins at Chitzén Itzá, but the first drama we encountered was a deadly coral snake on the road. Several vehicles ran over it and, although it writhed in agony, it looked far from being dead. We drove through flat but heavily wooded country and when we arrived at Chitzén Itzá, it seemed to us as if it were in the middle of nowhere. The Maya, the people who built the site between the 8th and 12th centuries AD, had a wonderful mastery of stone construction and building technique. The Castle and the Observatory dominate the ruins and, at the time Linda and I visited, tourists could still enter or climb the monuments. The steep climb to the top of the step-pyramid known as the Castle or El Castillo required the negotiation of over ninety steps, plus a further step to reach the temple platform at the summit, which is dedicated to a feathered serpent deity. Indeed, running down the northern side of the monument are sculptures of plumed serpents. Like so many other ancient sites in the peninsula – such as Uxmal and Tulum, which we also visited - the buildings marked and celebrated important dates in the Mayan calendar.

The old Mayan gods are those of fire, earth, wind, and water. When the Spanish arrived in the 16th century, they began the destruction of many Maya cities and of the people themselves. Once the Maya had been conquered, the Spanish attempted to convert them to Christianity, but found they could only succeed if they cast their own saints and Christian figures as the 'equivalents' of the Maya's old gods. Indeed, in Mani, we entered a Catholic church where the sculptured iconography was tilted very much towards the Mayan perceptions of deity, and where there was little sign of the Virgin Mary – Jesus himself was relegated to a small antechamber. Uxmal was even more dramatic than Chitzén Itzá; more grand, more powerful and mysterious, and even more hidden in the jungle. We climbed another set of steep steps to the top of the Pyramid of the Magician. The Mayans had been invaded at one point in their history by the Toltecs and their influence on the architecture of Uxmal can be clearly seen. As dusk fell, we had the Pyramid of the Magician to ourselves and that was indeed magical.

Leaving behind the ruins of this ancient civilisation, we arrived at the old colonial town of Mérida, a fusion of Mayan and Spanish cultural heritages. Despite the destruction of old mansions to make way for concrete offices for multinational firms, and despite McDonald's butchery of one particularly fine building, there remained many outstanding houses in the town centre. The local council puts on occasional concerts of traditional music and dance in some of the town squares, one of which Linda and I attended. It was hugely popular not just with tourists but also with local people. We were passing the town hall on our way back to our hotel after a wonderful evening meal in the garden quadrangle of a fine mansion, when an armed soldier on guard at the hall invited us to go in and look around. When we came out again ten minutes later, he invited us to go back in to see some murals he felt we had missed. He was clearly proud of that town hall.

Our return to Cancún was a strange affair. We took a privatised motorway and since it is privatised the police do not patrol it. The tolls are very expensive for most Mexicans and, consequently, there were very few vehicles on the road. This also meant that breakdown services were rare, and many service stations had closed making it difficult to get fuel. And finally, at night, armed gangs had been known to block the road, wait for the occasional car to arrive, and then rob the occupants.

Back in Cancún, Linda did some shopping, we lazed by the pool, we had a mediocre meal at Planet Hollywood, and then we did something much better by taking the ferry to Isla Mujeres, about thirteen kilometres off the coast from Cancún. Instead of booking a commercial package trip departing from the dock at Playa Linda, we took a bus to the ferry terminal used by locals at Puerto Juárez. The ferry fare was ridiculously cheap and we were even entertained on the crossing by two gentlemen playing guitar and trumpet. The island was immeasurably quieter than Cancún and exceptionally beautiful. The Mayan language was also more frequently spoken there. We found a quiet beach and did some snorkelling among shoals of brightly coloured fish that came near to the shore. On the bus back to our hotel, I saw a sign advertising beer for sale at one peso and thirty centavos instead of the eight or more pesos in resort bars. I was tempted to try and stop the bus to buy supplies.

Towards the end of our holiday in Cancún, we dined close to the hotel in a restaurant built on a floating pontoon moored at the edge of the lagoon. During our meal, I saw a two-metre crocodile swim up to the pontoon and then disappear below the water. The waiter assured me the creature was 'tame,' and that they fed it scraps from time to time. The next day, we were at the lagoon again to hire a jet ski. I was wearing shorts and a T-shirt to avoid catching any more sun that day. The man at the hire shop advised me to take out the jet ski on my own at first to get used to it, which I did with no problems.

However, when I went out again with Linda sitting behind me, my skills were not up to the job and the first bow wave from another jet ski turfed us both into the lagoon. Two thoughts immediately occurred to me as I hit the water: where was that crocodile, and had it been fed today? The jet ski was still chugging slowly away from us as we bobbed in the water in our life jackets. Eventually, someone arrived to rescue us, and to bring back the jet ski. Linda refused to have anything more to do with this particular adventure and was taken back to shore. I climbed back on the jet ski and completed a few circuits of the course but my heart wasn't in it as I found the vehicle difficult to control. I went back to the hire shop, falling off again on the way. A short while later, I was back in the hotel's impressively large lobby shedding water over its marble floor. Behind me followed two cleaners with mops taking care of the mess I had caused. And that was my last memory of Cancún.

Chapter Nine: Arid Wilderness – Kalahari, Namib, and Damaraland

It was the late summer of 1997 when Linda and I eventually returned to sub-Saharan Africa. On the day of departure for Windhoek, we spent the morning watching the funeral of Princess Diana. Less than twenty-four hours later, we were in the Kalahari Desert, having driven ourselves there in a two-wheel drive Toyota Corolla. The road from Windhoek, the capital of Namibia, ran south and crossed the Tropic of Capricorn. What a road! Very little traffic and mile after mile heading dead straight. It was our first taste of the compelling scenery, which changes quite frequently on a day's drive, and of the prolific wildlife of the country.

At Rehoboth, we stopped for a drink at an old-fashioned general provisions store and were served by two ladies in pristine dresses of a style right out of the 1950s. Later, we saw our first off-licence or drankwinkel, which often are so far from the nearest town that they pop up rather incongruously and appear to be deliberately isolated. At Kalkrand, we turned off the tarred road and drove on gravel for the first time. It's a pretty good surface though it can be dusty. The gate to Intu Afrika Lodge was opened for us by four small, smiling boys to whom we gave pens, and a few kilometres later down a dirt track we arrived at the lodge, pausing in sight of the place only to become stuck in the sand. Philip, the manager, greeted us and took us to our chalet - one of only eight on the site. No key to lock the room was considered necessary. We had a marvellous view of the red sand landscape dotted with a surprising number of green-leafed camelthorn trees.

After tea and cheesecake, we went for a late afternoon game drive with Raymond in a large, four-wheel drive former army Land Rover. In this part of the Kalahari, the land unfolds to the horizon in a system of parallel red dunes, much like medieval fields of ridge and furrow that can still be seen in the UK, only on a much bigger scale. We traversed from parallel dune to dune, seeing on the way oryx, steenbok, springbok, bat-eared fox, ground squirrels, a solitary blue gnu following the herd of oryx, ostrich including one male lying flat on the nest trying to disguise his presence, lilac-breasted roller, kori bustard, southern ant-eating chat, crimson breasted shrike, sociable weaver birds, plovers, and hornbills. We passed innumerable camelthorn and acacia trees all growing out of red sand in which yellow tufts of dried grass stuck up stiffly. All around us were thick black clouds, claps of thunder and intense bursts of lightning. Unseasonably, a great storm was breaking but for nearly an hour Raymond avoided all but a few spots of rain. Although we did return briefly to the lodge, we went back out again ostensibly to view a rather aggressive male ostrich protecting its eggs. Just before we arrived at the nest, Raymond stopped the Land Rover at the foot of a steep dune and warned us that we would have to take our photographs quickly and to stay well within the vehicle, as the ostrich was certain to charge. Raymond even told the busboy to move away from the left-hand side of the vehicle. Engaging four-wheel drive, we sped up the dune, swaying and bucking across the rutted path, and careened over the top where, instead of a large psychotic bird, we suddenly saw a man with a huge smile on his face standing behind a neat table set out with beer and wine and nibbles for a 'sundowner' drink. We had been royally duped! Our small party stood on the top of the dune, sipped chilled wine, took some refreshment from the white linen table, and saw the sun go down gloriously over the far desert.

Off to see the San or Bushmen as they were formerly known. They lived at a site separated from the place where we met them by several dunes. All of them were slightly built with sparse but tightly curled hair and with high cheekbones. They looked very different from all the other black people we saw in Namibia. An elder explained to us in the schoolhouse how their unwritten language is based on a series of clicks. A woman showed us how they made beads from ostrich shells, and the men demonstrated how they used poison arrows to kill their prey. Tendon is used not only to bind the arrowhead to the wooden shaft but also as a kind of 'sponge' on which the poison is spread. Small animals die quickly, but bigger ones linger for days becoming progressively weaker so that in the end the San can track their spoor and finish them off with spears. It was, however, a curious meeting with these twelve individuals; it smacked a little of a performance being put on. This was reinforced when we gave them a lift back over the dunes to their village where no one wore traditional San clothing but sported torn and dirty western-style attire. Given they can no longer roam as true nomads and given the high levels of alcoholism and anomie that exist among other groups of Bushmen, it was difficult to see what else these San people could do if they wanted to preserve as much of their culture and language as possible. Just before we left, we saw a big male leopard resting in the top most branches of a large tree. One of the San told us through an interpreter that it was the only animal they feared since it could track them better than they could track it.

We left Intu Afrika and drove west towards Zebra River Lodge, which we reached after a 288 kilometres journey, much of it on dirt roads. Some of the land en route was so dry and the trees and bushes so black that it looked as if it had all been burnt. It looked more inhospitable and forbidding than the Kalahari that we had just left. The worst part was the last five kilometres on the access road to the lodge, which was so uneven and strewn with rocks that I wondered how any vehicle successfully traversed it. At the end of our struggle, we were warmly welcomed by the lodge's owners, Ron and Marianna, and their niece Chantel. Zebra River Lodge was surrounded by beautiful mountains of striated limestone that were once under a shallow sea. Shortly after our arrival, we were allowed to walk the hills behind the lodge with the owners' three dogs: Masha, the greyhound; Winnie, the terrier; and Cara, the bulky 'hound.' We saw some fossils, small rodents (the main prey of the local eagles) and various birds and a nest complete with tiny blue eggs. Most of all we admired the view of the various steep-sided valleys and gorges. The air was dry and cool. On our return, Rob told us that some properties in the area had to drill 300 metres or more to reach water. His borehole was much less deep and had been located by a water diviner. While he preserves game on his land, youngsters in the area still think it is fun to go out with their .22 rifles to see how many steenbok they can shoot in a day. Moreover, some of the road signs in the remote areas had been used as rifle targets.

The canyon running through Rob's land had been formed by the Zebra River and by the wind. The river was now dry and there was only the sound of the birds in the various valleys around the main canyon. Rob and Marianna made an excellent job of beautifying the lodge. Outside our room - again no key considered necessary - was sweet smelling jasmine and fantastic views of the canyon. That night, ten of us dined together at one table in a very relaxed and enjoyable atmosphere. Just before dinner, all three dogs were crashed out on various seats around the main room forcing us to sit where we could. Rob, Marianna, and Chantel joined us after the meal for drinks when we found out from a guest who was a vet that in answer to our question about how many vets there were in Namibia, there are in fact forty-five; seventeen working for the government and the remainder in private practice.

The next morning, Rob was taking a party to Sossusvlei but before doing so he instructed me briefly on how to drive the Unimog. This bulky left-hand drive beast built by Mercedes boasts very large tyres, high ground clearance, four-wheel drive including two reverse gears, and even a hand throttle, and the ability to clamber over almost anything, even when it still had a tonne of sand in the back. This impressive vehicle also had an engineering marvel beyond conventional four-wheel drive so that, with the click of the special gear stick, it would continue to creep forward even if two or three wheels were off the ground. With Linda in the right-hand passenger seat looking a trifle nervous, no doubt on my behalf, and with Chantel as our guide standing with her feet on either side of the gear lever, and with me in the driver's seat with a slightly manic smile on my face, we set off to find some Bushman cave paintings deep into one of the adjoining valleys. We headed along part of the dry bed of the Zebra River and crossed several other river courses, the descent into and ascent from which were sometimes quite steep. On those occasions, I had to push hard on the brake pedal to ease the Unimog into the river bed, then engage a low four-wheel drive gear to creep across the bed, avoid the large boulders, scramble over the smaller rocks and, finally, gently but surely drive it up the other bank and back out onto the 'flat' where I could use third or fourth gear. I never did use fifth and sixth. At one point, I had to reverse in low gear to select a new route out of the river. Sometimes, we all had to duck to avoid the long sharp thorns on the white and yellow flowering acacias.

We followed the tracks cut into the plain of bleached yellow grass before climbing into one of the steep ravines that were strewn with rocks and dotted with copper-barked moringa trees. The edges of the surrounding valleys branched off in several directions, the tops of which were flat peaks composed of many layers of limestone looking like pages from an old and battered book seen from its side. Soon, we had to leave the Unimog and we walked along the course of the Zebra River itself where we saw the tracks of zebra, kudu, and steenbok in some stretches of sand. Again, all was silent except for birdsong and the hum of insects. As we walked through a patch of long grass, burrs stuck to our clothes in some numbers. At a small spring, we saw rosy-faced lovebirds with their brilliant green bodies and red heads, and dusky sunbirds, which are tiny black and white birds with curved beaks used for taking nectar.

We climbed further up the valley, marvelling at what a torrent the Zebra River must have been at one time to have carved out this riverbed with its tumble of boulders and sharp rock slippages. Part of the route was very sure underfoot; other parts were a bit of a scramble. Eventually, we reached a long narrow 'slit' two-thirds along the height of the valley wall, protected by a rock overhang, in which we found the Bushman paintings. They depicted two men dancing and another long-limbed man carrying a bow and arrow and showing the most exquisite detail of his hand. He was beautifully proportioned and painted in an elegant style. Under the rocks were many animal bones, but no one knows to what use this place was put or how many years ago the paintings were completed and for what purpose. I wondered what anyone would be doing out there in such a stark and unforgiving environment. I would never know, but I certainly have not forgotten that day when an implacable Namibian sun shone down on such a timeless creation.

On our return down the valley, lovebirds accompanied us for a while, flying ahead of us from tree to tree. It took four-and-a-half-hours to go there and back, including one-and-a-half-hours in the Unimog. It had been a wonderful walk but at times the terrain had been difficult. It would be easy to feel isolated in such a place. We were very lucky to see the paintings since they had only been re-discovered one month earlier by Chantel and a team of geologists. The former owner who had farmed the area had seen them many years ago, but only indicated their general whereabouts to Chantel and the team. We departed Zebra River Lodge wishing we could stay longer with this most hospitable family.

On our arrival at Namib Naukluft Lodge, Jessica, who showed us to our rooms, told us that if any gecko got in to let her know. The local people who normally clean the rooms would not do so until she had removed any gecko. They believed that they would die if a gecko bit them. One tour guide, knowing that their bite didn't hurt but that they do hang on for a little while before letting go, actually got two geckos to bite him on the earlobes and then, rather cruelly, walked into the lodge kitchen, promptly clearing the place of all local people.

To reach the lift-off site for our hot air balloon ride, we set out before dawn for Sesriem and Karos Lodge where a waiting driver took Linda and me, and three Spaniards along a very long and flat gravel track to the balloon. In the far distance in the pre-dawn light, we saw the burners being tested for the flight. As we arrived, the huge blue, red and yellow canopy was being inflated. Our pilot was a Belgian called Eric who owned Kulala Lodge and who spoke several languages. A Zimbabwean couple were the last to join us, and we took off just as the sun was creeping up in the sky. The noise of the burners was almost as intense as the heat we felt on the back of our necks, but the ascent was wonderfully effortless and we soon reached 800 metres. Beneath us was the huge gravel pan skirting the undulating, flowing dunes of the Namib Desert on one side, and the rugged Naukluft Mountains on the other. As the sun rose, the massive dunes seemed to change shape as the shadows lengthened and their curves became more accentuated, and their colours moved from yellow to orange, and purple to red. The Tsauchab River is normally dry but, in February that year, it had been a kilometre wide and had broken through the dune barrier to fill the pan at Sossusvlei with water for the first time in twenty years. By opening and closing side vents in the canopy, Eric spun the balloon slowly through 360 degrees presenting us with a fantastic panorama. Gently, Eric brought the balloon down so that we almost touched the canopy of a tall camelthorn tree that passed just beneath us. Eventually, we were able to pluck some leaves from a wild sage bush only a metre above the ground. As we regained some height, we saw the dark sinuous ridges of the dunes and the endless red sands stretching into the distance. As a finale, we landed gently on the side of a dune where we stuck fast until Eric found a willing Spaniard to jump out and drag the balloon out of the sand and down towards the flat by hauling on a rope over his shoulder.

When the crew arrived to pack everything away, we were taken off to a shady spot in the dry riverbed where we enjoyed our champagne breakfast. Eric's party trick was to open champagne bottles at the neck with a very long machete. As we sat and ate our food, we listened to tales of Africa - how the Spaniards had got caught up in a herd of elephants during their first day in Etosha; how the Zimbabwean couple encountered all kinds of nasty snakes; and Eric telling us of the ability of four-metre-long black mambas being able to rear two metres into the air and to strike downwards so that a person is bitten high up on the arm.

After breakfast, we went to Kulala Lodge, owned by Eric and his wife, and which was seemingly hidden in the desert overlooking the dry river running towards Sossusvlei. En route, we visited Eric's house, which is just like any other except that the TV is for videos only unless one installs a satellite dish. His male Rhodesian ridgeback dog greeted us and we saw some of his pet snakes. The workmen all ran away when Eric took one out to show them. We enjoyed our time with Eric and many years later I met him again. After lounging around the pool back at the Namib Naukluft Lodge, we went for a sundowner drive in the late afternoon to the Marble Mountain where the white marble has been smoothed and weathered by the wind. We enjoyed a bottle of white wine as our sundowner drink as dusk fell, and the last warm, red rays of the sun glinted on the marble. On our return, we caught a barking gecko, which has a rough pinkish upper side and a smooth belly and no suckers on its feet, unlike the ones in our room. We saw the Southern Cross and Jupiter, Venus, and Mars in the sky. Dinner was an outdoor barbecue followed by an impromptu song and dance session by the staff. The call was "make more dust" - very good fun.

The journey to Sossusvlei was another dawn start. We had to negotiate a segment of the road towards the very end of our journey that was very sandy and deeply rutted. The loose sand being thrown up by a car in front impeded my vision. Behind us was a very large lorry taking a group of people on an overland journey around Africa. Without warning, our car plunged into exceptionally soft sand and large clouds of sand and dust were being thrown up all around it, and a great deal was also coming into the cabin. Conscious of traffic in front and behind but mindful that the last thing I wanted to do in such conditions was to come to a stop, I put my foot down. The car slithered all over the place, then became caught in the ruts, but kept going forward. Although I could see very little, I knew the car had passed through the worst of the soft sand when it hit the hard gravel track and began to accelerate. The inside of the car, however, was fairly covered in the debris of the desert.

At the parking area for two-wheel drive cars, we saw a party from our lodge in a four-wheel drive vehicle and so we hitched a lift with them the four kilometres uphill to Sossusvlei. At the pan itself, still partially full of water for the first time in many years, the scenery was most impressive. Covering three sides of the vlei – the local word for a pan - were massive sand dunes and the early sun accentuated their shapely curves. Here are found the tallest dunes in the world, up to 300 metres high. On the ridge of the nearest dune, we could see a strong wind whipping away the grains of sand so that at times the view of the horizon appeared indistinct and hazy. The edges of the pan, where some of the water had evaporated, were now dried mud, full of the imprints of birds' feet and cracked like crazy paving. On the water were feeding avocets. Linda and I climbed one of the dunes towering above the pan; at the top, we could see some green trees dotted around the vlei and, beyond, an unfolding vista of apricot-coloured dunes stretching away into the distant unknown. The leeward side of the dune was exceptionally steep and completely smooth. It was tempting to run down it: many years later I did.

We ate our packed lunch at the side of the vlei before walking back to the car park, and setting off to Kulala Lodge where we enjoyed a sundowner drive through the 32,000 hectares of the property. Much of it was composed of wide plains with countless tufts of dried yellow grass. In addition to this veldt, the property also contained the very fringes of the Namib Desert so that the dunes nestled quietly at the edges of the grasslands. At one of our stops, Linda very nearly stepped on a large scorpion. In the dark, the driver negotiated the tracks back to the lodge at great speed and, with the wind tearing at our hair, we saw above us the clear outline of the Southern Cross. However, we now faced a 100 kilometres drive in the dark back to our own lodge at Namib Naukluft, which is always a little scary in this part of Africa where animals have a habit of suddenly running in front of the car or else trying to jump over the headlights and, sometimes, failing to do so with disastrous consequences. As it was, we had no problems except to wonder whether we might be caught in the storm that we saw off in the distance with its great flashes of lightning that momentarily threw an eerie light across the Namibian wilderness through which we were making our resolute way.

Our next destination was the Hotel Schweizerhaus on the coast in Swakopmund. The first part of our journey was accompanied by hundreds of lark-like buntings that the car 'flushed out' from the road verges and which then proceeded to fly around us in a maze of twists and turns. The drive through the Namib Naukluft Park was notable for small rounded hills rising from the plains, and for steep-sided passes with bare rock faces on either side. In Swakopmund, we had coffee and cakes in Anton's, the equivalent of Betty's, but with a strong German tradition. Our evening meal was at an Italian restaurant where they also sold Monkeygland Burger and chips, which we found out afterwards was actually beef with a special sauce.

Linda and I stayed only one night at Swakopmund before leaving early in the morning to drive part of the way along the Skeleton Coast Road as far as Henties Bay. The light was very flat and it was difficult to distinguish sky from sea and sand in the cloudy and misty atmosphere. The place gets its name from all the shipwrecks that came to grief along the coast, but I liked to think it had something to do with the actual skeletons of the poor sailors stranded there in the 19th century where, being beyond any kind of rescue at that time, and unable to cross the great expanse of the Namib Desert, they died of thirst. Increasingly, I found the drive along the coast claustrophobic as if the grey of the sea and sand were merging with the sullen, misty sky and collapsing around me. I was grateful at last to turn inland onto the gravel plains once more, and regain my depth of perception. At Twyfelfontain, we saw the San petroglyphs, or rock carvings. There were over 2,500 depictions of various animals and of people's hands and feet, some of them 6,000 years old. They could be seen very clearly for the most part, especially giraffe, zebra, rhino, elephant and oryx and their spoor; there was even a seal. The texture of the rock added to the beauty; for example, by imitating the reticulations of the giraffe's hide. After a picnic at the site, we resumed our long hot and dusty journey, eventually reaching the Veterinary Gate where we were to be picked up for the final transportation to Etendeka Mountain Camp hidden in the isolated depths of Damaraland. As we were early, we went for a beer at the nearby Palmwag Lodge where, as it turned out, we met the owner of Etendeka, Dennis Liebenberg, who was at the lodge on business. In fact, he had arranged with the lodge's manager for the bar to be open so that we could get those much-desired beers.

Etendeka means Stacked Mountains or the land of layered hills in the local Herero language and the track to it goes for eighteen kilometres through some rugged territory. We saw weltwitschia plants, Hartmann's mountain zebra, springbok, kudu and lots of birds en route from Dennis's large Land Rover. The camp consisted of ten walk-in shaded tents with solar-powered lighting and bush showers where very hot water comes from a solar-heated tank and is mixed with cold water before being suspended in a bucket over one's head in the shower. One night we showered in the dark with just the array of bright stars and the Milky Way overhead - far from being 'primitive,' in a land with so little water, it was a great luxury and privilege. From our tent, we had the most wonderful views of the layered hills composed of ancient basalt that had been weathered into flat-topped hills and boulder-strewn plains. Dennis's concession area was 45,000 hectares on the very edge of the Namib Desert. The place was pristine in nature's terms and very relaxing. A log fire roared at the communal dining area and we drank cold beer and wine with lamb and apricot casserole, coconut pudding and coffee, which we ate from trays quite informally as we sat around the fire, just Dennis, Guy (his assistant), a French couple, and ourselves. Through a small telescope, Dennis showed us the moon in incredible close-up and then we saw four moons of Jupiter and even more marvellously the rings of Saturn in quite superb detail. Brilliant end to a long day.

In the early morning, we left camp for a six kilometre walk with Dennis who led us down a valley into a dried-up river bed and then to the top of a basalt spur and thence back to camp. He showed us the butter tree, various acacias, the bottle tree (in flower), the shepherd's tree and its close counterpart the stinking shepherd's tree with its foul-smelling sap, and two kinds of euphorbia, which despite their poisonous sap are much favoured by rhino and kudu. We also saw harvester ants, termites, and twice we saw the rare black slender mongoose - the second time it 'scolded' us for being in its territory. The whole area was formed 130 million years ago from volcanic flows and there are lots of quartz and other crystals found in the basalt rocks. Part of the walk meant clambering up a volcanic dyke, one of the very last cracks in the earth's crust through which lava had been forced. When it had cooled, it left many different shapes of basalt in the dyke - some stepped and others like leaves in a book, and still others like crystals with long thin triangular shapes.

In the mornings, a warm wind usually blew from the north-east and if it stopped the temperature increased still more. By late afternoon, typically the wind had changed and blows from the south-west and cools things down since it brings colder air from the sea - the Damara Doctor. Dennis told us that occasionally they get flash floods. Once, he had arrived very late at the camp with guests to find it in darkness and a torrent of water flowing through the middle of it. Even so, the camp's cook had constructed a platform of wood and metal sheets over the main flow of water and was proudly standing there cooking the evening meal on this platform.

In the afternoon, we went for a game drive and saw the well-defined and elegant Hartmann's zebra. The sun striking the reddish rocks with their covering of rust from the iron-ore content gave the scenery a wonderful glow. That evening, we had roast chicken, cooked over a log fire's embers, and apple crumble. Once again, we saw Jupiter and Saturn. A Bomakarie bird, or Bokkie, came into the camp to take some proffered cheese. Another lovely evening around the mopane log fire; even the wood has to be brought to the camp since they cannot use the trees on site. Linda and I stayed talking until nearly midnight with Dennis and Guy and, later, in our tent we heard zebra clopping past the camp in the darkness.

Sadly, our time in Etendeka was over and we returned to Palmwag with Guy. It turned out to be more like an early morning game drive than a transfer and we got our best view yet of the zebra, giraffe, oryx, steenbok, and springbok. On our way to Etosha in our own car, we stopped briefly in Outjo, where we saw a Herero woman in all her finery in a costume that hasn't changed since Victorian times. Our three-bed rondavel at Okaukuejo, Etosha National Park, was very comfortable and spacious and had we had more 'camping' gear we could have made more of it. As it was, my Swiss army knife performed miracles! It even fixed the mount on my camera's mirror lens where two of the three screws had gone missing due to the constant vibration in the car. But it couldn't fix the one and only puncture we had on the entire journey. Luckily, we were only a few yards from the camp petrol station when we noticed it, and a man there fixed it for only fifteen Namibian dollars using the kind of techniques and tools that I used as a tyre fitter in the 1960s; techniques that are now illegal in the UK. Still, it held for the rest of the trip, as the man assured me it would.

Etosha was simply overflowing with animals and birds, and we saw many animals time and time again, often in large concentrations. Our first spectacular experience in Etosha was at the famous floodlit waterhole in Okaukuejo. Twenty-three elephants, a whole breeding herd, were walking towards the water along a well-worn path. There was even a tiny calf that hid behind its mother's rear feet at the edge of the water. After drinking, most of the herd engaged in simple play - wallowing and splashing for all they were worth Then, they moved off to dust themselves in the grey and white dust that is typical of

Etosha. At sunset, the lights were turned on at the waterhole and a little while later a small bachelor herd of elephant emerged from the distant gloom like white ghosts. In twos and threes, over thirty minutes or so, other bachelor groups joined their companions at the waterside until there were eleven male elephants in total. The biggest of them drank from a specific spot, where the pumped water entered the hole and therefore where the water was at its freshest. Occasionally, he asserted his authority and gently but firmly pushed other males away from his drinking spot. These large males drank for ages, for the most part standing very quietly at the edge of the hole. Only one male, much later, made a half-hearted attempt to 'play' in the water as the herd of females and young ones had done earlier. A few males had large collars around their necks as part of a study on anthrax. Suddenly, a lone black rhino came to the hole and the elephants appeared to ignore him. Incredibly, a short while later, a female white rhino with a suckling calf also turned up out of the gloom beyond the lights and then a fourth male rhino came into view. This large rhino was approaching the hole just as a bull elephant was making his way there. Suddenly, the elephant came close enough on a similar path to spot the rhino and after a short but somewhat animated contretemps the rhino ran off to circle all the way behind the drinking elephant and to lie down between us and the waterhole, not forty metres away. One South African seasoned visitor to the waterhole told us that in twenty years he had never seen a rhino that close on the spectators' side. The rhino simple lay there, as if asleep, until all the elephant had left and only then did it get up and go to drink.

Our next lodge in Etosha was Halali where we had a ridiculously large four-bed, two-bedroom cottage. That evening, Linda was unwell, so I made myself a cheese sandwich and opened a bottle of South African Swartland Wynkelder 1993 Shiraz purchased from the drankwinkel in Outjo. While Linda slept and recovered her health, I sat outside and lit a fire in the hearth outside the cottage. The wood, available from the camp shop, was mopane - very hard and dense - which gave off a good light and a lot of heat. Linda joined me later to view a total eclipse of the moon. During the eclipse, the clarity of the Milky Way was breathtaking.

The next day, Linda and I drove to Nuamses that had a deep crater for a waterhole, but there was no game. However, we were close to the immense pan at the heart of Etosha National Park – about the size of Holland - so we decided to go to the lookout point. At the pan, we saw springbok standing silently in line in the shimmering heat. As our gaze pulled back, we suddenly saw cheetah. First one, then two, then four; in the end, there were seven, and one of them flushed out a rabbit or hare, killed it, and ran off so that it could eat it alone. The cheetah crossed the dry estuary and walked slowly over the sweet scrub terrain with its yellow and ochre grass. Occasionally, one would flop down on the ground, raise its tail, and then slowly catch up with the others. Since the kill had been so small and only one of this band of brothers had managed to swallow more than a morsel, the group soon resumed their quest for food. They began to survey the plain and two cheetah walked on in front, climbed the estuary bank, and sat down. We could see them inspecting the area, looking left and right, and sitting close together but quietly. The others caught them up, the last one still having a piece of the hare in its mouth. As we left them, several were playing together and the others had settled back in the shade of a tree where it was almost impossible to pick them out so good was their camouflage. All seven looked sleek and healthy. One woman who had been coming to Etosha for twenty-five years told us back in camp that she had never seen cheetah. How lucky we were!

The next waterhole, Batia, was dry so we drove to Kalkheuwel which, although we did not know it then, was to become the undoubted 'star' of all our visits to waterholes in the park.

Kalkheuwel, or chalk hill, is a large drinking area with two holes about forty-five metres apart. Between them is uneven terrain where water can also be found among the rocks. One elephant was already there as we arrived and it was soon joined by four other males. There were lots of zebra, kudu, springbok, a black-faced male impala, oryx who were very skittish, and six giraffe - all waiting their turn to drink after the elephant. Thousands of lark-like buntings moved as a single flock and flew from tree to tree around the waterhole, sometimes swooping down to the edge of the water to drink en masse. We stayed for well over an hour - the elephant stayed even longer!

At Chudob, a large bull covered in mud from the waterhole approached our car and persuaded us that it would be better to reverse a little distance away from him. As he left this cone-shaped hole with a green floating reed island in the middle, the place was taken over by zebra that proceeded to get themselves very muddy indeed. The smell of the mud was very strong and unpleasant. A warthog tried to get among the zebra to drink as did a male black-faced impala. Giraffe came, looked at the zebra in charge, and left.

On our return to Kalkheuwel on the way back to our lodge, the elephants were still there. Then a mother and calf arrived, escorted by a huge bull in musth. There was a little trumpeting and jockeying around the waterhole among the males. However, when a herd of thirteen elephant with seven calves arrived, the males immediately ceded their positions at the hole. Another large male approached but was driven off by the bull in musth. Later, a big white-dusted male came and 'sparred' with one of the male juveniles in the herd. Two small calves were well looked after as the herd wallowed in the mud, but the matriarch had to discipline a second adolescent male for some misbehaviour. There followed lots of trumpeting and even more wallowing, accompanied by deep rumbling noises. Eventually, the herd left and only the adolescent male remained for a short while to spar with the big bull. Soon the whole herd had disappeared into the mopane trees scattered throughout the plain. On the way back to Halali, we saw another herd by the side of the road.

In the evening, we lit a fire with mopane logs and sat around it eating a Linda-special picnic after the Swiss army knife had managed to open a tin of tuna. The picnic was accompanied by Swartland Cabernet/Sauvignon, the music of Turandot, and the stupendous Milky Way.

The next morning, at Rietfontein waterhole, we spied a lanner falcon and then a continuous stream of zebra filing towards the water - over 600 we estimated. It was an impressive sight punctuated by occasional conflict and high-pitched squeals. Everywhere was a mass of legs and stripes moving backwards and forwards. On our fifth visit to Kalkheuwel, we again saw elephant - three bulls, one of which came within ten yards of the car forcing us to reverse. He stood there for over twenty minutes dusting himself, smelling the air, and appearing to eyeball the two occupants of a small red car directly in front of him who would have had no chance if the bull had decided to charge. Blue-helmeted guinea fowl arrived, each one running after the one in front looking like pantomime dames with full skirts and a silly hair-do.

We were unable to stay at Etosha for as long as we wanted because of the scarcity of bookable accommodation, so we stayed for two nights at Etosha Aoba Lodge, which was ten kilometres from the park gates. It was a very quiet environment, set in a wood and each of the eight rooms had its own veranda looking into the bush. We dined with two Austrian ladies (mother and daughter) and Jurgen and Elly from Munster. We had kudu for dinner, which was excellent, and were the last up drinking beer and talking to Helmut and his partner Christine who ran the lodge, whom Linda described as a 'jolly hockey sticks person.' However, at bedtime, we did not receive the armed guard to take us to our cottage. It was decided that last night's prowling lion had gone elsewhere. So, Linda and I walked off into the darkness on our own.

Our final destination in Namibia was Okonjima, a private game reserve dedicated to the preservation of big cats, especially leopards and cheetahs. No sooner had Linda and I arrived than we met a huge, tame warthog called Piggy and a tame lynx, called Shingi, with her three-week-old kitten, Max, who still had blue eyes. In the afternoon, we were introduced to three orphaned cheetahs, Chinga, Caesar and Choui, who joined guests on the lawn; while we polished off our tea and biscuits they ate chunks of impala. Chinga is the only female and the oldest, and the lodge's first tame cheetah. They came close enough to us that we could touch them and stroke their fur, which is surprisingly rough. Close-up, they are even more strikingly beautiful with large yellowish eyes, long tails, and tear drop markings on the face. They purred just like domestic cats when we stroked them. Wayne, the joint owner, turned up with Elvis, a large and very powerful male baboon - another tame creature.

On our way to the hide to see wild leopards, Wayne briefed us on the work and history of the Africat Foundation, which was dedicated to the preservation of big cats whose biggest threat came from local farmers who trapped and shot leopards since they saw them as poachers of their domestic cattle herds. However, when a farmer kills the dominant male leopard in an area, who formerly would have limited the number of other leopards in his territory, the door is then opened to a great many more leopards to enter the area so that more livestock are taken. At the hide, meat was laid out and we settled back to wait. Suddenly, a very large male leopard called Tyson appeared. He was the dominant animal in the area and weighed over seventy kilograms. Leopards can be individually identified by the collar of spots around the front of their chest and by the spots between their nose and whiskers. They are much more powerful than a cheetah. The leopard chomped on a bone and then effortlessly climbed a tree stump to take the meat left there. After thirty minutes he left, but hiding in the trees was another, Scar, who never plucked up the courage to come for any meat.

The next day, we were on our way to do the Bushman trail when we met the three tame lions at Okonjima who were being exercised by Wayne and his wife, Rosie, using footballs and a heavy medicine ball on a rope. The two-year-old male caught the ball and chased after it just like a domestic cat. Excellent Bushman trail, which was very relaxed and informative and involved no 'exploitation' of any actual Bushmen. It was a proper educational event, in which we learned – to our horror – that Bushmen could be legally shot until 1936 since the authorities looked on them as vermin to be eradicated. As we sat in the lodge reading and waiting to depart for the airport in Windhoek, Shingi came over and curled up right next to Linda. Several of those who worked there said how honoured Linda was since this lynx hardly ever bothered with guests.

In seventeen days, Linda and I saw and identified 102 different species of bird and travelled over 4,000 kilometres, mostly on graded dirt roads. Given all the wonderful creatures we had seen and the splendour of the changing Namibian countryside, I realized that I had stayed away from Africa for too long, and I chastised myself for not having visited sooner. That Namibian journey in September 1997 was the last summer holiday Linda and I ever took together. It was fully twelve years later before I returned.

Chapter Ten: Europe

Before I recount the long-haul travels to Namibia and elsewhere, I must first deal with my European journeys. I have already written about the skiing holidays, so I will not return there. Essentially, these city-based excursions were long weekends, except for a four-week study visit to Florence. After 1999 when my wife and I separated, these trips were no longer taken with Linda, but with family, friends, or lovers.

In the winter of 1991, I was fortunate to be invited to study as a visiting professor at the European University Institute in Fiesole, a village overlooking Florence. The Institute's director had an interest, like myself, in policing and the terms of my engagement required me to conduct comparative research on British and Italian police systems for which I would receive 2,400,000 lira for living expenses. However, the director omitted to inform me that the Institute's library had only two books on policing – both dated. Put bluntly, there was no possibility of me doing any kind of meaningful research, so most of my four weeks at the Institute turned into a month's holiday. Most mornings, I would take the No.7 bus from close to my hotel, the Adam, in the centre of Florence, and I would enjoy the twisting climb towards Fiesole with its commanding views of the terracotta roofs of the medieval city below. At the Institute, I would read the papers, speak to other academics and, generally, find ways to kill the time. No one ever chased me about the 'research' project, which suited me fine. In fact, the Institute paid my living expenses twice. Despite my strong protestations and insistence that

I had already been paid, I had another 2,400,000 lira literally thrust unceremoniously into my hands. That afternoon, I wandered around the market in Florence a lira millionaire with notes stuffed inside several coat pockets. I took special notice of the sign that urged people to beware pickpockets.

Occasionally, I would walk from the Institute with its grand mansions and fine gardens to the site of some Roman and Etruscan ruins where I could buy a coffee in a delightful café and watch birds squabble in the branches of ancient olive trees. After lunch, either at the Institute or in one of the small restaurants in Fiesole, it was time to catch the No.7 bus back to Florence. Tickets for Florentine buses could be bought at the main bus station and at hundreds of street kiosks. Tickets had to be validated by inserting them into bright yellow machines attached to poles inside each bus, which punched the date and time onto them. Few Florentine citizens did so unless a ticket inspector boarded the bus, in which case it was entirely possible to be trampled in the stampede to access the nearest yellow machine.

In the early afternoons, I went sightseeing and enjoyed easy access to the attractions because in the winter there were far fewer tourists. There were no queues to enter the Duomo, the Uffizi Gallery, the Palazzo Vecchio, and the Accademia to see the statue of David. I was able to walk freely across the Ponte Vecchio and do some window-shopping in the gold emporiums without the crush of people barring my way. It was marvellous in contrast to the insufferable summer swarms of visitors. But by far and away the best part was that the free time enabled me to create not one Mike's Bar but two! Not far from the Piazza del Duomo was a thriving street market composed of covered outdoor stalls selling woollen clothes, angora sweaters, suede and leather jackets, and many other leather goods. The area was a throng of small streets lined with stalls, behind some of which were permanent shops where most of the stock was kept. It was here I met Aldo, a shop owner, who gave me a thorough tour of his establishment. Later, when Linda had joined me for a weekend, we returned there and bought two gorgeous suede winter coats from Aldo. Not far from Aldo's place was a small corner bar. I could jump off the No.7 bus from Fiesole and be at the bar in no time at all. It was run by Marco and his wife and only operated during market hours since it was overwhelmingly for the use of the market workers, and not for tourists. I loved the fact that Marco threw down fresh sawdust over his floor from time to time, and seemed to know by name everyone who came in for an espresso or a grappa. This became the afternoon Mike's Bar No.1, and it wasn't too long before Marco knew my name too.

Mike's Bar No.2, mostly for late afternoon and early evening use, was Il Mio Bar on the Via Calimala, one of the broad streets emanating from the Piazza del Duomo, and only a short distance from the Hotel Adam. This small bar with modern and bright décor was run by Nico and Giovanni. I used to go there to have a coffee and later a glass of wine, and to sit in the corner and read the local paper. On one occasion, the place was rather full but as soon as Nico saw me, he politely but firmly moved a small group of customers so that I had a table to myself. At the same time, Giovanni was explaining to another customer with the paper that it was needed for someone else – me. Both Nico and Giovanni were great conversationalists and we spent some time chatting in Italian about the state of the nation, the high taxes, and the form of Fiorentina – the local football team.

At weekends, I saw my Italian friends that Linda and I first met in Kenya some years earlier. They lived in Prato, a city about an hour's drive from Florence. I went there usually by train, but sometimes Claudio would pick me up near my hotel in his very swish Mercedes. I had the most glorious lunches at their homes and, on one occasion, at the home of Paolo's mother. The evening meals were even better, often eaten at some restaurant in the Tuscan hillsides, or else in places we visited such as San Gimignano or Verona. Claudio always drove as fast as he could on such visits, which only made the memory of them more thrilling.

Another memorable visit to Italy occurred when my best mate, Allen Callaghan, arranged a package holiday with a south Walian travel agency to witness Wales's first game of rugby against Italy in April 2001 in a revamped Six Nations competition in Rome. We flew from London to Paris and then to Rome on a package put together by what turned out to be a dodgy firm. What a farce that travel agent caused us. There was no one to meet us at Rome Airport for several hours and all we had were match tickets and return air tickets but no accommodation. Eventually, a representative turned up and wanted us to wait even longer for a coach to take us and other clients to our accommodation, but Allen insisted she hired a taxi for us then and there to take us to the hotel, and she agreed. At the hotel, the manager, who spoke no English, at first refused to give us a room but by virtue of the fact I could speak some Italian, I persuaded him to do so. All we knew at this point was that our room was ours on a somewhat uncertain basis – would we have to pay again, would we be kicked out? We knew however that this travel agent was reportedly meeting people at nine p.m. at a church about three kilometres away to take people on a tour of the best drinking places. As Allen and I were about to set off to find him, a coach load of Welsh fans from the valleys had arrived, been checked in (sort of) and now were in the lobby in an angry mood and complaining like mad to the manager. Some of them had been allocated rooms with insufficient beds, others had yet to be given any room at all – it was chaos, and then the manager came over to me and begged for help to translate. Allen, seeing the disruption and being even more fearful for our own room, immediately took possession of our room key; one of the valley boys was saying there had been rumours of clients of this agency being turfed out of their rooms because no one had paid the proprietors. Allen took it on himself to find this church and have it out with the travel agent, leaving me to do the translating. I toured the hotel with the manager and the disgruntled fans sorting out what I could. Some lads were grateful for my intervention since it's always best if a party of four have four beds rather than one. The manager was even more grateful since the chaos might easily have escalated into force majeure. All this palaver took about two hours. Allen had not returned, and I began to worry since he had no map and only spoke a few words of Italian – yes, no, please and thank you. Near midnight, I was eventually back in the lobby, free of dispossessed valley boys but exhausted and even more worried about Allen and what if anything I could do now to find him, when suddenly the doors were thrown open and there was Allen with two of the biggest and coldest bottles of lager I have ever seen. The agent had not turned up but other disgruntled customers had, and Allen learned a great deal about this dodgy agent. Allen had been right to hold onto our key – people had returned to their hotels to find they had been locked out and their rooms re-allocated. I asked him how he found his way about – "Oh there are these street maps here and there," he said, matter-of-factly. "And there's this little bar around the corner which is where I got the beers. I thought you might need one." At that moment, there was no greater friend in the world.

The next day, we made our way to the Stadio Flaminio and sat outside at a café in a long, busy street leading to the ground. Suddenly, one group of Welsh fans came running out from a nearby bar shouting: "They've run out of beer." Within five minutes, there was a cascade effect, as other groups of fans in bars and cafés along the street were faced by café owners telling them they had no beer left - they had severely underestimated what rugby fans drink before a game. As distraught Welshmen ran further and further down the street to find a bar still selling beer, Allen and I, with a smug look on our faces, sat and drank our wine knowing that was the one commodity the Italians never ran out of. Just as in Paris as teenagers long ago and with so many of the other things we had done together, we were two great friends who had shared so much and we felt again to be kings of the world. Wales won by ten points.

There were other trips to Rome to see Wales play, not all of them with a successful outcome. The Stadio Flaminio, where Italy played, was a quaint but ramshackle heap; many of its seats were nothing more than shallow concrete bowls with no backrest and, if it had rained recently, fans had to sit in tiny puddles of water, if they couldn't dry the bowl. I soon learned to take plastic bags to sit on and an old paper to soak up the water. Welsh fans easily outnumbered the Italians in those early encounters and our European cousins drank a great deal less than we did. When Mark and I were at the ground, there were employees walking along the gangways with trays selling bottles of good Italian beer. All we had to do was call them over to get a drink; none of that dreadful queuing at the national stadium in Cardiff for overpriced alcohol. Rome's municipal police and the national Carabinieri in the first years of Italy's participation in the Six Nations both looked upon British rugby fans as another form of British football hooligans. They automatically associated heavy drinking with violence.

In 2003, the authorities became concerned at what the Welsh boys were putting away and ordered the bar owners near the stadium to stop the sale of alcohol. Within twenty minutes of the ban, Mark and I witnessed two teenage boys patrolling the perimeter of the stadium with a wheeled cart in which were litre bottles of lager. No sooner had Mark and I bought two bottles from them than a Carabinieri tried to confiscate all the beer they had bought from a nearby supermarket with such marvellous entrepreneurial foresight. One lad picked up three bottles and ran off, while the other scurried away pushing his cart for all he was worth with the Carabinieri chasing after him but losing the pursuit. Mark and I dined near the

Pantheon that night and then moved to a bar with outside tables and chairs. Next to us were a German couple but we had had no contact with them except when I returned from ordering more drinks. I had been inside no more than three minutes and, as I returned to my seat, Mark turned to the German couple with whom he had been trying to have a conversation and announced: "Here's my brother. He speaks German and will explain everything." It was amazing how much schoolboy German I could dig up when I had to. Much later, on our way back to the hotel near the main railway station in Rome, we spied a bar on a raised walkway above us that was still open in the early hours of the morning. We entered and saw one barman and four men in work clothes who were employed by the city cleansing authority. They were supposed to be outside cleaning the streets, but they were inside having a drink. They were surprised to see two tourists come in, but soon warmed to us when I spoke in Italian to them. I told them we were here to watch Wales play rugby; that meant nothing to any of them, but they became much more animated when I declared I was a fan of Milan football club. Soon we were buying each other rounds of drinks. Mark and I had lager and wine; they had Jack Daniel's!

Our 2005 visit was even more dramatic, but had nothing to do with the rugby or Rome and everything to do with the flight home. We were flying easyJet from Rome to East Midlands Airport and, at some point, Mark started to feel unwell. First, he requested some water; then he asked for oxygen as he was struggling to breathe normally; and, finally, he was in such a state that the captain declared a diversion and we made an emergency landing in a blizzard at Lyon Airport, France. At Lyon, several medical personnel, two members of the fire brigade with a stretcher, and a gendarme came on board. While the medics and stretcher-bearers carried Mark away, the gendarme more or less arrested me. I had to carry our cabin luggage and coats to the police post at the airport where I had to show our passports and explain what was going on. Very soon, however, the officer interviewing me realized this had been a genuine medical emergency, and he kindly escorted me to the airport's medical facility. As Mark was being taken off the plane, I genuinely thought he was suffering a heart attack. When I entered the cubicle where he was being looked after, he was sat up on a bed taking on some fluids. Immediately, he turned to the medical personnel and said: "Here's my brother. He speaks French and can answer your questions." Cue schoolboy French...again. For the next ten minutes, I was asked questions in French about my brother's medical history and health in general. These I translated for Mark and did my best to make coherent French versions of his replies. They told me his ECG showed no abnormalities. In fact, they did not know what had happened to him.

While Mark remained under observation, a very kind nurse with some broken English took me to the baggage reclaim hall to retrieve our luggage that had been taken off the plane; and then to the easyJet office to book homeward flights via Stansted Airport. EasyJet did not charge us for these flights even though the emergency landing must have cost them a lot of money, nor did the medical centre charge us anything for Mark's treatment. They would not even accept a donation. Later that day, we duly departed for Stansted only for Mark to experience exactly the same symptoms. The captain came to our seats, as Mark was using oxygen once again, and asked me if I wanted the plane to make an emergency landing in Paris. With such a short time to go before touchdown in Britain, we declined the offer. It was late at night when we landed and, by then, Mark was well again. We had to take a very expensive taxi ride to get home but at least Mark was fine. When Mark returned to Wales, he saw his GP, but nothing untoward was discovered and he has never had such symptoms on a plane since.

Throughout the 1990s and 2000s, I made several more visits to Europe, set out here in no particular order: to see Paolo marry his new partner, Sonia; to Kraków and the heartbreaking scenes at Auschwitz; to Berlin for a McCartney concert; to Venice in the depths of winter; to Montecatini with my girlfriend Mandi to see Paolo and Sonia; to Prague for Boxing Day only; to Budapest and the majestic River Danube; with my brother on several occasions to Montecatini, Florence, and Lucca; and, finally, to Paris in August 2000 with Zizi.

Now comes the difficult part of my story; difficult for the combination of happiness, sadness, sexual pleasure, and uncertainty that I experienced with Zizi. And difficult to write about those feelings while being fair to her. I had contemplated omitting this topic, but I will at least summarise the relationship for it was one that involved a great deal of travel, as well as much soul-searching. My relationship with Zizi was, put simply, elliptical – at times close and loving and, at other times, fragile. Most of the time I was on a firm footing with Zizi, but there were a few occasions when I was figuratively standing on the edge of a cornice, waiting for it to collapse. To call our relationship complicated would be an oversimplification: yet, when I was with her, I experienced so many delights.

I met Zizi through work and, after my separation from Linda, we became good friends. Zizi was always well-dressed in a stylish, casual manner, often preferring warm but slightly muted colours. In winter, which for her ran from September to June – so cold did she find the UK climate – Zizi loved to wear three-quarter length coats and thick wrap-around scarves or Pashmina shawls. Her home was decorated with shadow puppets from Southeast Asia and clown masks from Venice. Zizi's time in the UK was coming to an end, and in August 2000 she was returning home to renew her job at her old university. She had wanted to obtain employment at a British university but that had not materialised. She consoled herself in the knowledge that she would be much closer to her grown up children and no longer an active partner to her estranged British husband. She was flying home via Paris with a stop over, and it was typical Zizi – a woman who knew what she wanted and how to get it - that she asked me to go with her to Paris and sleep with her. Zizi had deep brown eyes, mid-length blonde hair with subtle highlights that changed from gold, to copper and to straw tones when she ran her fingers through it so alluringly. Her skin was a delicate shade of olive and soft and smooth to the touch. Added to this was an intoxicating smile and inviting lips, and the body of a woman who had once been a fashion model – I was not about to refuse. In Paris, we toured the Marais area, visited the Musée d'Orsay and other museums, but what I remember best was being in bed with her. And then the next day, she was gone; I thought I would never see her again. However, later that summer, Zizi emailed me to tell me she had, after all, secured a lectureship at a university in England. Four years of giddy elliptical movements through space and emotions started on her return. Throughout those years, Zizi endured job insecurity as many academics increasingly did at the start of the millennium. She had to apply for numerous jobs and move around the country to remain in work and in the UK. Zizi was often worn down and frustrated by the insecurity of her position, her fear of failure, the pull of wanting to go home, and the guilt she felt about the nature of her relationship with her husband, Paul. She also saw herself as an outsider. Most of all, Zizi was searching for an emotional nirvana, but whether that was happiness, fulfilment, or peace of mind (even all three), I did not know. I did know, however, that Zizi placed a great deal of faith in psychotherapy. Indeed, she told me several times I could benefit from it too. On one occasion, when I was visiting Zizi, I went with her to the psychotherapist's office and waited outside. She was in an emotional state when she went in and, when she came out, her emotional balance was worse. Zizi often spoke about psychotherapy as if it had more than just psychological advantages. To me, a sceptical onlooker, it felt like a quest for the Holy Grail. These sharp-edged topics came to the fore from time to time when Zizi and I were together.

Zizi liked to ask questions – very personal ones – and to act in unexpected ways. She would interrogate me about Linda, what our life together was like, why we parted and then condemn my response as being "too closed", or unsatisfactory in some way. A minute later, she would reach out to me, hug me, and breathe in deeply as if trying to experience some essence of me, and then say: "Be careful with me. I can be dangerous." My questions were often shunted off abruptly if I enquired about her estranged husband and why she hadn't left him. I asked her once if she still loved him and was met with "what is love?" Months later, her response was different: "I don't love Paul, but I feel guilty." Actually, I didn't give a damn about him. I was perfectly happy making love to Zizi whether he was on the scene or not, and yet I was curious. But I also assumed that one day she would leave him. Zizi wanted openness, but demanded more of it from me than I was allowed from her. I learnt that it was better not to criticize her behaviour for Zizi did not like to be judged in terms of right or wrong - to her, that was far too simplistic.

One of the things that Zizi liked about me was what she called my 'innocence.' She felt I had never been hurt whereas Zizi had felt great pain in some former relationships. I did not doubt her, but I could also see that she did her best to hide anything that upset her; her vulnerability was shown only briefly before she put it away and rebuilt the emotional shield. For all that, when she did occasionally confide in me, when she allowed some tears to flow, I loved her all the more – not because I wanted her to be vulnerable and dependent on me, but because such moments are the catalysts of strong, loving partnerships.

I met her as often as I could for weekends in a variety of towns and cities in Wales and England, in places where there were cultural attractions and entertainments. Despite our difficulties, we grew closer and discussed all manner of topics. She prided herself on being good at analysing people, their faces, and reactions. She liked the way that I looked at her; it made her feel wanted. I asked her once in some hotel bedroom in Bath what she saw us doing in a year's time. "You know we may not have a future together," was her reply.

Given that Zizi was an independent woman not given to romantic behaviour that she saw as unnecessary or meaningless, she could be delightfully coquettish. She used to flirt with me and tease me gently, and unexpectedly take my hand as we strolled together. Zizi put enormous time and thought into buying me presents for Christmas and my birthday; one of which was a soapstone carving of entwined, sitting lovers. Cards from her invariably wished me health, happiness, and peace, and were covered in a few kisses where she had pressed her lips against the card. Sometimes, there would be the intoxicating scent of her favourite perfume. Yet, she could also say: "You are not ready for me. I may send you away."

Discussions about Zizi's work often brought forward many complaints – nearly all of which were justified. She was a relatively junior and recently arrived colleague, and some duties (especially teaching and marking) were dumped on her. I saw it time after time at my own university. Her discontent was amplified by the chauvinistic attitudes frequently shown to her, and by her perception of belonging to a different culture, of being 'other' in the workplace. In these matters, I think I was genuinely able to provide some support, and at the very least to be a sympathetic listener – but not allowed to get too close. Once, something had happened at work that reduced Zizi to tears, but then she turned away from me and told me she was fine; she was in control again. Such was the tenor of our relationship and the concerns within it. On romantic visits to numerous European cities, we never fully escaped the concerns, but we did enjoy those moments free from the pressure of her work.

Our first overseas visit was to Berlin where we stayed in a bijou hotel close to Alexanderplatz. There was little talk of domestic matters, but even so Zizi had a gift for raising other issues that could be unsettling. She was fascinated by the remnants of the Berlin Wall and how some Germans had been outsiders in their own historic city. Zizi told me that's what she was - "an outsider." She warned me again to be careful with her because she could be "dangerous." I had heard it all before and, in fact, I liked the combination in Zizi of conservatism and permissiveness. She was conservative in the sense that she rarely showed public affection but, in private, the "dangerousness" was in reality about sex where she was very permissive.

In Montecatini, to meet my Italian friends, Zizi was at first anxious and unsure of herself. When she realized that no one was judging her, she relaxed and was soon on friendly terms with everyone. Our evening meal in the Tuscan hillsides was tender and affectionate. Later in bed she told me: "You are very precious to me." In Florence, we wore ourselves out trying to see as many of the city's treasures as possible, but I was delighted when Zizi told me that no matter what might happen in the future, she would always sleep with me which, admittedly, did not accord with the notion of sending me away. Inside the Alhambra in Granada, I thought Zizi more stunning than the Moorish palace itself. Judging by the looks she got as we walked through the place, many other men thought so too. She often teased me by saying that she was priceless, and I had to agree with her. We enjoyed an excellent meal at the Mirador in the Albaicín district. Later that year, I took a photograph of Zizi sat on the steps of the cathedral in Malaga; she looked so overwhelmingly alluring as she leant forward slightly to look into the camera that all I wanted was to take her straight back to the hotel and make love to her. In

Barcelona, I did not have to resort to that tactic for it rained for most of the weekend, so we stayed in bed for much of the time. In a moment of quiet pleasure, she told me: "I want you to know you are most precious to me." Naturally, when we were in Amsterdam, we tried the local 'pot' and then went back to the hotel to make love. I remember very little about our visit to Lisbon other than Zizi telling me: "Yes, we're lovers and you *are* the man in my life." At the Tivoli Gardens in Copenhagen, there was some further discussion of the shape of our future relationship. Zizi's response was a mixed one from my point of view, but perfectly correct from hers: "We have good sex; no, we have very good sex, but I'm not going to run into your arms." Even so, I felt bold enough to tell Zizi that I loved her to which she replied: "Well, that's your problem." But it was said gently and not meant to inflict pain. I persisted in telling her my feelings from time to time and got nowhere. Once, Zizi scolded me playfully: "You are a crazy man for loving me." She didn't say she was not in love with me, nor did she say she was. Until Genoa. There, in a small hotel along a narrow alleyway close to the port, we were in bed making love, with Zizi on top of me. She was subtly changing the angle of her body movements against me to extract every last spark of pleasure. Suddenly, she rose up and shouted: "I do love you; I do." It was the only time I ever saw her lose sexual control. Within a day of her declaration of love, Zizi insisted that: "Love doesn't matter; it's about difference." She never again told me that she loved me until fifteen years later in 2019.

The end came quickly and suddenly. A week before we were supposed to go to Brussels for a weekend, Zizi rang me and said that she couldn't see me anymore; that she couldn't go on as it was feeling guilty about the emotional tangle that was me, her husband and her in the middle. She didn't want anyone else but she felt she had to sort out her life, to be happy. She finished with: "This is about me, not you, or anyone else." It was 31st October 2004; a day, deep down, I always knew was coming. I had wanted so much to understand the complexity that was Zizi, and in large measure I failed. I don't think she fully understood herself or, if she did, was constantly in search of something and someone to change it for the better. After that, there were other girlfriends but few of these relationships lasted long. I became bored with them sexually – hardly a surprise after Zizi.

I had thought our relationship had come to a complete end, but I was mistaken on that issue as on many others. A year or so later there were tentative text exchanges, then a few telephone conversations and, eventually, the occasional visit to my house. Stripped of the sexual side of our relationship, and with enquiries about each other's love-life off the agenda, we once again became good friends, able to enjoy time together in a relaxed, if somewhat wistful, fashion. In March 2019, I sent a text to Zizi: "You should know that I never stopped loving you" to which she replied: "I can say the same. I always loved you. And regret losing you because of my stupidity. Please keep in touch. Xxx." When I saw that reply, my heart sank. All those years when we might have been together, now lost and scattered like strands of dry grass blown across the savannah. There's much more I could write about Zizi, but there are some matters best kept to ourselves.

I still travelled to Europe on skiing trips or weekends with friends and girlfriends, but I could not bear the thought of going away for weeks on my own on long-haul holidays. It was September 2009 before I went back to long-haul travel. Back to Namibia. I knew that even if I travelled there on my own, the majesty of the country meant that I would never feel lonely.

Chapter Eleven: Namibia

In September 2009, I flew from Heathrow via Frankfurt to Windhoek, Namibia, on an Airbus A343. The Air Namibia plane was relatively modern but it stood out incongruously on the apron at Windhoek's international airport. It was the only large plane there; the others were single engine light aircraft. There were no hydraulic sky bridges moving sinuously to connect to the aircraft doors of arriving international flights, only a set of steps and a stroll along the apron past the light aeroplanes to immigration and customs. There were no shiny glass and concrete terminals full of escalators, baggage carousels, and an endless array of shops, currency exchanges and restaurants. The unimposing airport buildings were brick and plain; there was one café selling food and cold drinks, and the small shops were outnumbered by car hire company booths. But the welcome to the country was overwhelming. At the Budget Car Rental booth, I was told that my pre-booked Toyota Corolla was not available. Before I could even begin to feel dismayed, the agent informed me that I was being upgraded for free to an eight-seat VW Kombi CDI with central sliding doors. I was now raring to begin what would be a journey of nearly 2,300 kms in seven days. Before we set off, it would be best to provide here a short digest of the logistics of driving in Namibia.

Namibia is big, very big. It covers approximately 825,000 square kilometres or, if you prefer, about one and a half times bigger than France and, when I visited, it had a population of less than 2,700,000. Many of these are subsistence farmers, especially in the north of the country where there is greater availability of water. Namibia is an arid country, and visitors are asked to limit their water use. It is disrespectful and wasteful to let the water run continuously when having a shave or brushing your teeth. Much of Namibia's foreign income depends on international tourism, but it has even more wealth generated by mining for large deposits of minerals, ores, and diamonds. The Namibian dollar is tied to the South African rand and within Namibia the two currencies are used interchangeably. In a country with a large divide between rich and poor, it should come as no surprise that over fifty per cent of the population must make do on the equivalent of US$2 per day – though how they do it, I cannot say. Namibia uses the metric system and they drive on the left. The major roads in Namibia are tarred and outside of Windhoek there is little traffic. One especially charming aspect of driving in Namibia are the laybys. Every few kilometres on the main roads, there will be a small layby – no shops or petrol stations, just a concrete set of table and chairs painted in green and white with a rubbish bin in the same colours, and usually situated under a mature tree in green leaf to provide shade. Naturally, there are petrol stations elsewhere and in the rural areas if you see one, you fill up - there may be no fuel at the next one. The minor roads, of which there are thousands of kilometres, are gravel or 'dirt' roads but they are very well maintained through regular grading and pothole repair. In fact, such roads are often so smooth that, combined with even less traffic, they are frequently dangerous as inexperienced tourists drive too fast over the graded gravel surfaces and sometimes overturn the car by taking a bend too quickly. On the other hand, it is possible to drive for a surprising distance and never encounter a bend in the road; and to drive for hours and not see another human being. That sense of isolation was just one of the reasons I fell in love with Namibia.

The B1 tarred road runs north towards Etosha National Park where I was to spend six days in two separate camps. En route, I stopped at a little town, Okahandja, for a coffee and to look at the dozens of makeshift stalls selling souvenirs, carved animals, and various trinkets. The stallholder I dealt with did not want to disclose the prices of items in which I was interested within earshot of his rival sellers. Accordingly, he used a sharp-tipped piece of wood to inscribe the amount on his forearm. His black skin turned a lighter colour for a second or two and then faded away. Of course, if I offered a lower sum, he had to scribble a new price to show me. It was all rather theatrical but effective since, eventually, I bought a carved elephant from him. Although I did not buy anything from these stalls on subsequent visits, I did always stop at the same café, *The Coffee Shop*; it was the start of a pleasurable pattern of events that were to be repeated over the next eight years. I continued north but at Otjiwarongo where I was meant to turn off the B1 onto the C38 to arrive at the southern Andersson Gate entrance to Etosha, I could not find the road. No one was able to direct me – I even ended up in an industrial estate – and time was pressing. At dusk, both entrances to the park would be closed and I now had severe doubts whether I could reach the park in time. I had no choice but to continue along the B1 in a north easterly direction and enter Etosha from its eastern Von Lindequist Gate. I got there with no further alarms, but now I was in Namutoni, one of the three camps in the park, whereas my accommodation was over 150 kms away to the west in Okaukuejo. It was now gone half-past-four and sunset was at seven o'clock. More to the point, the camp at Okaukuejo was supposed to close its own gates at sunset. Within the park, the speed limit was forty kph, and driving in the dark was forbidden. If I kept to the speed limit, I would never make it in time. I would have to drive at around seventy kph to have a chance; along a twisting dirt road in an inevitably gathering gloom while avoiding hitting any animals on the way.

I had driven along this graded road before on my first visit to Etosha with Linda in 1997, but in daylight and within the park's speed limit. We always encountered so many animals and, sometimes, had to stop if zebra, elephant or wildebeest blocked the way. In the local language, Etosha means 'Huge, White Place.' That evening it was anything other than white. Thus, on the journey, I could barely see the great pan in the centre of the park, nor the rocks scattered by the side of the road, nor the thorn trees and butterfly bushes, nor the heat haze that hangs in the air during the day, nor the various creatures seeking safety in the bushveld, nor did I see a night stalking-leopard – but then, no one sees the leopard even in daylight unless the leopard permits it. No, all I saw was the sun slipping towards the horizon with me still some way from safety. I did, luckily, see the herd of elephants in the road; they stood there simply eyeing me for what seemed like an eternity until they languidly moved on and I could recommence my journey. I reached Okaukuejo in the darkness but found the gates still open. Inside the camp were lights and people going about their business. I went to the administrative centre where the staff gave me a funny look as if to say: "Here's the guy we've been waiting for," paid my park fees, picked up my room key, and went straight to the bar for a beer – fitting behaviour because another version of Etosha translates as 'Land of Dry Water.' Indeed, the area was so meaningful to the original tribes that they named it three times.

Etosha, or 'Place of Mirages,' is one of the biggest national parks in Africa covering 22,270 square kilometres or, if you prefer, slightly bigger than the whole of Wales. At the heart of the park, lies a magnificent dry pan covering over 6,000 square kilometres and stretching for 110 kms in length and 60 kms in width. The vast majority of Etosha's waterholes are located like a life-giving blue ribbon along the pan's southern border. Some of the waterholes are artesian, and deep enough to encourage the growth of clumps of reeds. Others are known as contact springs and water-level springs where the flow of water is less reliable. A few, such as Kalkheuwel and Okaukuejo, have water permanently pumped to the hole. In the wet season, Etosha receives enough rainfall that animals can find water more easily, even on the pan, and can drink at many other waterholes that would otherwise be dry. Accordingly, animals are spread more widely throughout the park and, to some extent, are more difficult to see. However, in the longer dry season from April to November, there is little water on the pan and the wildlife must visit a smaller number of waterholes with reliable water supply and, thus, are much easier to view. It was no accident that I always visited during the dry season. The terrain in Etosha varies from the flat, silver sand of the pan, to mopane woodlands and open savannah. Fortunately, the dirt roads throughout the park are easy to traverse but taking a vehicle onto the pan itself is not permitted. Finally, the animals and birds. Millions of them! Over 100 different species of mammals, some quite rare, and over 310 species of birds - available to anyone with a car who wishes to drive themselves, and with three camps where you can stop for food and drink and fill up with fuel. To make it even better, in September it hardly ever rains, and the temperature moves imperceptively between thirty and thirty-four Celsius.

On my first morning in Etosha, I put my notebook, binoculars, and my guidebook *Birds of Namibia* above the dashboard and set off towards the Märchenwald, or Enchanted Forest, with my Olympus OM1 camera and telephoto lens on the passenger seat. I had the area entirely to myself but there was not much game, perhaps due to some parts of the forest being cordoned off to protect stands of copper moringa trees from over-grazing. The rest of the Märchenwald was scrub bush, dotted with stunted trees and, elsewhere, long, tinder-dry yellow grass. Leaving the Enchanted Forest, I drove east past Okaukuejo to Nebrowni waterhole, which frequently attracts lots of game, but is often deserted since it does not appear on all the maps of the park. To one side of the hole is quite thick bush, while in front stretching off into the far distance is open grass plain. When I arrived, there were some elephants far away on the plain, but three bulls drinking at the waterhole. A large group of zebra, some springbok, and a few oryx were stood off, waiting to drink when the elephants left. One bull detached himself from his companions and moved a short distance to a spot where he could dust himself. One shake of his head, sending his massive ears and trunk swinging back and forth, was enough to startle the zebra who sounded their screech-like alarm calls and became very skittish. As usual, with so many animals in the vicinity, a few black-backed jackals were sniffing around – indeed that night I even saw three *inside* the camp.

In the evening, after a dinner where impala was the main course, I went down to Okaukuejo's floodlit waterhole, itself only a very short distance from my bush chalet. This waterhole has frequently been described as the jewel in the Etosha crown and I saw why when five white rhino were present very close to the camp wall. Two male juveniles were sparring with one another, occasionally clashing horns quite noisily. A third, bigger rhino, stood quietly close by, as if refereeing the contest. The contestants were throwing up a lot of the white dust for which Etosha is famous, but their manoeuvres had taken them too close to a very large bull elephant drinking at the waterhole. He turned on them and made it clear that the rhinos should go away immediately; they did. Later, all five rhinos were actually in the water, which came up to the top of the legs of the mature animals, and up to the midriffs of the juveniles. When they exited the hole, the top half of the beasts appeared grey, but their lower half was a glistening jet black under the floodlights. It would have made a wonderful photographic print. In the distance, I could hear lions roaring. For me, it was safety behind the wall, and almost certainly death on foot beyond it. The lions were still calling to one another gone midnight when I reluctantly tore myself away and went to bed.

If I thought that night's experience at the floodlit hole was exceptional, the next night was even better. Present were three bull elephants, one with a radio collar. All of them had short and chipped tusks, as most Etosha elephants do. The condition of their tusks had a lot to do with having to use them to dig for water through tough rocky soil in the dry season and, possibly, because of a mineral deficiency that made them somewhat brittle. They drank quietly and other animals kept a respectful distance, even the nine white rhinos around the hole. Most of the rhinos moved off in various directions after drinking, and into the light came a single cheetah who disappeared very quickly when a pride of five lions arrived and took up residence under the only tree next to the hole. Two jackals were sniffing around but were understandably wary of the lions. The adult elephants, as usual, did not give a damn.

This was how I spent my days and nights in Etosha; touring the waterholes in the western part of the park by day, and settling down with a beer in the evenings to marvel at the prodigious array of arriving animals at the floodlit waterhole. The halfway mark between Okaukuejo and Namutoni was Halali where I would normally have lunch. Often, when I drew up at a waterhole, there might be little or no game but I was prepared to wait rather than drive off immediately. There were always birds to see and identify with the aid of my guidebook. Moreover, there were notes to make about previous sightings that day, and my camera and lenses always needed cleaning since the white dust of Etosha got everywhere. With my binoculars, I could see game from some distance and judge if they might be heading my way. No doubt, other people at the waterholes would have seen me doing these things, none of which mattered until, at the end of my holiday, I met a young couple at Okonjima, of which more later.

After three nights at Okaukuejo, I drove around seventy-five kilometres to Halali for another three nights. Halali also had a restaurant, petrol station, and a floodlit waterhole but the hole was located several hundred yards from the camp. At Okaukuejo, I could walk a short distance from my chalet to the waterhole to see if any game were present; at Halali, it was a bit of a trek but often worth the effort. From this camp, it was easier to explore the waterholes in the eastern part of Etosha and to take lunch at the old German fort, now converted tourist camp, in Namutoni. My bush chalet No.54 was in a secluded spot on the very edge of Halali camp and surrounded on three sides by bush. At night, it was sometimes possible for me to see animals moving nearby, the reflection from their eyeballs picked out clearly whenever they looked in my direction. I especially liked the nights at Halali for, after eating in the restaurant, I would return to the chalet, light a fire of mopane logs in the grate of the fire pit and sit back with a chilled beer or South African white wine. Mopane is very common in Namibia and is an exceptionally dense hardwood that burns for longer and with greater heat than many other types of hardwood. Being so isolated, the chalet saw little electric light from the lampposts sparingly scattered throughout the camp, but a small part of it was bathed in the glow from the mopane fire. On two of the three nights I stayed in the camp, there were short power cuts when the whole place fell into sudden darkness. I liked to think that the fire would keep any dangerous animals at bay, but of course I had no idea whether it would.

On the first morning of my stay at Halali, I drove along Rhino Drive and then Eland Drive away from the central plain and into mixed scrub and woodlands covering gently sloping hills. These 'drives' were still dirt roads on either side of which was a great deal of burnt and black vegetation. I was rewarded for my efforts to travel through what looked like a wasteland by the sight of four rare black-faced impala. In this part of the park, I saw no other vehicles at all. However, there was little game, so I decided to drive back towards the pan and then further east to Kalkheuwel, which was tucked away down a rough and narrow track off the main east-west route through Etosha.

Kalkheuwel was destined to be the stellar waterhole in the whole of Etosha as far as I was concerned. It became my spiritual home in Africa for no other place, save perhaps the waterhole at Okaukuejo, rivalled it. It was secluded, surrounded by thick bush from which at any moment great beasts would appear without notice, and a prime spot to view animal behaviour. The first time I arrived there that late morning, there were elephant. There were elephant present around the waterhole on my subsequent visits. In six stays at Etosha between 1997 and 2017, and numerous visits to Kalkheuwel, I almost always saw elephants there. What draws them and the other animals to this hole is a concrete water trough with year-round pumped water and, closer to the parking area, a shallow pan – often filled with water – where the elephants can wallow in the mud. I have spent hours there over the years watching youngsters play in the mud wallow while their mothers slowly drink from the trough. When a truly enormous bull arrives, he dominates everything, and completes his drinking and ablutions in his own time unbothered by any other animal, or by people like me hanging out of the centre door of my VW and taking dozens of photographs.

On the drive to Namutoni for lunch, I saw several pale chanting goshawks surveying the ground from tree branches at the side of the road. I also noticed that I was still getting waves and headlight flashes from drivers conducting private small group tours of the park. I couldn't figure out why, but I waved back anyway. At the fort, I filled up with diesel at Namibian $7.22 per litre, or roughly fifty-five pence at that time. For my last night in Etosha, I decided to join one of the night drive excursions run by the park authorities. Felix was our driver, in charge of an open-top lorry that carried about twenty passengers. As we left camp, the power went off but I could see that the cooks were still slaving away in the kitchen over their gas hobs. Felix drove for over three hours with one hand on the wheel and the other holding a small red-coloured spotlight with which to pick out any game. The spotlight caught the red reflection of a hyena's eyes and then those of a Cape fox. At Rietfontein, we dimly made out two rhinos at the waterhole, and at Salvadora on the very edge of the pan, two bull elephants. A spotted eagle owl was quite appropriately itself spotted on our journey, as was a comparatively rare skunk. The skunk was a timely reminder that in the cool of the night the scent of the many yellow acacia flowers was intensified so that most of our journey was passed in an atmosphere of pleasant fragrance. On our return to the camp close to midnight the power was still out. I made my way back to my chalet in complete darkness, picking my way home with a torch. Between the screen door and the thick wooden door of the chalet, a member of staff had left a candle and a box of matches. I sat outside for another hour or so with the last bottle of chilled white wine, and I leant back in my chair to let the Milky Way wash over me.

Last day at Etosha, and I had plenty of time to complete the drive south to Okonjima so I took a slightly circuitous route to the park's exit via Eland Drive. The one vehicle I met on that route flagged me down and told me there was a single bull elephant a few kilometres further along on the right. I assumed she meant her right, so I was driving very slowly looking at the thick bush to my left. I stopped to consult my map and retrieve my binoculars. When I looked up, on the *other* side of the road (my right) was the bull in question emerging through a mopane bush and demolishing most of it in the process. Had that creature charged, I would have had little chance of escape, and the damage he could have done to me and the vehicle does not bear thinking about. But, bless the old boy, he was more interested in plant destruction than causing me any distress.

My departure from Etosha was via the Andersson Gate where all vehicles must stop to complete certain formalities. In Namibia public transport is scarce especially in this part of the country, so it is no coincidence that at the gate there sit patiently a number of people hoping to get a lift to their family homes. When Linda and I left from this same gate in 1997, we happily gave a lift to three sex workers wanting to get to Otjiwarongo after their 'shift' in the workers' quarters. All three sat in the back and Linda offered them sweets; we took them all the way to their destinations in the backstreets of Otjiwarongo, and they proved to be courteous and fun passengers. On this occasion, the official at the gate asked me where my next destination was and recognised that for two waiting 'customers' their hometown of Outjo was on the way. The official asked me if I would take two female passengers with me and drop them off about ninety kilometres down the road. It was all done very quietly with no hint of pressure, and I was happy to oblige. On this occasion, my passengers were catering staff who worked at Okaukuejo, and they gratefully got into the VW with a staggering number of plastic bags full of their belongings. Luckily, there was ample room. They too were excellent company, and I was sorry when I had to drop them off.

I arrived at Okonjima for a one-night stay mid-afternoon. My chalet in Bush Camp was stupendous with a huge picture window with stunning views of the plains and the oryx grazing there. The interior was tastefully decorated with Africana and outside there was a small box full of bird seed that guests could spread near the water features that each chalet had. Within minutes of putting out some seed, I was joined by dozens of small, brightly coloured birds, such as Swallow-tailed Bee-eaters, Redeyed Bulbuls, Kalahari Robins, and Crimsonbreasted Shrikes. The old, and rather small accommodations at Main Camp when I was there with Linda in 1997 were now increasingly used for drivers and guides, and others were being renovated and enlarged. Guests could now stay in newly built 'palaces,' such as those in Bush Camp, and pay accordingly. The place had gone upmarket. Tea and cakes were served at four o'clock and a guided tour to find leopard started shortly afterwards. Tyson, the leopard I had seen in the wild in 1997 was now dead as was Piggy, the warthog. Moreover, no longer were cheetah paraded in front of guests at Main Camp. They had been relocated to huge fenced enclosures but, inevitably, Chinga, Chui, and Caesar were now dead.

Richard, our guide, took a small party of us on an afternoon safari to find leopard. Before too long, he located a magnificent fifty-seven-kilogram male leopard. With him was a tiny steenbok, about a fifth of the leopard's weight. The cat was playing with the antelope, pushing it around with his paw. It had already severely damaged one of the steenbok's legs, which looked like matchsticks compared with the huge limbs of the leopard. The cries from the prey were pitiful, but this was truly how nature worked. Shortly after we had arrived, the leopard took the steenbok in his mouth and disappeared into thick bush where we lost him. The rest of the safari was an anticlimax but we were still talking about what we had witnessed when we got off our vehicle to enjoy a sundowner drink on a small hill and to marvel at the spectacular and swift descent of the sun below the horizon.

At dinner that night, I sat next to Matthew and Lucy. Unexpectedly, Lucy told me how she envied my job and how wonderful it must be to guide tourists around Namibia. She and her husband, unknown to me, had seen me several times in Etosha in my large empty vehicle taking notes and surveying the terrain, and assumed that I was a professional guide scoping resorts and waterholes where, subsequently, I would take tourists. We laughed when the misapprehension was cleared up, but I would have loved such a job. It also explained all the waving and bonhomie from real professional guides in Etosha as they passed me on the roads. In the morning, Perreu, a proper guide, took myself and four others out into the bush to find leopard and cheetah. The cheetah, five elderly creatures too old to be rehabilitated, were found quite easily and were fed with small pieces of donkey meat – the cheapest available – thrown from the vehicle by Perreu. We spent a charming forty minutes with the cheetah, such beautiful animals, but we were not allowed to touch them. Memories of Chinga and his companions flooded back to me. Next, in a different and even larger enclosure, we tried to locate any of the radio-collared leopards who were not that keen to turn up automatically in front of the cameras. These animals were wild and killed their own food. Perreu told us that at least one of the leopards in the enclosure took to hiding in gullies as if they knew that might block the radio signals. During the search, we saw many antelope and one small oryx carcass wedged up high in a tree by a leopard. Just when it seemed as if we would not encounter a leopard at all, we saw two – a mother and cub lying under the cover of a tree with a kill hidden in the surrounding thick bush. After a short time, so as not to disturb the mother too much, we drove back to camp. There, I packed and was soon on the B1 to the airport outside Windhoek.

I had no problems when returning the car or at the airport. I spent the very last of my rand and Namibian dollars in the departure lounge's one souvenir shop and in the cosy bar. I had no cash whatsoever when I boarded the plane – the last coins had gone into the charity box by the departure gate. On the flight home, I made some notes about what to take next time I visited Namibia, and what I had taken that turned out to be unnecessary. Clearly, I had thoughts of returning; I had enjoyed long-haul travel on my own and been away for a reasonable period without any problems. I had no idea, however, when I would actually return until within days of getting home my brother, Mark, asked me if I'd be bored going back there again. He was enticed by my description of the holiday. I started planning immediately for a return adventure in twelve months time.

Chapter Twelve: The Fabulous Stephens Brothers on Safari

This trip to Namibia covered much the same ground as the year before in 2009, but there were also new elements. Long-haul travel was much cheaper when there were two travellers, and to avoid the hassle of settling up between us when we had to pay bills, we agreed on a kitty. I was to hold the kitty! Mark and I were due to meet around midday at Heathrow Terminal Five for a latest check-in of one p.m. but at twelve-thirty there was no sign of him – his train having been delayed. Fortunately, I had spoken to a BA employee who told me to come directly to her if my brother arrived in time so we could bypass the queues at the check-in desks. Just in time, Mark did turn up and the BA woman checked our bags through at a separate terminal – I already had our boarding cards pre-printed. We were most grateful to her. Frankfurt Airport, where we boarded our overnight Air Namibia flight, was as confusing as ever but pleasant enough to while away a few hours. We were away from Windhoek Airport just after dawn in a Golf 1600cc heading north on the B1 for Okahandja where we stopped at *The Coffee Shop*. Much later, but still on our way north to Etosha, we pulled into one of those charming spots where a green and white painted table and bench and a rubbish bin are situated under the shade of a reasonably large tree. At the pullover was Stanley, waiting for his mate. He was very proud of the fact that he was the driver for the regional governor and went to his car to show us his ID card. In the UK, Stanley would have been at a motorway service station having agreed a set time to meet his friend, but here Stanley just sat in the shade waiting patiently and knowing his friend might yet be hours away.

Our chalet in Okaukuejo in Etosha National Park was very comfortable and near the waterhole, but we spent five minutes looking for the towels until we realized they were on the beds folded like swans. By mid-afternoon, Mark was driving to the Ghost or Haunted Forest via Leeubron waterhole where we almost ran over a sleeping jackal on the road. It gets its name from the number of deformed moringa trees growing there with their tangled shapes. I had chosen that secluded route so that Mark could get used to driving on graded, dirt roads. He took to it like a trooper. That night, two bats flew tight circles around Mark's head, as we sat outside our chalet, but didn't bother me at all.

On our first morning safari, we saw more elephants than cars, including one freshly dusted bull who appeared like an apparition by the side of the road, covered as he was in the distinctive white dust of Etosha. We had an excellent oryx stew for lunch at Halali at whose waterhole we also saw twenty-three elephant. In the afternoon, we visited Salvadora, Sueda and Homob and saw a very large lone bull just off the main road. At Nebrowni there were six lions, three of which were right by the waterhole so that none of the other animals dared approach to drink. On the road back to Okaukuejo, we encountered for the first of several times some Namaqua sandgrouse who were lined across the road as if trying to pull off a hold up. Nearby, some ground squirrels were either trying to bury themselves in the sand while shading their bodies with their bushy tails, or standing erect on their hind legs and thrusting their testicles in our general direction. In the evening, a more decorous performance was put on by the Okaukuejo Primary School Choir who sang and danced for us at dinner.

It was time for Mark and me to re-locate to Halali camp and, en route, we saw a white rhino walking along by the side of the road –

one of the few I had seen in daylight. At Halali, our travel agent had booked the only accommodation available - the biggest place at the camp. Sekelbos VIP lodge had a palatial lounge, large bathroom and toilet and two separate bedrooms each with two double beds, and with two sitting out areas on different levels, plus our own barbeque or braai. The place was full of every utensil needed to host a barbeque party but the supplies in the shop were meagre, so we settled for burning mopane logs on our two evenings when we sat outside gazing at the stars of the Milky Way.

Our last afternoon in Etosha was our final chance to visit Kalkheuwel. The road to the waterhole had been recently regraded so that it was now an easier drive than before when it was a hell of potholes. I admit I felt somewhat apprehensive as I drove there. Would there be elephant as there always had been? I needn't have worried for as we pulled into the parking area both holes were full of elephant – we counted over 50 of them, some drinking quietly at the top hole with the freshly pumped water, and others (including calves and juveniles) having fun splashing around in the mud at the bottom hole. There were elephants all around – some covering themselves in dust, or wallowing in the mud, or playfully sparring with one another, which meant foul-smelling water being kicked all over the place.

On our way back to Okaukuejo, en route to the Andersson Gate and then to Okonjima, we encountered a few cars parked at the side of the road, which from a distance we thought had halted to allow some springbok to cross. In fact, the passengers were watching a cheetah stalking that same herd, its brother or male companion hiding elsewhere close by. I knew this might prove to be a marvellous photographic opportunity, so I got out of the car – against all the rules - and rested my camera on the roof. For a good few minutes, the cheetah lay still not moving even its ears, allowing the herd of springbok as they grazed to come naturally closer. Then, it exploded into action, and the herd flew off amid the sound of clattering hooves and the sight of dust flying up everywhere. I had the camera set on continuous shoot so obtained some good pictures of the cheetah's pursuit. However, it had not got close enough and the attack ended without a kill, whereupon its partner sauntered up as the attacker lay in the shade of a butterfly bush breathing heavily and recovering from its exertions. The springboks were still running and pushing up a dust cloud so energetic that it looked like a squadron of tanks on manoeuvres.

The drive to Okonjima was very pleasant and we were allocated View Room No.1 close to the main dining area. The concession had now increased significantly in size through buying neighbouring land, and had added other attractions such as opportunities to view hyena and wild dogs. Our afternoon game drive with Martin, our guide, and an Italian couple was to see three cheetah, eventually found lying down in the shade to avoid the heat. Here in Okonjima, we got much closer to kudu and giraffe than was the case in Etosha. Later in the Kalahari, we noticed how oryx, kudu and especially springbok were much more wary of the approach of a vehicle. The springbok would often take off in full flight as if pursued by a cheetah, jumping into the air in a pronking display and keeping this up for some time when all they had to do to put distance between themselves and the vehicle was to turn off the track, either left or right. Just before dusk, we saw two adult male giraffes engaging in what is known as 'necking,' a form of sparring where opponents swing their necks with immense force against the other in the hope of landing a knockout blow. At the finish of our cheetah drive, we enjoyed a sundowner drink and watched the sunset. At dinner, we had the most delicious cuts of oryx, which fast became our favourite bush meat, and later sat on the veranda picking out any animals in the blackness with our torches.

I awoke at five a.m. and went outside into the pitch blackness; I heard not a sound but a few eyes were caught in my flashlight in the distance. Tea and muffins were served at six-thirty, and then we set off to find leopard with Martin again and a French-speaking Swiss couple. Eventually, we found a seventy-kilogram male leopard called Mafana and, on this occasion, we saw him several times out in the open and not as is usually the case with leopards behind a blizzard of tall grass and bushes. I took one photograph just as Mafana turned and walked down a narrow gulley right in front of our vehicle. There was a distinct green reflection off his eyes that made him look especially menacing. After brunch, we drove the short distance from Main Camp to Bush Camp for our second night at Okonjima and settled into room No.4 or 'Lapa'. While Mark sat by the pool that afternoon, I put out seed by the bird bath and watched any number of different species swoop down to feed. Then, the third time I put down seed, a group of warthogs arrived, bent down on their front knees and proceeded to hoover everything up. The front part of Lapa was open to the elements – at night a tent flap was pulled down and secured – so I got up and shouted and waved my arms at the warthogs. The females and juveniles ran off a little distance, but the male simply turned, looked at me, walked purposefully to the low wooden rail in front of our room, squirmed under it and came directly at me. I was just about to scarper to the toilet, the only place with a door I could close to keep away from his tusks, when suddenly he stopped, stared at me for a while, turned and then carried on eating the seeds. So, no doubt who won that contest.

In the late afternoon, we went with Paul and a black tracker, called Sunday, who was working the radio equipment, to find hyena. This was partly by vehicle and partly on foot. It was on foot that we approached one of the three hyenas (called Poo) in their enclosure, after walking through the bush for some while, mindful of the terrifically sharp thorns on every bush around us. Basically, it is not a proper bush with hopes of growing up into a tree in this part of the world unless it has a thorn of some description, some of which can puncture tyres – as we found out later during our travels in southern Africa. We approached within three or four metres of the hyena, and he was very relaxed about our presence. I had not realized until then just how muscular and heavy they are – eighty kilograms. I think Paul and Sunday were winding us up a little when they told us how powerful the jaws of a hyena were, and how it could literally rip us apart, and how they had forgotten to bring the gun with them. For our sundowner drink of dry white wine, we again left the vehicle and walked to the edge of a steep escarpment on which were a troop of baboons about to sleep in the trees hanging over the edge of the drop for safety. That night we dined with an American medical doctor who could have won a medal for talking.

The next morning around seven a.m., we set off on the Bushman trail with two white guides and one black guide who had been taught by the San themselves how to make fire and rope and how to prepare traps for hunting. Mark and I tried to evade the string snare snapping shut on our wrists as the trap was triggered, but to no avail. Mark kept the actual string that one of the guides had made in front of us from a certain type of grass, the strands of which he twisted together by rolling them into a strong cord along his leg.

After breakfast, we began our 550-kilometre journey to Bagatelle in the Kalahari, stopping again for coffee at Okahandja. As the B1 passed through Windhoek, where it became a dual carriageway, people just sauntered across the road in front of us, and along the wide verges there were people selling firewood and fruits from flimsy stalls. Baboons too frequently patrolled the verges. Just before Mariental, we turned onto a dirt road and soon found the entrance to the ranch. The road was a one-way system of about three kilometres of very narrow, sandy tracks to the ranch itself. Our two-wheel drive Polo just about made it, but a four-wheel drive truck had to take us and our luggage to our room – a wooden affair built on stilts and overlooking the red sand parallel dunes of the Kalahari Desert. Almost immediately, Mark set off into the desert to explore until he came upon a game fence by which time he looked a very small dot in an enormous expanse of red sand. Around the dining area of Bagatelle, there were sitting out areas, a pool, and two rather small enclosures housing one female cheetah and three males in the other. They had all been orphaned as youngsters and so did not know how to hunt for themselves. Captivity and some sort of life was all they now had, but the enclosures were in effect too small, and the female could often be seen pacing around the perimeter fence. I felt sorry for them and did not go inside the enclosures to see them close-up. The ranch also had a few other 'pets,' including peacocks, a domestic cat (Rasti), an oryx, and a female springbok called Skank who had a tight-fitting sleeve of green hosepipe over both her horns. This was just as well, as that night Skank followed Mark and I almost to the door of our room, admittedly encouraged by some food offerings, and when I appeared to be withholding said food, she promptly nutted me in the balls with her horns. That's when you are thankful for the hosepipe! The main course of oryx that night, eaten outside, with an excellent bottle of red Scaramanga, was the best of the whole trip.

For the first time on holiday, we were able to lie in and just lounge around drinking the free tea and coffee, and reading books from the library, until it was time for our afternoon game drive into the Kalahari, which although called a desert is full of life and animals. In the camp, just before departure, we saw a very shiny black millipede crawling through the sand, and by the pool there were hundreds of white butterflies some being caught and eaten by Cape sparrows. Peacocks were displaying right in front of us too, and occasionally Rasti and Skank put in an appearance. On the game drive, we saw wary oryx, kudu, zebra, eland, a big lizard, two bat-eared foxes, lots of vultures, and springbok, which often tore away from us at full speed. There are also many leopard in this area but we saw none. We drove up over the crests of the dunes and then along the straw-coloured 'valleys' in between, where we saw a lot of sociable weaver bird nests and were told never to walk under them since snakes often try to get inside the nests but, having a precarious hold, they sometimes fall onto unsuspecting people below. Dinner was springbok that had been shot earlier on a neighbouring ranch – the chef and waiter being at first a little reluctant to divulge this fact in case anyone might be upset. They stressed that it had not been shot on their land – as if this made any difference.

Our next drive was towards the Namib desert and Kulala Desert Lodge about 360 kilometres away on what we thought was all tarred road. Just on the outer edge of Maltahohe on the C19 – a small community where Mark drove up and down a few times looking for our turn-off - we eventually stopped so I could take over the driving. We noticed a small shop selling snacks and decided to get something to eat. As we sat in the car about to eat our food, three ragged and bare-foot boys approached us and stood by the car windows. They were clearly hungry, so Mark and I got out, gave them what we'd bought from the shop, and dug out some sweets from the boot of the car to hand over to them. We were met with big smiles and many thankyous. Fifty metres after I set off, the road turned to dirt and stayed that way until days later when we reached Rehoboth. Mark had certainly chosen the best leg of the journey to drive. Going through the Tsaris Pass was spectacular and as we came down the other side, we encountered a European cyclist. Mad. I joked to Mark that having travelled this road in 1997, I knew that just around the corner was a café. Damn me, just a few moments later, in the middle of nowhere, there was a sign by the side of the road, saying 'Why not take a break?' That was how we pulled in and met Philip, a tall lean man who had been travel guide, driver, farmer – you name it. He had acquired this old cottage, renamed as Zaris Roadhouse, only in July and had transformed it in a few months. He had only opened a few days previously, but now he had guest rooms, a wonderful garden and vegetable plot and he served all kind of drinks with delicious home-made biscuits. He had several dogs there with him, which hunted rodents for most of their food. Philip told us that the whole area was fully booked at this time and that by accident on a visit to the Hammerstein hunting lodge – his nearest neighbours – he had found out about a Canadian couple making enquiries on the internet who wanted wedding photos in front of the great Namib dunes. So, he offered them accommodation, which they accepted and then they came back to him and asked him to arrange the actual wedding – he succeeded and has got a reverend driving over 400 kilometres to officiate when the couple fly in from Canada. We stayed and chatted to him and a local ex-school teacher called Cora who had called in for coffee and who was carrying some of the belongings of the said cyclist we had seen earlier to be dropped off much farther down the road.

The fourteen-kilometre approach road to Kulala was awful – rutted and with some potholes - but as we pulled up three waitresses emerged with cold drinks for us. It was only later that I understood the slight look of surprise on their faces when they saw us. In our room, Chalet 15, there was a welcome message written on hand-made paper and addressed to Mr and Mrs Stephens. They corrected their mistake when they left a goodbye message on the bed addressed to Dr and Mrs Stephens. We kept one each as a reminder. But they really did look after us very well at the lodge. One night the whole staff came out to sing and dance and to play traditional drums. Mark slept out on the flat roof one night where there was only room for one, and there was no bother about the staff going to our chalet and making up a bed for him. We heard jackals calling to each other in the night.

The next morning just after dawn, we set off to the huge dunes at Sossusvlei through the lodge's private entrance into the Namib-Naukluft Park. The road to Sossusvlei was now tarred all the way to the two-wheel drive parking area – not like in 1997 – and there was even a shuttle service from the parking area to the vlei or dry pan at which there were toilets surrounded by wooden stockades and full of flies and noxious smells. Even so, it was not too crowded despite the changes. We came across a German couple walking back towards the car park because their four-wheel drive had got stuck in the thick sand. We helped to get them out but it was clear the driver hadn't a clue about how to drive in these conditions, and there was even some doubt as to whether he had engaged four-wheel drive in the first place. We got them moving but never saw them afterwards at the pan. We saw the dunes known as Big Daddy beyond Dead Vlei, and Big Mammy which surrounds part of Sossusvlei and which Linda and I climbed in 1997. Our guide, Mark and myself and one member of a couple climbed a dune directly overlooking Dead Vlei – his wife declined the offer. We walked steadily up the ridge or arête and, when we were some distance along the vlei, we plunged straight down the sand onto the white-coloured floor of Dead Vlei itself. Our guide descended the last part in reverse, jumping backwards to lose height. The vlei is filled with trees that died over 600 years ago and which stick up in all manner of strange and twisted shapes. One of them is called 'Old man falling over.' When we returned to our vehicle, it had a puncture so we helped the driver change the wheel, Mark being especially helpful. We drove the short distance to Sossusvlei where we had lunch. Our guide laid out all manner of very good food on a table under the shade of a large tree from which pied crows looked down in anticipation of some leftovers. There is more vegetation on the pan than I remember from 1997 but no water as there was then. In this part of Namibia if you mention 1997 everyone speaks of the heavy rains that enabled the rare flooding of the pan, just like we refer to the hard winter of 1962/3 or the drought of 1976.

It had been unusually windy in Namibia for the time of year, but thankfully there was not enough wind to prevent our hot air balloon ride this morning. The pilot was Dennis, the son of Eric who took Linda and me up in 1997 and invited us to his home afterwards to see his snakes. It was Eric who drove Mark and me back to Kulala Lodge after the trip and who told us that he had sold the lodge some years ago but had now set up a new ballooning venture in Zambia. His base there was 3,000 kilometres away, a journey he took three days to complete by vehicle. Although there was some cloud and haze the flight was fantastic. We did not skirt the huge apricot-coloured dunes but flew over the rockier parts of the Namib, our balloon finally landing perfectly on its own trailer. The eight passengers were driven to breakfast at Springbok Point. Dennis did his father's old trick and opened the bottles of champagne with a machete. What a feast it was too with tables and chairs and clean napkins and tablecloths in the middle of the desert, and we even had zebra meat but it was a bit too 'gamey' for my taste. We saw leopard spoor on the way there, and Dennis had seen a cheetah outside his home only a day or so earlier. We left Kulala (siesta in the local language) late morning and drove on dirt for a long way over passes and twisty roads, seeing many rickety old carts pulled by sad-looking donkeys, until we hit tar again at Rehoboth and the main B1. An uneventful journey back to the airport and home.

Mark and I returned to Namibia in 2012, again in September, but on this occasion, we visited more places than our old favourites and, for the first time, we explored Botswana. This time there was no last-minute, frantic arrival at Heathrow Terminal Five and our flight to Frankfurt was uneventful. Still unable to fathom the workings and layout of the airport there, so once again we formally entered Germany and went to the usual restaurant to eat. The Air Namibia flight was on time and the food on board was good, as was the red wine.

We landed at Windhoek around six a.m. – dressed in T-shirts and light jackets – to find that the air temperature was minus one Celsius and, as we walked along the airport apron, we could see our breath condensing. Just after seven o'clock, we were driving away from the Budget car hire in our Toyota Corolla – a vehicle we soon came to dislike for its prissiness. It wouldn't start unless the clutch pedal was pressed all the way to the floor, and it kept making increasingly insane noises if you so much as drove ten metres without one of us not having fixed the seat belt, and its axle height was far too low, which caused us problems later. The Polo was much better the time before. We stopped at Okahandja on our way north along the B1 at our usual place. By now the temperature had risen to plus thirty Celsius. At Otjiwarongo, we bought some supplies of wine and beer and by mid-afternoon we had arrived at the Andersson Gate and driven through Etosha National Park to Okaukuejo Camp and bush chalet No.79, a short walk from the waterhole. Shortly after leaving our stuff in the room, we were out driving west towards the Enchanted Forest. We never got there for, shortly after Leeubron waterhole, we came across a rare and wonderful sight. About ten metres from the dirt road was a carcass of a recently dead springbok. There were no marks on it at all and it looked as if it might have died of natural causes. As we pulled up, a few vultures were just beginning to open up the carcass in which there was no sign of rigor mortis. Three jackals appeared, and two of them (seemingly a male and female pair) drove the third one away. Then, as more and more vultures flew in and settled on the corpse, the pair drove these away. For the next forty minutes, these two devoured about two-thirds of the animal. Even when one rested a little way off, the other continued to eat and to defend the carcass from vultures – a crow did occasionally sneak in and make off with a morsel. When they had finished, they walked away with very full stomachs and immediately a feeding frenzy of vultures descended on the remains. We had never seen such an event so close-up – often the kill is a long way off or hidden by thick bush. We were lucky that this happened right by the side of the track, and that no other car came by at all during all the time we were parked there watching this natural behaviour. What an incredible first outing at Okaukuejo!

The oryx at dinner was very tasty and afterwards Mark and I sat outside the chalet drinking some red wine, and planning the next day's excursions. Two jackals walked right past us on the hunt for scraps of food inside the camp. Mark went to bed around ten p.m. so I went down to the floodlit waterhole where I saw seven rhino and five bull elephants all drinking and getting along without too much trouble. The water level was lower this year than before.

Mark and I went to the waterhole at Okaukuejo after breakfast, and saw a tawny eagle sat high up in the tall tree that overlooks the waterhole. It hardly seemed interested in any potential prey but suddenly it swooped down from its perch and attacked a dove about to land by the water. The initial dive missed its target, but the eagle was able to turn sharply in the air, land close to its victim and pounce on it. Then it flew off to sit atop another tree and started to pluck its prey. The seventeen-kilometre approach road to Halali was having major repairs done to it as were parts of the C38 running east-west through Etosha. Here, we encountered one side of the graded dirt road covered in dumps of rock and earth at regular intervals. If anything came towards us, we had to pull into one of the gaps between these dumps. There was a man with a rifle too, presumably to protect the workers on foot from any dangerous animals. It was amazing how much progress they made on the roads while we were there. At Rietfontein waterhole, we saw a small bird taking seeds from a huge roll of elephant dung. The dollop of dung was much bigger than the bird that stood underneath it reaching up for undigested seeds from a rather precarious position if the roll had toppled over. Unable to identify this heroic creature, Mark and I decided to name it the Stephens Shit-eater Bird.

The next morning, we called at Nebrowni where there was mixed game. We could not get through on the track to Homob since it was selfishly blocked by several cars whose passengers were intent on watching some lions asleep behind a bush. We had no desire to jostle for our own position to see such a non-event so we drove to Rietfontein where, as luck would have it, we saw two lions in plain view lying down close to the water's edge. There is a limit to how long one can watch lions doing nothing, so after a short while we left and drove to the Etosha look-out spot over the pan. Many of the barriers designed to keep traffic on the track had been broken and there was a lot of evidence of four-wheel drive cars cutting up the pan's surface. The track itself was in a much poorer condition than two years ago when we last visited. At Nuamses, there was only one car with a South African couple who told us that they had seen a leopard walk behind a bush where it was now lying in wait. It was difficult even with binoculars to spot the leopard so effective was its camouflage, but then amazingly it came out of hiding and remained almost always in full view for forty minutes – unheard of luck and only the two vehicles at the waterhole throughout. At one point, it hid again behind thick bush before some red hartebeest arrived at the hole. However, its ambush position was too far away as it broke cover and the animals easily avoided its attack. Then the leopard walked back along the water's edge growling as if scolding itself for missing an opportunity. It lay by a rocky outcrop in full view for quite some time until a matriarchal herd of twenty or more elephants arrived with five small calves. Our car was blocked in at the right by the waterhole itself, and in front of us and quite close was the vehicle of the South African couple. This wasn't a problem until the herd had finished drinking and playing in the water and moved off to dust themselves. I looked in the car's rear view mirror and could see nothing but grey elephant hides, and then a large cow came right up to the passenger side of the car and simply stood there motionless looking directly at Mark for some minutes. I was busy taking photos over Mark's shoulder when he casually said to me: "Don't you think it would be a good idea to at least start the engine?" There was still nothing but elephant hide at the rear and a big cow stopping us from going left, and going forward would mean driving through a narrow gap between the other vehicle and the stationary cow; so, we were effectively stuck. Luckily, after a few minutes all the elephants moved off and left us alone; it was then the leopard suddenly came back to the side of the waterhole and just lay down in the sun. On our way back to Okaukuejo, we saw a spotted hyena right at the side of the road which allowed us to stop a few feet opposite him from where we got some great close-up photographs. At Nebrowni, we photographed from the main road six bull elephants drinking at the hole. In one day, we had achieved a kind of 'Triple Crown' in seeing lion, leopard, and hyena – sadly no cheetah, so no 'Grand Slam.'

The next afternoon, now based at Halali, we drove along Rhino Drive and part of Eland Drive on our way to Goas and then down towards Springbokfontein - wonderful undulating country through which to travel with many trees and bushes but little game at first. Then on Hartebeest Drive we encountered a small herd of elephant and left them two over-ripe bananas that had been stuck on the backseat of the car too long. We saw more elephant at Springbokfontein and later a single very large grey-dusted bull walking down the middle of the main C38 dirt road forcing us to stop to see whether he would walk right by us. In the end he turned off. As we returned to Halali, we encountered some elephants crossing the road including two young ones playing together. They had come out of nowhere. As big as they are, we certainly did not see them coming through the thick bushveld. That night, we got some bags of mopane wood from the shop at the camp and sat outside after dinner with our glasses of wine and a good fire going in the braai.

In the morning, we left some bread crumbs for the glossy starlings outside our chalet door. We drove to Kalkheuwel but much of the bush to the right-hand side of the main road to Namutoni before the Kalkheuwel turn-off was blackened with fire. The same sight greeted us as we took the Kalkheuwel track, and in places there were still patches of grass burning or smouldering. We went to Namutoni for lunch. All three camps served ham and cheese toasties and chips as a staple, but the best version was to be found at Namutoni. Mark and I bought some presents from the shop there and did a short tour of the castellated ramparts of the old fort. It was delightful and refreshing to sit in the shade of the inner courtyard and relax over lunch.

It was time to leave Etosha, but at the exit gate at Namutoni the ranger there asked us if we would give a lift as far as Tsumeb to an elderly San woman and her grandchild. Perhaps she had been taking the child to see its mother who worked full-time at Etosha. Who knows? In any event, it was clear that without a lift from people like us, she would be waiting there by the exit gate indefinitely. The old lady had a very few words of English and the baby simply gurgled and laughed its way through the 120-kilometre journey. Briefly, we lost our way in Tsumeb after we had dropped them off, but soon we were back on the road to Rundu in the far north of the country and at the western edge of the Caprivi Strip. We made excellent progress but had to slow down frequently after Grootfontein because of the large number of villages straddling the B8 road. Every few miles, there was a school - usually the most solidly built of any of the buildings we saw along the way. It was also that time of day when the children were leaving school and we often saw them a long way off playing in groups on the road, but as our car approached, they all unfailingly moved to the side. They all looked very smart in their blue and black uniforms. At a veterinary gate, we were stopped by the police who were most polite and friendly. Tired looking donkeys pulling heavily laden carts by the side of the road were frequent sights, but the man striding along in large Wellington boots in the midst of a parched landscape was a one-off.

At Hakusembe River Lodge, we found a lovely camp where they originally intended to give us a double-bedded room – the old Mr and Mrs Stephens confusion again that as brothers with the same surname, we had encountered before – but quickly handed over a family room with three beds in it and more space. In this western end of the Caprivi, a narrow, fertile strip of land running east towards Zimbabwe and Zambia, the Okavango River is known as the Kavango River and for much of its length, before it turns south towards the Okavango Delta in Botswana, its course forms the boundary with Angola. Indeed, from Hakusembe Lodge's well-manicured lawns, we could see Angola. The far bank, only some fifty or so metres away, was full of local people and children, either collecting water and washing clothes or else playing in the shallows. Within minutes of our boat journey from the lodge, we could see that the waters were home to crocodiles and, further downstream, hippos. This was a little gem of a boat trip because we had swallows landing on the prow of the craft, children waving to us from the Angolan shore, crocodiles slithering into the current down the embankment, Angolans looking after their cattle and goats or bathing in the water, and most of the time a great sense of stillness as we often drifted along on the current. It was the first time that Mark or I had ever seen flowing water in a river bed in Namibia. That night we had an excellent meal of eland and spent some time talking to a Portuguese woman and her daughter. After sunset, the frogs made a very loud noise indeed. It was always a delight but a slightly strange sensation to be able to look across to Angola and to watch the locals going about their daily lives. It was clear that in this part of the world, there were no border controls and we were told that it was common for Angolans to cross into Namibia to find work close to the border.

Our journey continued east along the Caprivi Strip to Mazambala Island Lodge which sits alongside the Kwando River. Once again there were many clusters of villages along the route until the B8 enters Bwabwata National Park where there are very few and where the vegetation is very dry and clearly has been extensively 'cut back' by elephants. The lodge was owned by Andre who was born in Namibia and who spends three months of the year in Washington DC and by Tom, an American resident in Washington who visits the lodge twice a year for a few weeks each time. Both were very welcoming hosts. The main part of the lodge itself was a fantastic wooden structure that incorporated a first-floor dining area, a viewing lounge above it and, off to one side and above that, a more Spartan top-most viewing platform with a basic wooden handrail to keep guests safe while taking in the great views of the river, the floodplain, and the various animals grazing nearby. No sooner did I approach the handrail, than my foot went through the floor of the viewing platform as a short plank broke in two.

Our arrival at the lodge had been by boat. We had been driving around the campsite owned by the lodge looking for a road we believed existed to take us further on to the lodge itself. Eventually, an employee found us, explained that there was no such road, and ordered a launch to take us to the lodge. The launch followed the twists and turns of the Kwando River between banks covered in cane and papyrus reeds. At one point, the driver accidentally ran the boat over the shoulder of a submerged hippo he had not seen. Instantly, as we had just gone past him, he rose out of the water and made his displeasure known by opening his jaws menacingly and 'barking' at us. That evening, our sundowner boat trip was marvellous and we saw many kinds of birds, crocodiles, hippos, red lechwe, and hundreds and hundreds of elephant feeding greedily along the banks on the tall lush reeds, or else wading across the river right in front of us. Mark and I had never seen so many elephants in one place. After dinner we sat around the fire until late, chatting to Tom. We were the last to go to bed but before we did, we checked to see if any elephant or hippo were close by. The lodge had a small barrier less than half a metre high which was apparently an effective obstacle to hippos but not to elephants. We heard both in the distance and, earlier, staff with whistles had been outside near the lodge driving off some elephants that came too close.

In the morning, we drove the 180 kilometres from Mazambala to Muchenje Safari Lodge in Botswana. There was very little traffic on the B8 road but we still drove with our headlights on as we realized that in the heat haze nothing allowed us to pick out approaching vehicles better than their headlights. There were a number of small villages, schools, and medical clinics close to the road. Most of the dwellings were made of wooden poles sunk into the ground and then the spaces filled in with smaller sticks and mud to form circular walls topped with conical sloping thatched roofs made of dried reeds. Supplies of thatch for repair or for new dwellings could often be seen tied up in neat uniform bundles by the side of the road together with smaller bundles of chopped wood, stacked together in a square tower. Sometimes, we saw earthenware pots of various sizes for sale, and occasionally various carvings of different animals for sale to passing tourists. In a few of the bigger villages, we often saw stalls groaning with fruits and vegetables. However, always the most substantial buildings, made from breeze block, brick and cement and often with tiled or tin sheet roofs, were the schools that were laid out in quadrangles and frequently contained small houses on the grounds for the use of the teachers.

Both boys and girls attended school and virtually all of them wore decent, clean uniforms. The medical clinics were often equally as substantial as the schools but smaller in scale; one or two buildings to the six or more that a school might have. Most noticeable, however, were the shabeens or bottle stores that many of the larger villages seemed to possess. Our impression was that the customers of these drinking places were overwhelmingly male. Somewhere within walking distance of a group of villages would be a source of clean water, usually pumped from an aquifer. We frequently saw women and children carrying various containers of water on their heads, and sometimes having to walk several kilometres to fill them. At Ndhovu, later in our journey, we were told that the pump there was only unlocked for a few hours each day so that people did not 'waste' the water. It seemed that many people in Namibia in the rural areas have decent but basic facilities – and we saw many people with mobile phones – yet to survive here as farmers or through animal husbandry required very hard physical work.

At the Namibian and Botswanan borders, we exchanged polite formalities with the officials and had to fill in various forms and have our passports stamped, but there were no fees of any kind to pay. A little while after we crossed into Botswana, we turned off the Chinese-built tarred road and drove along the sandy approach to Muchenje Safari Lodge where disaster soon struck. The Corolla got firmly stuck in a stretch of deep red sand, a section we later came to know as the 'Red Zone.' Mark and I put twigs and branches and any rocks we could find under the front wheels, but the damn thing would not come out – the wheels simply spun uselessly and threw more sand into the car's air-intakes so that the seats and cockpit were now covered in a mixture of white sand from Etosha and this new red sand from Botswana. My mobile phone would not connect with the lodge, so I consulted our travel documents and concluded that the actual lodge was not that far away along the approach road.

While it had been my driving that had got the car bogged down, it was Mark who offered to walk in search of help. I let him go! First, however, I strongly reassured him that this close to the lodge there was no possibility of encountering any dangerous animals. I watched Mark stride away while I 'guarded' the car. Twenty minutes later, an old Land Rover rounded a bend in the sandy track and I could see Mark sat in the passenger seat; he had come across two workers employed by the lodge just off the approach road. From our conversation with these two, it became clear that a good number of two-wheel drive cars had got stuck in this precise spot over the years, so much so that our rescuers called it the 'Red Zone.' Most people came to the lodge in the lodge's own four-wheel drive vehicles having been picked up from Kasane Airport. The two workmen attached a long metal chain to the front of the Corolla and then reversed a good thirty metres down the path on to ground that was firmer and less sandy. Only then did they attempt successfully to pull the car clear. We gave them a good tip for their effort and kindness and then drove the rest of the way to the lodge, thinking that there was no other significance to this little episode. How wrong we were.

JJ, the manager, met us on arrival and provided cold drinks and wet towels with which to refresh ourselves and then showed us around and told us what was on offer. What a place! It sat on a high ridge overlooking part of the Chobe River and its floodplain, while being surrounded on its other sides by thick bush. The main part of the lodge consisted of high sloping ceilings partially covering the dining and communal areas, which were packed with the most exquisite large carvings of local tribes-people and animals. Our thatched cottage was almost the furthest away but with the same elevated views of the plain and the animals. At lunch, we enjoyed a fantastic cottage pie and then went out on an afternoon game drive with our guide 'KB' who did not return until after dusk, by which time it was dark. We drove through the parched bush, with much elephant damage in places, onto the plain below where we saw elephant, giraffe, impala, Cape buffalo, and a troop of baboons, some of which were wading upright but gingerly across a tributary of the Chobe. We also saw mekoro, wooden canoes, to the same design as those on Namibian rivers being used by local people to fish. These dug-out, pencil thin wooden craft seem very precarious to us and would offer no protection against an attack by a hippo. Mark and I, and the two Australian couples with us, enjoyed an excellent white wine sundowner drink on the edge of the forest bordering the floodplain. That night at dinner the beef was mouth-wateringly good and afterwards we sat by the teak-burning fire on the platform overlooking the plain and a flood-lit waterhole and we talked to Clinton and Lips who were to be our guides for the next three days on early morning game walks. Later still, JJ joined us and was always the solicitous host – going to the bar for us to refresh our (all inclusive) drinks.

We received a pre-dawn wake-up call, went to the restaurant for tea and coffee and set out with Clinton and Lips on a foot safari just after dawn. Clinton led with a rifle and Lips came at the rear with Mark and me in the middle – the chief point of the safety briefing was 'don't run.' We stayed out until after eight a.m. before returning to the lodge for breakfast. Our trip on foot revealed a great deal we might not have seen from a vehicle, such as a host of different insects, spoor, dung, spiders, termites, and birds. It soon became clear, however, that a good part of our route that morning – accompanied by a man with a rifle because of the prevalence of leopard, elephant, and buffalo in the area – was the *same* route that Mark had walked on his own the afternoon before when he had set off to find help to extricate the car. Moreover, to our surprise, we saw the carcass of a large dog stuffed high in a tree that had clearly been placed there by a leopard. Mark stored this revelation for later use!

After breakfast, we spent some time on our wooden balcony overlooking the Chobe, listening to the birdsong, and watching the smoke rising from the many fires away in the distance that had been lit by Namibian farmers. A special early lunch was prepared for us, and then Lips drove us into Kasane to the pick-up point for the boat ride on the Chobe River where it became a much more vigorous and wider force of nature. Within twenty metres of the flimsy jetty, which was the pick-up point for the boat, was a hippo lounging by the water's edge and about 100 metres in the other direction was a large bull elephant browsing on the leaves and branches overhanging the river. At this stage in the holiday, such proximity to dangerous wild animals that may decide to approach even closer seemed perfectly normal to us, so Mark and I just sat there between the two animals and watched an official in a delightfully smart uniform who occasionally got up and spoke to a driver of a boat docking at the jetty to ensure he had the necessary permit. KB took us out into the main channel of the Chobe where we saw literally hundreds of elephant, buffalo, crocodiles, and hippos. Many of the elephant we were able to approach closely as herds of them swam the various channels to get to good food on one of the many islands. Invariably, as they gained the far bank, they would dust themselves. Some of the bulls were tall enough to wade the channels, but many cows and all the calves had to swim at some point when they would use their trunks as snorkels. There were also many birds, all of which KB could instantly recognise. We also saw some relatively rare puku grazing at the river's edge. This was one of our best days in Africa if only for the quantity of game on view.

That night at dinner – a wonderful beef 'stew' with roast potatoes – Mark struck! The subject of our being brothers had come up and Mark proceeded to tell the company at dinner that I was such a 'loving' brother that I was prepared to order him off into the lethal bush to find help for the stuck car having assured him it would be safe. “Next day,” Mark continued, ”we walked the same route with an armed guard and found a leopard kill, and my brother hasn’t even apologised for putting me at such risk.” He had them in stitches with his mock indignation. We ended the evening drinking wine around the fire at the same look-out spot. JJ told us that he had struck a deal with the Chinese company that had just finished the major roads nearby to fix the Red Zone before all their machinery and workers returned home. Within a few days all the offending sand was to be dug out and the strip filled with concrete and then back-filled with a top layer of sand only a few inches deep. Thus, the track would look the same but any car wheels would not be able to sink too far down.

Once more, we set off with Clinton just after dawn for another walk in the bush. Clinton was training some lodge employees to conduct such walks safely so, in addition to Lips, there were two other guides with Mark and me. This time we saw much larger animals such as kudu, impala, banded mongoose, giraffe, and a herd of elephant walking parallel to us but up wind so they never came to suspect our presence about 100 metres away. A great few hours, followed by a breakfast of omelettes and fruit, after which KB (Kabalo) drove us to a local village near Muchenje where we visited a family home. The family - a grandmother and two grandchildren, one of whom was crippled, and a grandfather who briefly appeared later – lived in a semi-enclosed compound inside which was an old abandoned rondavel, a newer more solid family home, and various ‘sheds’ for animals. There was also a separate out-kitchen in which the utensils hanging up around the semi-circular wall were all spotless. Most of them were heavy thick steel or cast-iron pots and pans that looked as if they could have been handed down the generations so solidly built were they. The floor of the kitchen was compressed mud. One of the little boys was playing outside with a small tyre while his disabled brother pulled himself after him. When our vehicle arrived, it became an object of great interest and they both tried to pull themselves on board but to no avail. We gave them a few sweets; we had nothing else with us. We learned later that the disabled boy was being assessed by the various authorities and would shortly start school, probably in a specialist boarding school elsewhere in Botswana. We also learned that his mother was abroad studying medicine and sent back money for the care of her children; hence the brick-built house and the abandoned one made of wood, mud, and thatch. Their grandmother emerged from the main house and urged us to inspect the chicken coop before re-emerging and putting down an assortment of woven baskets she had made. Several of these excellent pieces of work were immediately selected and paid for, much to everyone's satisfaction. As we were about to leave, the grandfather appeared – he had been looking after some goats close by. It seemed he was asking us for beer or money to get beer, whereupon the old lady shouted at him and made it clear we were to give him nothing.

KB then drove us a little way to Mabele Primary School. In the playground there was one little and very persistent boy who followed me all over the place as we were looking around. Eventually I gave him a sweet. It soon became clear that many eyes had been upon us for no sooner did this boy start to unwrap the sweet than an exuberant, jostling crowd of expectant children surrounded us. Immediately, I gave the bag of sweets to Mark and started to film as around twenty youngsters mobbed him. They were all shouting something that sounded like 'kwakwee' which we took to mean 'please, me,' as they all jumped up to try and get a sweet. The look of absolute delight when they received a sweet was humbling – that a tiny sweet should generate such joy. Completely devoid now of all sweets, Mark and I were taken to meet the headmaster in his study. KB suggested that there should be a formal photograph of me handing over some pens to the school. I politely suggested that donating some biros was hardly worthy of any recognition. The head took them, said thank you, and laid them on his desk and invited us to see the rest of the school. The large library was full of books, mostly in English, donated from people and organisations from around the world. They ranged from detailed technical manuals to learn-to-read books for the youngest pupils. We later saw the rules of the school posted up on a wall that commanded that children speak in English at all times in the classroom. There were also seven dated yet serviceable computers in the room, but the headmaster told us they worked only as glorified typewriters because they could not afford any proper software programs for them. Outside again, we were told by KB that we could simply pick any of the buildings and go inside to see a class at work. The one we entered had twenty-five children in it aged about nine years old. The teacher was a big disappointment, and I suspect to the children too. Almost his first question was why people like us "with money" would want to come to a "dirty place like this." When we told him we came to see wild animals, he could scarcely hide his disbelief. I found such a lack of imagination in a teacher shocking. He barked some order and the children all got out their exercise books and we were expected to inspect them. Many of the children wrote with exceptionally precise handwriting. One of them wrote about the shebeen in his village and how excessive drinking caused many problems there. Mark told the teacher I was also a teacher in a university, so the next thing I knew I was expected to give a mini-lesson. I thought I would do it on geography – about where Mark and I came from, but no one could find an atlas or a map at first. Instead, I told them what Mark and I did for a living. When a map did turn up, it was so small that you could cover Wales with a finger nail. I then took photographs of all the children sat in their groups around banks of desks – the teacher insisted on holding my hand when Mark took our photo. Hard copies were sent to the school later with the help of JJ from Muchenje Safari Lodge.

The 'dinner ladies' were a great treat. After we left the classroom, we had a tour of the kitchens which consisted of a storeroom containing sacks of maize and kitchen equipment, and a cooking area with large metal cooking pots and a pit for a wood fire. Outside was a big stack of hard wood used for cooking and although the kitchen had windows, there was no glass in them. The senior dinner lady was very jovial and teased us saying that the children always seem to get photographs sent to them, but the kitchen staff never! We took several photos of her and her assistant and promised faithfully to forward hard copies, which we later did. Finally, we visited a cultural centre at the school and bought some more woven baskets. All of this was a delightful change from what had hitherto been a steady diet of game drives. KB took us back to the lodge where we had an early lunch and then we set off again with KB for a sundowner game drive.

In Chobe National Park, we saw the carcass of a young elephant being eaten by vultures including some rare lappet-faced vultures and, later, we got within a few feet of a herd of elephant one of which made a half-hearted mock charge. On the floodplain close to the river, we saw a big leopard; it came out into the open and walked along for some distance before the bush swallowed it up again. From there, we drove no more than one kilometre and got out to have our drinks at a picnic area. Chilled white wine and South African lager went down a treat. On our journey back to the lodge, just as the sun was about to dip below the horizon, we had to stop for a breeding herd of elephants with calves to cross the road. The fading rays of the sun cast them all in a pale pink and red light as they rumbled off into the bush to feed.

With great reluctance we left Muchenje Lodge after one more early morning walk with Clinton during which we again passed the large domestic dog stashed halfway up a tall tree by a leopard. Killing a domestic dog would hardly have been any effort at all for such a powerful creature, but it almost looked as if the leopard had 'arranged' the dog's carcass purposefully, so perfectly draped was it in a fork of the tree. At the end of our final walk, I asked Clinton the calibre of his gun. Point 458 he replied, which means a bullet of that size in the right place would stop anything, "but it's never loaded" he added matter-of-factly. He argued that it was safer to have the gun unloaded and to practise quick loading technique when required. On our departure, it was JJ himself who drove the Corolla out of the lodge and past the Red Zone lest we get stuck again. His technique was very interesting and consisted of hurtling towards the offending stretch of sand at eighty kph, hitting the deep ruts and simply keeping his foot down until we came out the other side. On the road to Kasane, we saw herds of elephant on either side, and two dead elephants whose carcasses had been burnt to decrease the spread of what was suspected to be anthrax. At Kasane immigration, we filled in some exit forms to leave Botswana and had our passports stamped, and then met Charles from Impalila Island Lodge who took our luggage to his boat at a jetty very close to the immigration centre. We then drove to Chobe Safari Lodge to leave our car and Charles met us at that lodge's jetty on the Chobe River.

Charles took the boat out into the Kasai Channel that links the Chobe and the Zambezi rivers. Within minutes we saw a magnificent fish eagle perched on a bush on the bank. Just when Mark and I were assuming our next stop would be Impalila Island Lodge itself, Charles turned the boat towards a very rickety-looking jetty on the other side of the Chobe River, which was the southern tip of Impalila Island. Charles told us he would stay with the boat and our luggage while we were directed to take our passports and the Namibia arrival forms Charles had supplied and to walk towards a large baobab tree some distance down a rough track along which a few islanders were strolling. When we reached the baobab, we were to turn left and then we should be able to see the police station where entry formalities would be concluded. The officers there were friendly and soon we were back on the boat for a thirty-minute journey to the lodge. Our chalet (No.4) overlooked the Mambova Falls on the Zambezi River. The public areas of the lodge itself were a typical mix of wooden platforms, look-out points, and fire pits. It turned out that Mark and I were the only guests there and so we had the place to ourselves. With so little for the staff to do, we needed only look as if we desired another drink for one to be brought, or to seem the slightest chilly for more wood to be placed in the fire pit. Indeed, that night the staff placed a single immaculately laid table on the wooden dining platform right up close to a look-out point over the river. At breakfast, staff had obviously been waiting around for us to appear and then descended to take instructions on what we wanted and how it was to be cooked. It seemed very luxurious to be treated thus.

After settling in on our first day, we went out late afternoon not for a sundowner drive but a sundowner cruise with Kelvin, our new guide. The cruise took in the four channels of the Zambezi in these parts and a close view of Zambians working and fishing along the river's banks. The flimsy-looking and unstable mokoro boat was much in evidence as were some fishing villages where the fishermen live with their families during the season until the water rises too far and destroys their temporary dwellings. Then, they returned to their permanent villages to do other work, and come back when the fishing season resumes. Very soon, we saw crocodiles, usually lying along the banks, and hippos often with only their snouts showing above water. There were so many birds, including African skimmers, fish eagles, egrets and even a pied wagtail just like the ones back home. As the sun dropped quickly towards the horizon and the sky turned a deep throbbing red, Kelvin cut the engine so that we drifted gently on the current towards the Zambian bank, served us our chilled white wine and allowed us to enjoy the simple peace and the wonderful majesty of the place. As we sipped our wine and looked along the main channel of the Zambezi River towards the huge ball of red now slipping below the horizon, there lay before us an expanse of reeds and swirling eddies. In that moment, it felt as if this place was beyond the possibility of all change; I hope so for it would be a pity to lose such a beautiful spot to over-fishing or crass exploitation. We had an excellent chicken for dinner and spent some time talking to the joint managers, Anna and Peter. Finally, Mark and I took a bottle of wine to our chalet and sat outside mulling over the day on our balcony accompanied by the constant soft sound of the waters of the Zambezi flowing over the rapids. The camp generator was switched off at ten o'clock plunging everything into complete darkness, but what a view we had then of the stars in a coal-black sky.

Breakfast cooked to order; still no other guests. Mark and I fed some bulbuls that hopped right onto the dining table to take the bread directly from our hands. Immediately below us, a water monitor suddenly slithered down the bank and into some thick undergrowth near the river. At eight o'clock, Kelvin took us on a walk to a local village and school and told us something about the way of life and customs of the people on the island. He told us that when a young man and woman are romantically attached to one another, they do not tell their respective parents but rather their uncles and aunts or grandparents. It is these people who assess the suitability of the potential wife and husband. If the extended family have any doubts about the man, they will negotiate very hard indeed for the prospective husband to pay twenty cows or more in compensation to the woman's family. This is to compensate for the fact that she will leave her village and live in her husband's village and, thus, will no longer carry out all the duties she used to perform in her parents' home. However, a well-thought of man who is considered reliable may only have to pay five or six cows. Kelvin apparently paid seven cows and was very pleased to be thought of so highly. Each village is occupied by extended family members and groups. A reed fence around a rondavel denotes a married couple. The villagers grow many of their own vegetables on their own land and they all own cows, which can be sold for cash if needs be. Some villagers may catch and sell fish, or gather wood and reeds for sale, or they may cut poles from mopane trees to use in constructing dwellings. Virtually all the hard money earned comes from doing these 'natural' activities. Moreover, one part of the extended family may have tomatoes but few onions so they will swap with other family members. Primary schooling is to all intents and purposes free.

After lunch, our speed-boat safari soon travelled the considerable distance to the park area where we had been before from Muchenje, the only disadvantage being the lack of any shade from a ferocious sun. We saw hundreds of elephant and one big bull in particular crossing a channel. Kelvin got the boat right up behind the bull as he waded through the river. Once he checked on us, decided we were not worth any further bother, and carried on his way powerfully pushing aside the water to gain the far bank. On our return, six other guest had arrived for what was to be our last night at the lodge. The staff gave the new guests a table out of the way while we kept our spot overlooking the river. That night, we sat by the fire-pit with two employees of the lodge, the kind we did not often meet because they are not front of house but are nevertheless the essential workers who keep the generators going and the kitchens functioning.

We left Impalila Island Lodge after breakfast but had to visit the police station again by the baobab tree and fill out forms and have out passports stamped, and then the same thing all over again in Kasane as we re-entered Botswana. Before ten o'clock, we were driving away from the Chobe Safari Lodge where we had left the car but, a short while later, we had more forms to fill and passports to present at Ngoma Bridge as we left Botswana, and the same on the other side of the bridge as we entered Namibia...again. Namibians by law must present themselves physically at the one office in Windhoek when they obtain or renew a passport - a difficult, expensive, and often time-consuming task for many. Hence, both the Namibian and Botswanan authorities are very careful to cram as many arrival and exit stamps to a page to lengthen the life of passports – they did the same for us, but even so we had ten stamps spread over two or three pages. Most surprisingly and pleasantly, we had to pay nothing in either country for such processing and no visas were required and no payments for cross-border vehicle use. After immigration on the Namibian side of Ngoma Bridge, the police wanted the vehicle's engine and VIN and chassis details. The copper on duty summoned me to his little hut ahead of the patiently waiting truck drivers, and read out all the long numbers from the car hire paperwork so I could more easily and quickly enter them into a battered old book, which I am prepared to bet was never consulted afterwards.

Bwabwata National Park, through which the latter part of our journey took us, showed a lot of evidence of burning on either side of the road, but we did see two herds of elephant on this second visit. We reached Ndhovu Safari Lodge by three p.m. and soon after Mark bought up what seemed like half the gift shop. Monica, the manageress, told us that since we were doing a four-wheel drive tour of Mahango National Park tomorrow, there was no need to pay extra to do the boat trip that afternoon since it would add little to our experience. We appreciated her honesty and settled into our well-appointed tents overlooking the Okavango River. Here the river was so broad and the current so strong that it was difficult to believe that it literally all ran out into the sands of the Okavango Delta many miles to the south. In effect, we now had about twenty-four hours to relax and to watch hippo and elephant from the wooden balcony in front of our tent. The previous week two young French people had gone swimming in the river and had to be hauled out by the managers before the hippos or crocs got to them.

The evening meal was en famille and we sat close to a German and an Austrian couple who asked me to write down the 'best' waterholes for them to visit when they got to Etosha. Later, Mark and I took a bottle of white wine from the honesty bar and sat chatting on the tent's balcony. It was surprisingly cold overnight and there were also loud noises made by hippos that seemed very near but which we assumed came from the *far* bank of the river. In fact, at breakfast the next day, we learned that they had been wandering around *inside* the camp. One, some years ago, had even got itself stuck in the swimming pool.

Just after dawn, I crept outside and took some photographs of a crisp sunrise over this iconic river. Mark and I enjoyed an excellent breakfast at which I handed over my 'reports' of where to go in Etosha to the two couples, and then Mark lounged by the pool while I got rid of a lot of the dust all over the inside of the car, wrote some letters, and listened to Joni Mitchell on the balcony overlooking the Okavango. After lunch, we left for a sundowner drive with Johan through Mahango National Park in a Toyota Land Cruiser – only Mark and me aboard. The park is very small and part of it can be driven in a two-wheel vehicle but to get the best out of it you need a four-wheel drive. There was a dirt road through the park that provided one of the few land crossings into Botswana. We saw buffalo, hippo, impala, zebra, giraffe, several small herds of elephant, bushbuck, roan, tsessebe, many birds, and a 1,500-year-old and very large baobab tree by which we had our sundowner drinks. The very last elephant we saw on this holiday was in this park – a bull who was very displeased with us and the way we just sat there looking at him. So, he gave us a mock charge. He only covered about ten metres – we were a few more than that from him – but he completely uprooted and demolished one small tree in the process while all the while shaking his head vigorously, swinging his trunk from side to side and flaring his ears wide. Johan reversed the vehicle a few metres and the elephant was satisfied by our backing down. Johan mentioned that young bulls like this were rather 'stroppy' and often acted this way because in this particular park there weren't enough older and mature bulls to show them how to behave properly.

We enjoyed another good meal that night, still sat next to the German-speaking couples that allowed me to practise my own German a little more. Mark and I again enjoyed a bottle of wine on our little balcony and began to chat about some of the things that had made us laugh on the trip. We recalled the strange 'elephant trees' seen in the hazy distance, especially in Etosha, that trapped the unwary into shouting 'look elephant.' Of course, *we* were far too experienced to fall into this trap – well not after the first few days anyway. We started giving marks out of ten to the most convincing elephant trees. Later, we found out that there were also rhino and giraffe trees to trap the inexperienced. There were also a lot of laughs about the communal kitty that I held to pay for petrol, incidental expenses, etc. According to Mark, *he* kept on putting money into the kitty and I was the one spending it on *my* souvenirs – a total slander on my character. Indeed, the competitive buying of artefacts and then commenting: "you must have enough now to open a shop back home" were also matters that made us smile regularly, as was finding that new species of bird – the Stephens Shit-eater. We also laughed at how through a misunderstanding at Impalila Island Lodge we had moved away from free house wine to expensive a la carte wine, bottle after bottle of which we had for dinner and on our sundowner cruises. Well, we laughed a little less when the bill arrived. The biggest laugh came a few days later when we left Ndhovu and drove to Ghaub Guest Farm via Rundu. We thought we would get some wine in Rundu to defray our expenses at Ghaub and at Okonjima but the Spar there only had a tiny selection. I bought two bottles of Tassenberg red wine for the entirely reasonable price of twenty-two rand each or less than £2 a bottle. Mark found it so awful as to be undrinkable whereupon, on our last two nights in Ghaub and Okonjima, I would 'taunt' him with the one opened but unfinished bottle, suggesting that we should finish it off and not buy any expensive stuff from our hosts. Mark's response was to make a face like a man sampling a most unpleasant concoction. In the end, I finished the bottle myself, but as we left Okonjima on our way to the airport and home, we left the second bottle with the gateman along with a tip. Mark insisted he would think we were real cheapskates to hand over such rubbish; I insisted that's all they had in the Rundu Spar! There were three beds in our tent but when I woke in the morning the bed in which Mark had gone to sleep the night before was now covered in cases and presents and in the free bed was some unknown shape. It turned out that Mark had been woken in the night by ants crawling all over his face, neck, and upper body – fortunately not biting ones – so he had changed beds.

We left Ndhovu in the early morning and drove the 500 kilometres to Ghaub Guest Farm via the infamous Spar in Rundu. There was still a lot of burning of scrub going on as we headed west along the Caprivi Strip. We got some lunch at the Spar and drove outside the town to eat it at one of those charming 'rest stops' set by the roadside. Near Ghaub Guest Farm, we accidently drove into a workers' accommodation area, then into the *actual* farm with cows and pens and farm machinery, but eventually we found the guest part, passing a dry-stone wall on the way that could have come directly from the Lakes in the UK. The area was quite lush and green here because there is underground water, and the guest farm was expansively laid out with various walks. It was a very relaxing place in which to stay. I had fancied going horse riding but it was not available. Mark went pot-holing. The caves were close and Mark went with a guide (Abrams) from the farm. Inside it was incredibly hot and the deeper they went the more the shortage of oxygen. Mark enjoyed the short while he spent underground but I had never seen him look so hot and bothered as on his return. We had excellent kudu stew for dinner accompanied by music from the 1940s after which we sat outside our room with Mark nursing some Windhoek lager and me drinking the by now accursed Tassenberg.

The following day, we arrived at Main Camp, Okonjima, to be told there that they were full and, therefore, they were giving us a free upgrade to Bush Camp. At the chalet, Mark chose his own little area with bed, other furniture, and fridge, which he referred to as the 'servants' quarter.' We took tea and cakes in the main part of the camp, and then went out on a leopard sundowner drive. Our guide, Rohan, found a female leopard without too much difficulty and we saw her quite clearly for several minutes. We returned so late to camp, long after sunset, that we had the bonus of a mini night-drive with Rohan picking out various animals with the red spotlight. Dinner, however, was still served perfectly despite our late return and we enjoyed an excellent steak and spent much of the evening talking in English and Italian to an elderly couple, Giorgio and Clara, who were originally from Italy but now lived in the USA. The crockery, I could not help but notice, was the same black and white pattern as I had at home and which was bought in the 1990s.

Just after dawn the next day, Mark and I went out with Rohan and a black tracker called Peter. After an hour or so, we came across three wild cheetah that had recently killed a juvenile oryx. One of them was on the carcass just opening it up at the rear and already the face of the cat was smeared with bright red blood. The other two lounged nearby. Our very first day in Namibia had included seeing animals on a kill, and now our last day was ending in similar fashion. Even in reasonably thick bush, Rohan had managed to get the vehicle quite close so we had excellent views of the cheetahs.

Mark and I were not expecting the next development for Rohan informed us that if we did as we were told, we could approach even closer on foot. In fact, there turned out to be only one main rule, beyond no sudden movements or noises, and that was under no circumstances run! Rohan produced a pick-axe handle from the vehicle to serve as some kind of defence, if needed, and invited us to follow him on foot with Peter bringing up the rear. Within a few minutes, we had circled the cheetahs and approached them slowly from a different angle until we were only fifteen metres or so away. From here, we started to take photographs for the cats seemed very relaxed about our presence. What a fantastic end to our journey of over 4,200 kilometres.

By now we had become addicted to life in the bush and to safaris, so back we went to Namibia in 2013. Our hire car was a Nissan with much higher road clearance and stiffer suspension than previous cars – a factor that made our long journey much more comfortable, especially on the dirt roads. After no more than fifteen kilometres, a low tyre pressure warning light came on and we had to return to the Budget depot at the airport. The 'fault' was quickly fixed, or so we thought. In fact, when we were over sixty kilometres away the same light came on again and stayed on the whole journey. After we had checked the tyres twice during that day and found them to be fine, we simply ignored it. We arrived at Bagatelle Ranch in the Kalahari Desert before noon to find that Skank, the tame springbok who had nutted me in the balls two years earlier, was still alive. She had had seven offspring, all of whom were wild, but Skank preferred to hang around the breakfast and dining tables in the hope of easy vegetarian pickings rather than join her progeny in the desert beyond. This is the place where we first encountered Scaramanga red wine and then singularly failed to find it anywhere else in Namibia. We had barely settled in before Mark and I were anxiously examining the wine list to see if it were there. It was not. What disappointment. Then,

Mark found a dusty bottle sitting on a shelf in the breakfast room. Further enquiries revealed that the lodge did have it, so we ordered two bottles for dinner, and another one to take away with us when we left the next day. We should have taken the lot.

There was quite a crowd later that afternoon for the sundowner drives and one vehicle was soon full up. So, Mark and I got into the other vehicle with a French couple and Andre, a South African living in Namibia. It turned out, we had joined the 'wrong' group and, therefore, in addition to our drive through the Kalahari spotting game on the way and ending with a sundowner drink at sunset, we were also taken as an unexpected bonus to see three cheetah being fed in a large compound close to the lodge. The Toyota Land Cruiser was adept at muscling itself up the steep red dunes of the Kalahari and then plunging down the other side into flat valleys mostly strewn with dried yellow grass and various acacia trees. Quite a few of the trees were festooned along their thickest branches with the large and heavy nests of sociable weaver birds. While we did see one majestic male giraffe stood all alone at the top of one of the dunes, most of the game was in the valleys in between, including a great many vultures that took off in all directions as Pedro, our driver, approached them. We returned to the lodge to see the three male cheetah, which had been orphaned when very young and thus had not learned any hunting skills from their mothers. They are such graceful cats, but it was a pity to see how of necessity they were penned into such a relatively small space. We then drove back out across the dunes to come over a certain ridge to find a table with a crisp white table cloth and groaning with various drinks, and there we enjoyed our sundowners.

The next day involved a five-hour run from the lodge to Mariental and then south down the B1 to Keetmanshoop and eventually onto the dirt roads C12 and C37 to Canon Lodge near the Fish River Canyon, the second biggest canyon in the world. We crossed over a narrow-gauge railway line a few times on our way but never saw any traffic. Stations are no more than halts, marked only by a small sign, and sometimes seemingly miles from anywhere. Canon Lodge consisted of about thirty well-appointed chalets 'sunk' into a kopje-strewn landscape of huge rock forms and steep basalt hills over which rock hyraxes roam in large numbers. The swimming pool was without doubt the furthest away from any accommodation or dining area I have ever known – it was a hike into the countryside. There was also a bar with a refrigerator at the top of one of the steep hills overlooking the lodge.

In the morning, Timo, our driver from Canon Lodge, took us in an open top vehicle to see the Fish River Canyon along with a young German couple. Mark and I had never been so cold in all our time in Africa. Even though Timo was not driving quickly, it was freezing. One of the Germans moved into the driving cab with Timo, and Mark and I covered ourselves with as many blankets as we could get hold of. It was not very pleasant but the view at the end of the hour-long journey was magnificent. Snaking tightly into the distance was this 'scar' cut deeply into the layered rocks. It was impressively steep and deep to reach the actual river, which because of very poor rainfall that whole year was barely flowing at all. The approach down to the valley floor, which authorised and guided hikers take, is accompanied in places by a metal hand-rail, so steep is the descent. In the afternoon, we spotted a lot of birds back at the lodge and climbed the kopje overlooking our own chalet to inspect the 'bar' on top.

We had been talking to a young barman and waitress at dinner the night before and the young man had wished Mark a good journey as they wouldn't meet again, as he put it. Just before noon today at Keetmanshoop, some distance from Canon Lodge, we met them both again at a petrol station where they were waiting for transport to Windhoek. They had left before dawn to get this far and were going home for a few weeks – many people work six weeks on at a lodge and then two weeks off when they usually travel home to see family.

From Maltahohe, we drove through rough terrain to the Zaris Pass, hoping to find if Philip were still in business at the old Zaris Roadhouse where we had first met him and where he had regaled us with tales of all his exploits. There was to be no repeat of two years ago for Philip, we learned later at Zebra River Lodge, had gone back to guiding and the old farmhouse was shut up. After seven hours and over 600 kilometres on the road, we were tired when we got to Zebra River Lodge but the excellent sundowner drive to a hill overlooking the lodge soon perked us up. At dinner, we sat outside on the terrace and thoroughly enjoyed oryx and fine red wine. Guests ate at various tables and Louis and Geraldine, the new owners, made us very comfortable. Louis knew about the Bushman paintings Linda and I had seen there in 1997 in a remote valley under a rock overhang, but surprisingly did not know where they were. From my description of our original route and some photographs I sent later, Louis was confident he could pinpoint in which valley the overhang was located.

At breakfast, we fed some of the birds that frequented the shaded terrace and then Mark went off with Job, a guide, on a long drive and then walk around the property. I chatted to Louis, who breeds his own herd of horses, which put in an appearance at the waterhole. We were apparently Louis's first ever Welsh guests and we got on so well that by the time we left the next morning, he had given us a free bottle of wine with dinner, a free trip in the Land Rover to see the billion-and-a-half-year-old stromatolites in a dry river bed, and two free Zebra River Lodge fleeces. These came in very handy at a cold Swakopmund by the sea.

The dirt roads from Zebra River Lodge to Swakopmund on the Atlantic coast were poor. Swakopmund looks a much bigger and more prosperous place than in 1997, but also one with more crime for almost the first thing we noticed on driving into town was the razor wire or small electric fences around the tops of high walls surrounding many houses. On the streets, we also saw 'armed response units.' In addition, there were uniformed 'parking attendants' – young men you tip to keep an eye on your car. At the Cornerstone Guest House, they even gave us a mobile phone with the numbers of the owners should we need to summon help. We toured the town a little and had lunch in the centre but, in the evening, we drove to the Jetty Restaurant at the end of a long thin pier sticking out into a very cold and rather choppy ocean. There, we met the young parking attendants, who were very solicitous and guaranteed the safety of our car. We enjoyed an excellent change from mainly bush meat in the form of sole and salmon and a brilliant KWV Sauvignon Blanc. They sold us two more to take away with us. As we made our way along the pier, the wind and waves had become much stronger and we felt the structure sway under the Atlantic onslaught. We met our friendly parking attendants, gave them a few dollars, and returned to our lodge, where Mark and I drank the wine from the restaurant outside our room behind the high walls and the razor wire.

The first part of our route from Swakopmund went along the Skeleton Coast where we saw a wrecked fishing boat quite near the high tide mark. The rest of the route from the coast to the north west and Etendeka Mountain Camp in remote Damaraland went through some staggering geological features, including some ancient volcanic 'flow' country with what seemed like interlocking fingers of rocky clumps. It appeared to be almost impenetrable. In the background was the Brandberg Mountain, the highest in Namibia and very dramatic. We also drove through some mountain passes with steep and twisty dirt roads. Just after the Palmwag veterinary gate, where government officials control the movements of vehicles and animals, we met two guides from Etendeka who took us to Palmwag Lodge where we left our car. On the twenty-four-kilometre route to the actual camp in the four-wheel drive vehicle, we were joined by two middle-aged Belgian couples, one French speaking, the other Dutch. Both were such avid photographers and video enthusiasts that what should have taken about ninety minutes took nearly two and a half hours, arriving in camp just as it was getting dark. We did however see two black rhino en route, so well worth all the stopping to take photos of every Tom, Dick, and common springbok! The driver pulled over on one occasion and asked us if anyone could identify the bird close by perched at the top of a small mopane tree. "Pale Chanting Goshawk," I replied immediately to his and everyone else's surprise. Later, the driver asked the same question of another bird – a bird that Louis and I had been viewing and discussing at length just a few days earlier at Zebra River Lodge. "It's a Mountain Chat, or more accurately, it's been officially reclassified as a Mountain Wheatear," I said. I think the driver 'hated' me at that moment but the others all looked very impressed. Not Mark, of course, for he too could recognise a Pale Chanting Goshawk and well-remembered the conversation with Louis who had originally supplied all this arcane information. He was very amused by the fact that there were probably over 200 *other* birds the driver could have asked about and whose names I would not have known. However, the Belgian video enthusiast was very impressed by my apparently encyclopaedic knowledge and at the lodge came over to me and enquired if I were there as an expert ornithologist just to see the bird life.

The camp – all tented – had stunning views of the surrounding hills with their clearly layered rock strata. Our shower was a bucket suspended by a rope with a valve to let solar-heated water run through, but was more than adequate. Dennis, the owner, did not receive the Beatles tape Linda and I posted to him in 1997. "Things go missing out here" was how he diplomatically put it. He was just as passionate as ever about keeping this pristine part of the world protected and unspoilt. But it had cost him three marriages.

In the morning one of the zips on the front of our tent became stuck, so we had to roll out of the tent along the floor through a narrow opening at the bottom – someone soon fixed it for us. Bonnie, the chief guide, took guests on a three-hour morning walk through the countryside, highlighting many plants and insects as well as animals. After tea and cakes in the afternoon, we set off on a game drive, again with Bonnie. We passed through very rugged terrain and visited some springs that bubble up in a few places on an almost permanent basis. Indeed, all the water we had at the camp came directly out of one of Etendeka's aquifers, so pure and safe is it to drink. The land was dotted with large euphorbia bushes, some the size of caravans sitting there in their silver, light green colours among all the orange basalt rocks and boulders. Euphorbia bushes are poisonous to many animals, but not black rhino and oryx, and the thick white 'puss' that secretes from a broken branch can blind a human if the fluid gets into the eye is not soon treated. Among the euphorbia were mopane bushes and trees. We saw few birds but lots of oryx, kudu and mountain zebra, and two more black rhino. That night, after an excellent dinner, Dennis got out his telescope and we all saw distinctly the rings of Saturn. He also showed us how to work out due south from the stars of the Southern Cross. Mark and I took a bottle of wine from the free bar back with us and sat outside the tent flaps for a while chatting.

We left the next morning to collect our car at Palmwag, rather disappointed not to have seen desert-adapted elephant at Etendeka during our stay. Then, marvellously, on a high and steep escarpment, we saw four of them, gathering what sparse food there was on the side of the mountain. Even at a distance, we could see that the elephants were completely sure-footed and at ease despite the steepness. What a farewell to this lovely and remote place!

We drove on dirt through some very interesting countryside for over 100 kilometres until we reached Outjo, where we had lunch in the charming Farmhouse Bakery, and then on to Okaukuejo, where we unpacked, got in fresh supplies and some mopane wood for the braai and relaxed for a few hours until we went down to the waterhole just before sunset. We saw over twenty-five elephants kicking up a lot of dust as they eagerly approached the water in the warm orange glow of the setting sun. After our meal of kudu, we lit the fire outside our bush chalet where a jackal walked right up to our car in the darkness. Mark, with only his binoculars, was able to find both Venus and Saturn whose rings we could just make out. Later still, I went to the waterhole alone and saw two pairs of black rhino, and was able to get a few decent photographs. Back at the chalet, as the mopane wood had been reduced to glowing embers, I heard lions roaring in the distance.

In the morning, we worked our way to the Etosha lookout point on the very edge of the huge expanse of the dry pan. The road there and the barriers keeping drivers on the road were much improved from the previous year. Indeed, the main road through Etosha had been upgraded and is the better for it even though there are still a few rough parts between Okaukuejo and Halali. At the lookout point, there were numerous stones lying around that we used to spell out 'Wales' on the pan floor. It was hard work under the blazing sun and high temperature.

After lunch in Halali, we journeyed to Rietfontein where there were many elephants, including a 'middle-aged' female who was struggling horribly with a problem with her front right foot and a very pronounced limp. She would stagger a few steps, stop, stagger a few more, stop and then stretch her leg, and so on. But she was still with her herd and they had not deserted her, so there was hope for this animal. Previously, we had seen a single zebra with an injury that restricted its mobility. The equation for this latter animal was simple – get better before you encounter any lions or leopard, or else. On our way back to Okaukuejo, we had a very strange but enchanting experience involving two zebras. They were standing very close together side by side in the middle of the dirt road and would simply not move away. Eventually, as Mark took some photos, we squeezed past them at the side of the road at a walking pace and still they held their ground.

No sooner had we left the chalet in the morning than we returned since we had forgotten to leave a tip for the cleaning lady. She was very pleased to see us. At lunch at Halali, a waitress asked us why we had both taken off our wristwatches and put them on the table. Was it some obscure Western custom? No, we replied, we simply got a lot of dust and sweat under the straps. All three rest camps inside Etosha seemed busier to us than ever before, especially at meal times; yet out in the park itself, it rarely felt crowded at all. There were also many more German holiday makers than last year and more big buses and backpacker 'cattle trucks' (as we called them) in evidence around the place. I saw Mark later in the camp shop where the electronic till had broken down. Everything was now being done with forms made out in triplicate, which took so long that at one point Mark returned his Magnum ice-cream to the freezer and selected a new one because the original had melted. After dinner, we drank the very last bottle of Scaramanga that had been driven all around Namibia in the boot of the car since the Kalahari Desert. Mark and I kept an eye on one another to see that there was no cheating in the portions poured.

We had set off in the morning from Halali towards Namutoni and had been driving for a while without seeing either animals or other humans when in the distance two black shapes came into view. We soon realized they were black rhino, a mother and calf. They approached us slowly walking along the dirt road, but they did not seem at all bothered by our proximity. We had them all to ourselves as they ambled past us and then turned inland. Within an hour, just before Ngobib waterhole, we saw a herd of six bachelor elephants off to our right in open scrubland, all taking the same line to cross the road. We positioned and stopped the car where we thought they might cross. We could not have judged it better for they all went past very close to us, and one was so close that it could have placed its enormous trunk on the bonnet of the car, or much worse if it had chosen to do so. Fortunately, large bull elephants are usually relaxed around cars in Etosha.

The long and circular drive to Ngobib was worth the effort for there, under a tall tree close to the water, was a pride of lions. Even though they were half asleep and possibly digesting an earlier meal, their presence alone prevented some red hartebeest from drinking. It was on this journey that a classic rookie error was unexpectedly made by Mark. In our previous inexperienced days, there were a few craftily designed bushes, seen from a distance, that would make us cry out "look, elephant!" Those innocent days were long gone until Mark, straining to see if ahead there were some sign of Ngobib, mistook a white termite mound for one of the marker stones in the park. He was not allowed to forget this error in a hurry.

On our return to the chalet at Halali, we found that someone had taken the plastic table from outside by the braai. After accusing some German neighbours (in German) of pinching it, which they denied but not convincingly, I managed to get housekeeping to deliver a new one. It arrived on the back of a small truck and was heaved into place by one of the workmen – this one was too heavy for anyone else to cart away casually. Later, we were very lucky to see two adult female lions at the waterhole. The restaurant put on an outside barbeque that night and afterwards Mark and I burned some mopane wood and chatted around our newly delivered table. Around ten o'clock, to the far west there were flashes of lightning and the distant rumble of thunder, but no rain came our way.

By mid-morning, the next day, we had driven back to Okaukuejo having checked out at Halali. At the waterhole, we saw a tawny eagle take off from the tall tree to our left and swoop onto one of a pair of passing dove-like birds. Then, with its prey in its talons, it flew to a plucking post at the top of a tree in leaf about 200 metres away. But this was *exactly* the behaviour we had both seen at the same spot last year. If this was not the same bird then it was surely the offspring. A splendid end to our time in Etosha.

All that remained was to make our way slowly south to Windhoek and the overnight flight home. We stopped again at the Farmhouse Bakery in Outjo and at our usual café in Okahandja. The outside of the car was a real mess. It even had some dried mud splashes around the wheel rims where we had passed through some puddle or other in this immense land. At the petrol station at Okahandja, one of the young lads there saw the splashes and wanted to know where we had encountered rain. He was disappointed when we told him it was not caused by freshly fallen rain. Inside the car were several shades of dust and sand from all the regions we had travelled through – in total over 3,800 kilometres. The country was crying out for rain – a few days after we got back Louis emailed to say a few millimetres of rain had fallen at Zebra River Lodge and that already the desert was flowering. We would have liked to have seen that. Mark and I have now seen many faces of Namibia, certainly all the classic ones, but we shall never see them all, I suppose, so vast, so instantly changeable is this land.

Chapter Thirteen: The Stephens Brothers go East

In March 2013, Mark and I 'abandoned' our safari love affair and travelled to Egypt. That was also the month when I treated myself to a Mercedes 'A' Class Sport. I enjoyed the drive to Heathrow, playing with all the new electronic driving aids. However, the Air Egypt experience was not pleasurable at all. The seating was a three-by-three configuration, and the seats not that comfortable given that the direct flight to Luxor took six hours. What came as a bigger shock, however, was that no alcohol was served and precious few other kinds of drinks come to that. Mark and I arrived around eleven p.m. the worse for the wrong kind of wear.

Sadly, our very first experience of Egypt was the kind that annoyed us most – the driver of our minibus wanted an immediate tip just for loading two bags into the vehicle. The twenty-minute journey from the airport to *Ra 11*, our riverboat berthed just outside the centre of Luxor, was interesting for the flagrant traffic offences committed by the driver, who was still rabbiting on about getting his tip. Traffic lights on red were clearly only advisory and traversing any roundabout was largely chaotic – at least to our untrained eyes. We found wrapped sandwiches and fruit in our cabin on arrival, along with towels on the bed made into the shape of swans, which were nice touches. However, Mark and I soon abandoned the room and headed for the bar where we had a few drinks until gone midnight. The capacity of the boat was 150 but there were far fewer passengers on board – mostly European. During the night, the boat set sail north along the Nile to Dendera.

We left the by now berthed boat around eight a.m. at Dendera to see the temple dedicated to Horus. Our permanent guide on the boat, Salah, was informative and well-organised – he called the small group of us in his care the 'mashy-mashy' group, which means 'okay-dokey' in Egyptian Arabic. We had an excellent explanation and mini-tour of the temple from Salah before he left us to our own devices at the site until it was time to sail slowly south back towards Luxor. Mark and I sat on the comfortable sundeck and watched the villages along both banks of the Nile slip by, where often we saw fishermen going about their work in their sailboats, and noticed how the women washed clothes in the shallows of the river. We also saw lots of different kinds of birds, and quite often young children would call to us from the bank – sometimes the older ones told us to "fuck off." At the rear of the boat on the sundeck and shielded by a sheet draped across a rail were two teenage boys, whose sole job on the journey to and from Dendera was to man an old Second World War machine gun, possibly a Vickers, mounted on its own heavy steel frame. This was one of the security precautions deemed necessary to protect tourists. For a few Egyptian pounds, the boys would let tourists 'play around' with it even though it was loaded with ammunition. Much later in the tour, we found out that many of our fellow passengers hadn't even known it was there and, as we neared Luxor, it was deemed no longer necessary and I saw it being carried down into the bowels of the boat for storage. There were other members of the crew with much lighter hand-held machine guns who always got off first when the boat berthed somewhere, but instead of looking and acting in a military fashion to discourage any attack that might take place, they invariably strolled along the bank and found a spot in the shade to sit down and have a smoke. That seemed perfectly reasonable to us since, other than the maniacal driving, we never felt threatened or unsafe at all while we were in Egypt.

We left very early for our journey to the Valley of the Kings from our berth on the outskirts of Luxor. There were long queues of vehicles trying to fill up with diesel at the fuel stations where supplies were severely restricted. We toured the valley long before most tourists had arrived and we entered three of the many tombs open to the public and saw some very well-preserved wall paintings. As usual, the entrance to such sites involved first having to traverse either a gathering of hawkers trying to sell an assortment of tourist trinkets or else a row or even an arcade of densely packed shops and stalls where the owners do their utmost to entice people in. Mark and I adopted a heads down, say nothing, and walk on approach, which is a pity as we would have liked to speak to many of them, but their only interest was to sell us something – things we just did not want. Later, we visited a village close to the Valley of the Kings that is almost entirely given over to shops selling nothing but alabaster. We entered Morsey's Shop where an entertaining 'pitch' was delivered explaining about alabaster before we were invited to tour their various products and to buy. It was almost impossible to browse alone as is the custom in the UK because as soon as we looked at a product an employee was offering to wrap it, and then to sell us something else – but at a special price!

After Mark and I made our escape from Morsey's – minus alabaster – we were driven to the Temple of Queen Hatshepsut, which was very impressive and which we were able to explore without any fuss. On our way back to *Ra II* for lunch – both lunch and dinner were always buffets but with excellent food and presentation and presided over by a jovial and proud head chef – we stopped briefly at the Colossi of Memnon by the side of the road. After lunch, we had an evocative two-hour horse and carriage drive into the centre of Luxor and through a local market full of tiny, tightly packed stalls selling everything under the sun. There was barely enough room for the carriages, but the people politely stepped aside to let us pass. The stallholders did not seem to mind that many of their colourful samples of cloth and garments were hung so low across the narrow alleyways that we frequently had to brush them away. We stopped for a while to rest the horses and to see the continuing excavations of the Avenue of the Sphinxes that runs from Luxor Temple to Karnak. The row of sphinx after sphinx was impressive even then, so it should be wonderful now the excavations are completed.

That evening, after dinner, Mark and I were the only ones left on the sundeck as the boat sailed on through the night. We heard the last (Isha) call to the faithful to come to prayer, broadcast from the minaret of a mosque. Although we could not see the mosque, the muezzin's voice filled the whole of the riverine expanse. Despite the impressive width of the Nile, we could clearly hear the rise and fall of his captivating chant. We two atheists found the whole experience strangely spiritual. The singer certainly had an excellent voice and would have graced any Welsh choir. It was a haunting few moments before the boat carried us away.

The boat was cruising south towards Kom Ombo. It was clear that we had left behind urban Egypt for now and we were sailing through farmland, but we also saw some areas by the banks where stone had been quarried in ancient times for temples. Occasionally, a few sparrows landed on the sundeck looking for food, and we also saw lots of herons, egrets, and swallows, but most of all we saw young and old, men and women working in the fields along the Nile. Every piece of land, including small islands in the Nile, were used to grow some produce or other, even if a few of those islands looked decidedly temporary. After we docked at Kom Ombo and toured the temple, we returned to the boat trying to mind our own business and the attentions of various hawkers. Two eight-year-old boys approached us with a young donkey in tow. They were trying to get us to be photographed with the donkey and then to hand over some money. We did not exactly tell them to bugger off but we were not very approachable either. Back on board, Mark and I watched these two children for some while as they walked up and down the elevated quay in front of the boat. Gamely, they accosted nearly every tourist returning to the boat and tried to convince them of the virtues of the donkey but all to no avail. Mark now ventured that he thought I had been too hard on them, and that we really should have given them something. Given that the boat was about to depart, it was too late physically to hand them any money. In a flash of inspiration, I called to the two children who saw me by the side of the sundeck clearly putting some Egyptian pound notes into a half-full bottle of water. They saw me screw the top on tightly and then watched me expectantly as I hurled the plastic bottle off the sundeck, over the crew below preparing to take up the gang-plank, over the men carrying the machine guns, and land it behind the children on the upper quay. In an instant, they were on the bottle, opened it and retrieved the money. They waved and shouted at Mark and me, during which time the donkey took the opportunity to make a dash for it. It raced away towards its mother followed by the two boys who ran past them both and up to their own mother to show her what they had received. Then, in a flash just as children do, they ran off again, caught hold of the exasperated baby donkey and dragged it back to the quay – from which the boat was now departing - where they shouted and waved and smiled at Mark and me and held the donkey up on its hind legs. One of the boys ran his hand along the donkey's mouth to make it 'smile.' I suppose they were saying thank you to us for the money. It was, without doubt, our finest moment in Egypt to see the joy on the faces of those two boys.

We again enjoyed some wine after dinner on the sundeck, aka Mike's Bar. In fact, such was the size of the bar bill, we had clearly been enjoying quite a lot of wine. Every purchase on board was signed for and the customer then received a coloured chitty. We had so many pink chitties for alcohol sales that it was painful to add them all up. A bottle of very ordinary Egyptian white wine cost about £17 on board. Outrageous!

Our next boat trip was by sail on a traditional felucca to the Botanical Gardens, which is a small island in the Nile near Aswan. There were lots of local families enjoying themselves in the well-tended gardens and others singing and praying inside the mosque at the end of the island. The day also included a trip to an aromatherapy centre. I did not go inside since I dislike the scents and aromas, so I sat just outside the centre in the shade. After some moments there, a young man came and spoke to me. He owned the alabaster shop next door with his brother. I was very much expecting him to try to tempt me into his shop, but no such attempt ever came. Rather, we sat there together for about thirty minutes talking about which football teams we supported and the political and economic situation in Egypt. At one point, he introduced me to his brother with whom there was a little tension as he was not a Morsi supporter whereas my new friend thought that President Morsi was doing a good job. How ironic that only a few months later, the military coup removed Morsi from office and probably increased those brotherly tensions. Occasionally, some of the young hawkers who were waiting for tourists to come out of the aromatherapy centre would come over and nag me to buy their wares. My friend would tell them in Arabic I was not interested in buying and immediately they would ask me in English what football team I supported, had I been here before, what did I think of Egypt, and so on. Free from the often intense and annoying ritual of hawkers dancing around tourists trying to sell largely unwanted goods, it was much easier and informative to chat to them. All too rare an opportunity. When Mark came out of the centre, they tried to sell him stuff too, but when I told them he was my brother and didn't want anything, they relaxed and started to ask him about ordinary things.

In the late afternoon, we had yet another tour – this time a motorboat trip through the Nile 'rapids' in the Cataract National Park to see various kinds of birds and even a brief stop further along the river in what was hailed as the Nile's only 'beach.' It was indeed sandy and there were a great many camels at the back of it, mostly waiting for local people to hire them as part of their day out. Later still, we visited a large hilltop mosque near the centre of Aswan and then drove to a much more impressive hill just on the outskirts of the town, where we saw the sunset over the Nile and sat and enjoyed tea and cakes. Finally, we toured on foot a small but very active street market where, among a lot of other things, they sold all kinds of intensely coloured spices. To enter a spice shop was magical for both the sight and smell of the spices all piled up in baskets everywhere.

The *Ra II* spent the whole day heading north back towards its base in Luxor and we relaxed most of that day on the sundeck. A few days earlier, I had given a decent tip to one of the familiar waiters who served us on the sundeck. Later, when I returned to the little bar on the deck to order some more glasses of wine, he poured them, looked at me conspiratorially, and told me they were free to his 'friend.' I gave him a few US dollars for the freebie and he seemed to appreciate the gift of foreign currency. That night he called me over to his bar, produced a large plastic bag in which were some cans of lager and bottles of wine, and told me to put it in the minibar in our room. He did not ask for money, but after I returned from the room and had spoken to Mark, we decided we would give him a few more dollars on the quiet. Well, after that, our bar bill hardly increased at all for, apart from bottled water, we barely bought anything officially; instead, our drinks were supplied at knock-down prices by our new waiter friend. It was an arrangement that not only saved us a lot of money since wine especially was very expensive in Egypt, but also suited both parties very well. Mike's Bar was now operating at maximum efficiency!

On Easter Sunday, all the passengers received lovely chocolate eggs, and the lunch and dinner buffets were especially lavish and included various 'floral' decorations, many of which were carved from vegetables. Having passed through some huge lock gates earlier, we eventually arrived in Luxor about noon and tied up alongside the original *Ra* on which Linda and I had travelled many years previously. The afternoon tour of Karnak was magnificent but for the first time we felt the intense heat and it was hard work walking around the site. The place where they showed us how to make papyrus – and then encouraged us to buy it – was at least air-conditioned. Mark and I bought some small pieces there. Luxor Temple was even better (and cooler) than Karnak. We returned to Karnak that evening for the son et lumière, where we walked through parts of the temple as the story of the ancient monument was told and, eventually, we ended up sitting in a large stand overlooking the sacred lake.

To get to the shore as we left our boat for the last time, we also had to walk through *Ra*, the original. All along the river banks at Luxor, there were dozens of boats moored side by side permanently as there were not enough tourists to fill them all. Our flight to Cairo was so hazy we hardly saw anything below. We arrived at Le Meridien Hotel in Giza, close to the Pyramids and on the very edge of Cairo just after noon, and found that the price for lager and wine was even more expensive, and little chance here of acquiring an understanding and crooked friend. We had an afternoon to ourselves so we recruited a taxi driver, Kaled, who for 150 Egyptian pounds spent over two hours with us, took us to the Pyramids and the Sphinx, drove us around those sites and explained everything, warded off the hawkers, kept me company when Mark went climbing inside one of the pyramids, showed us small places where only the locals go, and even took us at the end of our trip to the Giza equivalent of an off-licence. To get there, we first turned off a very grand highway until we ended up in a narrow dirt-covered passageway so close to stalls, work places, houses, and shops all mingled together that it was barely possible to open the taxi doors. As we got out, Kaled ushered us to a small square hole in a wooden façade and, as we peered in, we could see two rather startled Egyptians standing next to a row of four tall glass-fronted fridges full of cans of beer and lager. I doubt very much they had seen many (or any) Western customers peering in through their small serving hatch. Lagers duly bought, we drove back to Le Meridien, emptied our room's minibar of the hotel's contents, put our own in and then retreated to the hotel pool with a couple of cans to cool off. We gave Kaled a good tip!

In the morning, our booked tour with Maha, an attractive, divorced and very independent Egyptian lady, had the benefit of a seventeen-seat bus just to ourselves, but the driving was as bad as ever. At one point, on one of the four-lane Cairo ring roads, there were six cars abreast, and amazingly people actually crossing the road on foot as best they could. The Egyptian Museum in Tahrir Square was magnificent though very tatty in places. The Tutankhamun rooms were stunning. In other parts of the museum, workmen were climbing over scaffolding and handling heavy poles with no protection set up for any of the exhibits. Then, we returned to Giza to have in effect our second tour of the Pyramids and the Sphinx and, finally, we attended the son et lumière in front of the Sphinx as our last piece of cultural activity on the holiday.

Our next eastern excursion was to Thailand, Cambodia, and Vietnam in 2016. Mark and I were members of a small group among which we soon built ourselves a reputation as 'daring and adventurous.' Our first group activities were in Bangkok, the City of

Angels, where we toured the Grand Palace, which was as exhilarating and colourful as on my previous visits. The so-called 'Death Railway' came next. We travelled into the countryside with its sugar-cane plantations and rice paddies and, then, further into the jungle to see the Bridge over the River Kwai and the infamous railway where so many prisoners of war were worked to death by the Japanese or died from neglect, ill-treatment, and tropical diseases. Trains still run on part of the line and tourists are allowed, indeed encouraged it seemed to me, to clamber all over the bridge and to walk along the sturdy wooden 'scaffolding' that, in parts, skirts the river and prevents the precarious railway from slipping down steep slopes and crashing into the water. The old carriages are noisy but undeniably quaint, and usually full of tourists. In the carriage where Mark and I enjoyed our slow but short ride along the river and over the bridge was a neat sign written in Thai and English, which indicated that certain seats were 'Reserved for Monks, Disabled, Senior Citizens.' Our group had found it a struggle for all of us to get into that carriage, but even so, the one monk present in his orange robe sat serenely alone. Mark and I found that the only place anywhere near the bridge that was not swarming with tourists was the Commonwealth War Grave site. Inside the immaculate grounds could be seen very few visitors, but there were rows of ramrod straight pristine headstones. My god, how young those prisoners were.

After that, while the group made off to visit floating markets and any number of temples, Mark and I detached ourselves until we left Bangkok. One of my former students, Sunida, was now living in Bangkok and she had kindly agreed to ferry us to the kinds of places tourists do not normally visit unless they stumble upon them by accident. One such place was a covered food market close to the Chao Phraya River. It was crowded and noisy but full of produce that intrigued the untutored Western eye. The signs were in Thai; the chatter of shoppers and stallholders was in Thai; and in all the while we were there, Mark and I saw only two young Western backpackers. Suddenly, there was a terrific downpour that clattered across the plastic roofing sheets and made such a noise, as if an express train were punching through the throng. Sunida patiently explained to us the names of various fruits and other food products and how they were used in traditional Thai cooking. Sometimes, as we passed a particular stall heavy with spices the aroma made my mouth water in anticipation, for Sunida had promised to take us to her favourite restaurant for an early evening meal.

Sunida's favourite restaurant had no roof, no door, and no walls for that matter; indeed, it wasn't really a restaurant. It was no more than a small booth with a few tables and chairs in a sea of other such booths at a local night market. The elderly woman, whose stall it was, greeted Sunida in a very warm and touching manner. Sunida explained that she had regularly eaten there for many years, having first being taken to the market as a child by her mother. Sunida introduced us and then ordered for everyone a hot and tasty mixture of fried chicken, rice, and other ingredients I could not recognise. Behind us was a large Buddhist temple, its stupa glowing a dark orange, and all of it framed by an angry grey sky. Sunida assured us that this temple was almost exclusively used by people who lived locally. We visited it later and it was as she had promised. It was a completely different and better experience to stand back in a quiet corner and to witness the prayers of the devout without the click and whir of cameras and the abuse of their flashlights.

All too soon, we had to say goodbye to Sunida. Mark and I were back on the coach with the group on our way through the countryside to the border crossing into Cambodia, and then to the French colonial town of Battambang. Close to Battambang is the so-called Bamboo Railway. It was a twenty-minute journey on a decidedly uneven and wonky single track through thick bush on either side. The vehicle that Mark and I shared with two female passengers was nothing more than a raft of bamboo poles lashed to a low-slung, four-wheel metal chassis, while at the rear was a small engine and a driver. During our relatively short journey, we picked up some good speed and as there were no seats, we were all bounced around. Occasionally, we had to swipe away protruding branches to avoid being hit by them. While it was possible to do the whole trip without interruption, we were not so lucky. Shortly after passing over a rickety bamboo bridge, we had to stop, dismount, and help the driver to lift the vehicle off the rails and set it down by the side of the track to allow traffic to pass in the other direction. As we stood by the side of the track, the passengers on the vehicles that had claimed right of way gave us a perfunctory and ironic piece of applause. At the end of the journey were a few stalls selling souvenirs, and a dozen children who, ideally, should have been in school.

Our hotel in Battambang, close to the Sangke River, was a decent but very quiet place. Our fellow group members were not prepared to venture out after dinner, content to chatter together in the bar or go to bed early. Mark and I were not so disposed. We learned that there was night market, which we thought would be in good place to visit to see ordinary Cambodians going about their business. Outside the hotel was one taxi – so limited was demand. I say taxi, but in fact it was an old, very skinny, man on a tricycle on the back of which was mounted a single flat board. It was here Mark and I sat cross-legged rather precariously since there was nothing to hang onto except each other. We asked to be taken to the night market, but the gentleman had no English. Nevertheless, we asked again. After a moment or two, our driver took off as if the penny had dropped. For the next fifteen minutes, we marvelled how this man could possibly propel the two of us along in such a determined fashion. However, he dared not slow down on any slight hill for fear of not getting underway once more, which led directly to a near miss with a car as he cycled straight through a red light. By now, we had also noticed there was no sign of any night market. We were traversing very dark streets, where all the shops and businesses were barred and shuttered, and piles of newspaper pages and other debris were being blown swiftly along the road. Our driver might not be lost, but Mark and I would never have been able to retrace the route back to our hotel. Finally, there was a small sign of minimal activity and the dim light of a bar, which was the only place open in an otherwise dark and strangely threatening area. It was there he dumped us. Sat outside at a table playing cards and swigging greedily from bottles of beer were four young men, who immediately turned to survey what the taxi driver had dropped off. Mark and I stood there on the pavement, thinking this was not a night market, and wondering even more what we should do next. We might have crawled back on top of the tricycle but he had now gone. The scrutiny of the young men seemed more severe, but a woman sat just behind them got up, and beckoned to us to come and sit down. Her young daughter came to this woman's side – reassuring, we thought - so we sat down and ordered two beers. It was the little girl who went to get them but her mother re-directed her daughter to the fridge so that we could have cold beers. The young men returned to playing cards, the woman who ran the bar told us in broken English that the tricycle man would return, and Mark and I began to savour our drinks while still anxiously turning around from time to time to see any sign of the tricycle.

We ordered another round of drinks in what now seemed to us to be a more relaxed atmosphere. Mark had to use the toilet and the woman in charge directed him to the back of the bar and into a small yard. There, he encountered a young woman with a long knife who made it very plain that he was to follow her to her room to conduct amorous manoeuvres. Mark made it back to me unscathed to recount what had happened. It was, therefore, with some trepidation that a while later, I too needed the toilet. It was all true; there she was with a knife, giving me come-on signs as I quickly peed against the wall that served as the bar's urinal. The tricycle man had delivered us to a small brothel, no doubt in the belief that was what we had asked him to do. We were on our third beer when the tricyclist returned. The woman approached him and gave him some money, probably not as much had both of us gone on manoeuvres, but we had had some beers so the old man was worth a small sum. We drank up and returned to the hotel where we paid our driver. In the hotel bar, a few guests were still in evidence. Naturally, we told them what had happened and, unwittingly, cemented the legend of the Stephens Brothers among the group.

The next destination was Angkor, a gigantic twelfth-century complex of temples originally dedicated to Hinduism but later converted to Buddhism. The whole site extends over 161 hectares and the temple of Angkor Wat itself is surrounded by a wide rectangular moat. There is also a long impressive avenue lined with naga balustrades. Our group arrived by coach before dawn, for our guide insisted on obtaining the best position by one of the moats from which to view and photograph the sunrise. Most people had already entered the temple complex but our guide maintained that there was plenty of time for that after we saw the sunrise from our present position. He was right: the view was stunning, and could not have been seen from most places within Angkor. I was not prepared for the immense scale of the temple complex, let alone the enormous ambition of the creators of Angkor Wat who built the temple with such precision, elegance, and overwhelming beauty. Visitors were allowed to climb the many uneven and steep staircases at the temple to gain marvellous views of the extent of the complex and, closer still, the intricacies of the innumerable carvings. Given its age and the damage that years of incursions by nature had caused to the stonework, the temple was in good shape – the fractured lines, uneven terraces, and the misshapen ruin of an occasional monumental carving made for an even more beguiling experience. Trees taller than anything I had seen in the UK with tangled lattices of buttress roots had embedded themselves over the centuries into some of the buildings so that the brick and the bark seemed as one.

The whole complex of many hundreds of buildings was so big, our group moved between the most important points of interest by coach. Thus, we toured the famous Bayon Temple with its many examples of serene stone faces of Brahma, and Ta Prohm Temple where there were so many trees organically welded to the building that I felt without them the temple would collapse. Every now and then, Mark and I would turn a corner and come across a Buddhist monk in his saffron robe quietly making his devotions, and reminding us that this was much more than a tourist site. Our guide told us that in Thailand and Cambodia monks move through their communities and are not confined to their temple as is mostly the case in Vietnam. Hence, families are very proud if a son becomes a monk, even for a short period as is often the case in Thailand and Cambodia, but in Vietnam such a son is 'lost' to the family.

After our final visit of the day, we had quite a long walk back to our coach. When we were within sight of it, the heavens opened. Our busboy could be seen running helter-skelter towards us, several furled umbrellas held in his hands as best he could manage. The lucky few took possession of said umbrellas and soon we were all back on board. Some of the women guests took especial care of the busboy, insisting he dried himself off and sat next to one of the bus's heaters. We returned to our hotel in the charming and bustling town of Siem Reap for a dinner and a show of traditional Cambodian dancing.

The next morning, we set off to Tonlé Sap Lake passing many rice fields of the way. Our guide informed us that although Cambodia produced the best rice in the area – and the best silk in the world with a natural yellow tone to it – only one crop a year could be grown, whereas in Thailand and Vietnam, they would grow two or even three crops per year. At the lake, we transferred to a diesel-engine boat and soon found ourselves among many of the villages, some built on stilts and others floating, where people lived and worked. Tonlé Sap Lake forms part of the Mekong River system and is the largest freshwater lake in Southeast Asia. The fish caught there provide over fifty per cent of the protein intake of Cambodians, so productive is its output. During the rainy season and when the Mekong River floods the lake, the waters of Tonlé Sap can rise by nine metres. The floating villages and all their houses and shops can be moved closer or further from the shore as the receding and rising waters dictate. The stilted houses stay in place because they are constructed to remain above the high-water level. Unsurprisingly, in the wet season, everyone travels to the shops, to friends' houses, and to school in small wooden boats. To the eyes of tourists, such villages look rather rickety but, in fact, each house or shop is exceptionally well-organised so that ordinary daily activities can easily be carried out. At one point on our cruise, Mark and I saw some young children playing on the floor of a stilted house, and we offered to give them pens and writing materials. Immediately, the older children dived into the lake and collected some pens from us; the younger ones approached us in any craft they could find, including a large washing up bowl being erratically steered with a long wooden spoon, in order to collect pens and paper. On our way back to Siem Reap, we stopped at Bakhong village where we discussed aspects of Buddhism with a monk, and received a blessing. After dinner, Mark and I enjoyed our last night in the centre of Siem Reap in *Island Bar* from where we could hear the impromptu street band outside.

Our next transfer was to the capital of Cambodia, Phnom Penh, on the banks of the Mekong River. There, we visited the Cambodia National Museum and the Tuol Genocide Museum. The latter vividly and movingly depicted the horrors of the killing fields, imprisonment, and torture that the Khmer Rouge inflicted on so many Cambodians in the 1970s. The same night, the group dined at the Foreign Correspondents Club. As everyone piled back onto the bus after dinner, Mark and I waved them off and found a bar to prolong the night's pleasures – the first one of which was a rat that scurried under our table as we were raising a glass. We saw it again on a few occasions, but stopped caring about it after our third round.

The next day, our group boarded the boat that would take us along the Mekong River to the Vietnam border crossing and to the town of Chau Doc. The craft moved swiftly through a changing prospect of rice paddies and fields full of fruit trees, where Vietnamese farmers could be seen toiling in the hot sun in their conical hats. We passed the occasional floating market, and all manner of flat-bottomed boats making their way along the river whose banks were sometimes bedecked with bougainvillea. We also saw in family plots the outline of grave stones erected in a corner of the field, something we hardly saw at all in Thailand and Cambodia where, apparently, cremation rather than burial was the norm. The wide Mekong River was rarely devoid of activity on our journey; it bristled with capitalism. In theory, communism had emerged as the winner after the war against the USA but, in reality and especially in the south of Vietnam, it was individual and corporate striving for profit that had won the day – the apotheosis of which could be found in Saigon.

Chau Doc was a border town with a thriving floating market, and many of the houses along tributaries of the Mekong were brightly painted and built on stilts to cope with seasonal changes in water levels. The immediate area outside our hotel appeared to offer little of interest so few of our group ventured out after dinner. Of course, Mark and I were among the few exceptions. We found a most interesting bar cum restaurant, which consisted of walkways built on wooden piles driven into a lagoon and seating areas where customers could order food and drink. Mark and I enjoyed some beers there and, later, saw two other couples from the hotel and called them over to join us. Our next port of call was Can Tho, which unsurprisingly had its own floating market. The one that we saw was slightly different in that it was a wholesale market, which meant that the boats were much larger and brought for sale substantial amounts of various produce. Just as trees in southern Africa must have fearsome thorns, so it seems any village or town on the Mekong and its tributaries must have a floating market.

After a few more visits to temples, another floating market, and one more boat ride, we eventually reached our final destination – Ho Chi Minh City or, as every inhabitant of the city calls it, Saigon. No sooner had we arrived than we set off to the Cu Chi tunnel complex, a lengthy underground maze of low, narrow tunnels that had been used by the Viet Cong during the war and was now both a monument to those killed in the conflict and a tourist attraction. It was here I learned that the Vietnam War did not exist; in Vietnam it was called the American War. In places, tourists could crawl through parts of the tunnels which, it was said, had been enlarged to accommodate larger European bodies. Whether true or not, the tunnels were the stuff of claustrophobia, as Mark could testify although in his case the constrictions caused him no problem. At the very end of the walk through the complex was a café and a live-fire range right next to it. Coffee could be enjoyed to the painful sound of Kalashnikov AK-47 assault rifles being fired by anyone – young, old, psychotic – prepared to pay for the bullets. It was cheaper to fire a couple of rounds from a breach loading rifle, and a fortune to go through a machine gun belt. No matter what, the noise was overwhelming. The War Museum in Saigon also offered a different perspective on the Vietnam/American War, particularly the deprivations suffered by the Vietnamese. The wreckage of shot-down USA fighter jets and other military machines were proudly on display.

The area outside our hotel in Saigon was bustling. Mark and I had never seen so many two-wheel vehicles in one place. At red traffic lights, they looked as if they were lined up for a mass start to see who could reach the next red light first. After dinner, Mark and I found a place to drink literally above the din and smoke of the mopeds and scooters on the first-floor outdoor veranda of a bar cum restaurant. The venue overlooked what seemed to us to be *the* nightclub in Saigon to visit. A regular supply of expensive Mercedes, Ferraris, and other sleek items of envy pulled up outside the club, to be immediately whisked off to be parked elsewhere by club flunkies, while the passengers flounced through the doors in their Dior and Armani outfits. It was impossible not to recognise the wealth of these people who were living the Vietnamese (capitalist) dream. On our last night on this holiday, Mark and I found a different bar in which to while away the evening. Suddenly, from the street outside the bar, we heard a woman shout out: "Look John, it's the boys. We've found the boys. It's safe to drink here." On that enhanced reputational note, we left for home.

In January 2017, Mark and I went to Sri Lanka. We covered many of the places that Linda and I had visited years before but, on this trip, there was no Menika. Instead, we had our own car and driver throughout the tour of the island. We arrived in Colombo via the Maldives where the sea, as we came in to land, turned from deep blue to green to turquoise. It seemed a place in which I would have liked to stay. Mark and I visited Sigiriya Rock, Dambulla Cave Temple, Kandy, Pinnawala elephant orphanage, Yala National Park, a tea plantation in Nuwara Eliya, and Galle. Many of our experiences in these places were similar to my earlier visit, so I will not describe them again. Touring Sri Lanka often meant early morning starts and sometimes only getting back to our hotels barely in time for dinner.

While this certainly applied to the other members of the group with whom we were touring, it did not apply to us. Having our own driver meant Mark and I could still be enjoying a leisurely breakfast as our other group members drove past us in their coach, only to return much later in a hurry to shower, change and go down to dinner, to find us delighting in a pre-prandial drink on the terrace. Eventually, one of them asked me why they were all in a coach and we had a personal car and driver. "I booked it in advance. It was quite cheap," I replied. The person told me he had not seen it online when he had booked. "I couldn't say. I saw the offer in the bottom right corner of the hard copy brochure." Undoubtedly, an example of when the internet does not know best.

Our final journey in the Far East was a brief visit to Hong Kong in April 2017. Gone was the hair-raising landing at Kai Tak airport, which closed in 1998. Moreover, the island was no longer a British colony, but effectively under Chinese control. We stayed at the Excelsior Hotel, itself now gone, and made ample use of the Executive Business Lounge, where they served free drinks in exchange for membership. The hotel lost out on that exchange. Mark and I enjoyed the rides on the old-fashioned trams and, of course, the Star Ferry crossings. The MTR (underground) was comfortable and peaceful whereas one of the bus rides we had out to Repulse Bay on the No.65 was akin to a grand prix race with a double decker for a vehicle that pitched and swayed on the twisty road. We liked our trip to the Peak with its fantastic views of the city and harbour, and equally good was the evening light show seen from Kowloon side. Somehow, we got lost and could not find our way out of the SOGO Department Store in Causeway Bay, until eventually we opened a fire exit to make our escape. In essence, these were many of the familiar things that Linda and I had done on our three earlier visits, although she would never have become lost in a shopping store. Thus, I shall recount only the actual journey from the UK to Hong Kong in any detail, for that is the part I remember most.

The transfer started in style as Mark and I were driven to Heathrow in a Mercedes 'S' Class, laid on by Emirates Airlines. As business class passengers with Emirates, there were naturally no queues to negotiate at check-in, and no frustrating delays at security since we had special access to the fast lanes for business customers. The Emirates business lounge put into stark contrast the experience of the thousands of passengers milling around in the departure area looking for a spare seat or a table in a bar or restaurant. I did not want to avail myself of the lounge's work area; nor its beds where you could have a short nap; nor did I need a shower or massage. But I was interested in the complimentary and high-quality food and drink, especially the champagne. Mark and I entered our Airbus A380 plane via a separate sky bridge for business and first-class passengers. We settled down, champagne and stylish amenity bags in hand and quickly realized how spacious, comfortable, and privileged were our surroundings. At the back of the upper deck was a small bar and, shortly after take-off, we were ordering cocktails from the attendant. Later, another attendant came to the bar to tell us our meal was about to be served. The food and drink, and entertainment, were excellent as was the fully flat bed when it was time to get a few hours sleep before our change of planes in Dubai. The business lounge in Dubai was stupendous; it was almost as long as the platforms at Rome's Termini railway station but without the graffiti. We boarded our Boeing 777 directly from the business lounge. What a disappointment. There was no bar, and some seats did not have unrestricted access to the aisles and, most damning of all, our seats did not truly transform into fully flat beds. We had enjoyed one, just one, business flight and already we had become expert critics. Whatever the failings of that 777 plane, the trip to Hong Kong had initiated in us a desire for more business travel.

Chapter Fourteen: Tanzania and Zimbabwe

In September 2014, Mark and I flew to Nairobi with Kenya Airways and then took a short connecting flight to Dar es Salaam (Abode of Peace) in mainland Tanzania. Dar es Salaam, or Dar as locals call it, is the financial centre and largest city in Tanzania. Soon after landing, our group was being driven through the chaotic morning rush hour traffic where drivers had a particular propensity to lean on their car horns; it certainly was not a place of peace and quiet. We went past large shanty towns largely built of crude breeze blocks and corrugated metal sheets and through into an area with rather grand mansions where white-suited and unarmed policemen and women directed the traffic at the interminable junctions. Along the stationary vehicles walked men, women and children trying to sell all manner of goods, including one man who had a good line in rather large fire extinguishers – so bulky he could barely carry one under each arm. Other sellers favoured large and brightly coloured maps of Tanzania that they sometimes struggled to control if the wind got up. Once, we saw two soldiers in khaki slowly cross the street carrying machine guns that seemed like a burden to lug around, so bored did they look. Before ten o'clock, we had arrived at the Slipway Hotel on the coast and began to explore its modern but clearly 'Moorish' layout and architecture. It was an upmarket area with not only a hotel but also several boutiques, restaurants, a book shop, and a pedicure palace.

There was a group meeting and meal at six p.m. at a place by the shore for the seven of us in the group and Hassani, the leader for the first part of the tour. Mark and I left them to their meal about thirty minutes later and dined outdoors in a restaurant near the hotel where the beef medallions and the red wine were most satisfying. We ended the evening in a courtyard café next to the Slipway talking to Olive, our waitress.

In the morning, we drove to the railway station on the other side of Dar for a ten o'clock departure. Our train did not even arrive on the platform until gone ten o'clock and it left even later. In the interim, we sat in the First-Class Lounge, which sounds magnificent but was in fact a very down-at-heel place with an assortment of birds that flew in through the many broken windows to nest and scavenge for food from passengers. The floor and furnishings were very shabby but the toilets were dirty beyond belief. Not casual yesterday's dirt, for a cleaner was there working hard to clean the whole area, but rather the dirt of accumulated years – thick and persistent. We laughed at the state of the toilets, but were too polite to condemn their woeful state outright since this was not a first world country. Little did we know then that the toilet at the end of our carriage on the train made the First-Class Lounge arrangements look positively wholesome, indeed even desirable if only from a physical safety point of view. A large hole in the floor of the carriage as the train sped along was all that the journey into the Selous Game Reserve had to offer!

As we waited for our narrow-track train to arrive, another came into one of the otherwise deserted platforms and disgorged such a throng of people that it was difficult to believe they had all got off a single train. Indeed, when ours arrived and the barrier below was lifted to allow passengers onto the platform, there was yet another surge of humanity with many individuals balancing bulky containers on their heads, or dragging huge canvas bags, and in one case carrying sawn lengths of timber – all of which somehow were manhandled into very crowded compartments. Despite there being over twenty carriages, the train was packed with people and goods and even the odd animal here and there. Although we had to ease past the throng of people as best we could along the train's corridor, our reserved compartment was reassuringly empty. However, by the time we had heaved all our luggage onto the upper folded-down sleeping bunks and fitted seven of us on the lower berths, the compartment began to resemble all the others for lack of space. There was a light that did not work; there was a small fan that did not work; there was a window that did not shut – but this did not matter since there was no glass in it. The seats were very hard and sticky and then the real nightmare began when the train moved off. Minutes later, the whole carriage went into a troubling swaying motion with a distinct up and down component – a bit like sitting on the top of a pneumatic road drill operated by a drunk - that made it feel as if the springs were completely broken. Mark was able to explain precisely in engineering terms how and why this violent motion came about, but even so it still felt as if the whole train would soon catapult itself from the rails. Within ten minutes, I had found and taken some travel sickness pills – the first time I had ever done so on a train. Our journey was to be a non-stop four hours but the full journey for many passengers was seventy-two hours all the way to Zambia.

The journey, however, towards the Selous (pronounced Seloo) and then to the reserve near its northern boundary was fascinating. The land changed from a more open aspect to one with a much greater density of trees and bushes. We passed close to several villages and saw many different wild animals en route. There was suddenly a man at the compartment door taking orders for lunch. The brave opted for the chicken, which turned out to be the only choice left anyway, and after about thirty minutes four plates were passed into the compartment each containing the scrawniest pieces of chicken imaginable and surrounded by a dubious dollop of rice or a portion of polenta accompanied by a small dish of some sauce or other. I think one plate was chicken and cabbage. The full complement of knives and forks turned up a little later so that the food had time first to cool and congeal. The three of us, blessed with enough sense not to have ordered anything, settled down to watch the diners try to eat this fare while balancing the plates on their knees as the carriage bounced violently up and down. Dirty plates with a lot of uneaten or possibly inedible food were laid on the floor under the seats for later collection as Hassani now informed us that we had to get out of the train as it approached Kisaki village. All the luggage was pulled down from above and, as the train came to a stop, it was pushed out through the window into the hands of the driver sent from Sable Mountain Lodge. All of us had to exit via a door rather than a window, but since there was only a short stretch of platform a good 100 metres away, we had to descend to track-level using the poorly positioned footholds. Poorly positioned because even exiting the door backwards, it was impossible to see where to place one's feet. After a gingerly and awkward exit, we found ourselves amongst the dozens of local villagers walking along the length of the train and offering all manner of things for sale to the passengers. One of our group gave a few children some sweets and they were decidedly suspicious about them, possibly because they were of the sour variety. Fifty metres away, I could see my bag bobbing up and down on someone's head as it made a very wobbly path to a long wheelbase Land Rover. Somehow all our luggage ended up being loaded onto the vehicle and we left behind the scenes of apparently chaotic activity for the twenty-minute journey on dirt roads to the lodge from where we would explore the Selous in the next few days. The short journey through the centre of the village was a delight as everyone was happy to wave and smile at us, even the adults. There was so much activity going on there; the various domesticated animals such as goats and chickens seemed to know to keep out of the way of the few vehicles, as did the children playing along the dirt road. We learned later that an adult elephant had been hit by a train not too long ago. It may have been sick or even surprised by the speed of the train but, after being hit, it managed to walk off some distance before it collapsed and died.

Sable Mountain Lodge consisted of a small number of stone-built cottages spread out some distance from each other and all located on steep terrain over which it was easy for wild animals to roam – hence the armed guard to escort us to our rooms from the central dining area and bar at the end of the night. In fact, Mark and I, armed only with torches, often had a chat with whomever our guard was as we returned to the cottage after dinner, and always gave him a small tip, which was much appreciated.

In the morning, we had a walking safari with Hassani. We saw little game but the walk was nevertheless remarkable for the steepness of the terrain and for how often we were in deep shade under a thick canopy of leaves. Getting back to the dining area for breakfast was particularly demanding for me, given I had only recently recovered from Guillain-Barré Syndrome but, encouragingly, it was also the furthest I had walked in over nine months. After lunch, Mark and I sat on the small veranda of our cottage, from where we could see the impressive Sable Mountains in the distance and the unmistakable smoke from the fires set by the local farmers to burn off the dry grass. At night, we could see the lights of those fires flickering against the dark mass of the mountains and, as the grass was consumed, the lights moved slowly along the mountain flanks in the direction of the wind.

The following day at three o'clock in the afternoon, we left for a vehicle safari. We entered the Selous Game Reserve via the Matambwe Gate and, en route, we saw colobus monkeys, impala, zebra, giraffe, and a solitary male elephant moving quickly away from us towards the setting sun. The skittish behaviour of most animals was clear evidence of how few tourists visited the Selous and how unused to vehicles they were. It was also, sadly, indicative of how much poaching went on there. The tsetse flies, however, were certainly not shy of us and frequently bit us even through our clothing. Fortunately, they did not, apparently, carry sleeping sickness in this area. Hassani had a little heap of dead flies in the footwell, which he had killed as he drove along. At one point, we had to change the right rear wheel when the tyre suddenly deflated after being punctured by a thorn. Not only were the animals much more wary than in Etosha but there were also many more mature trees, at times so dense that it was impossible to see beyond the first row of greenery. The tall stacuria trees with their incredibly smooth and shiny magnolia-coloured bark were very impressive. They thrust up towards the sky effortlessly, straight as an arrow and higher too than everything else; their smooth trunks were undisturbed by any offshoots or branches until the very canopy itself.

Today, we were on an all-day vehicle and boat safari, penetrating deeper into the Selous than before. Along with our picnic lunches, the Land Rover also carried the outboard motor for the small boat we were to use on Lake Tagalala. Once again, we were rarely far from tsetse flies other than on the lake itself. We saw little game at first but, suddenly, I saw a long, curved tail in a patch of sunlight to my left about forty metres from the dirt road along which we were travelling. Even as I called out to stop the vehicle, I was looking back from the tail to see the shape of a large male leopard lying in the shade of an impressive termite mound. No sooner did we reverse and everyone got a glimpse of it than the animal made off. Behind the three-metre-tall mound stood a tree and draped along a thick branch was the disembowelled body of a warthog that the leopard had killed and safely stashed for later consumption.

The highlight of the trip came later when we caught a brief sight of an elephant in a dry, sandy river bed. We all exited the vehicle and walked for over a hundred metres along a narrow ledge some seven metres above a steep drop into the river bed itself from where we saw not one elephant but a matriarchal or breeding herd of about seventeen elephants. Four adult elephants were digging into the soft sand with their tusks; they were clearly finding water because juvenile members of the herd were coming to the holes and reaching down with their trunks to drink. Senior members occasionally sniffed the air with their trunks held aloft as if they were picking up our own scent, but the herd was calm and apparently unconcerned about us silently watching them from above. As soon as the herd left, other animals approached the holes and they too were able to drink. On our way back to the Land Rover, Hassani told us that on an earlier visit, just at this spot, a pride of lions had walked right past him and his clients while everyone was still on foot.

Close to Lake Tagalala, we encountered a well-fed pride of lions with one big male and six females, all lying under various bushes near the water's edge and hiding from the sun. Two younger lions were still exhibiting the reticulated patterns of youth on their coats. We drove to the far side of the lake where a small boat had been hauled up onto the shore and chained to a nearby tree. There was no undergrowth anywhere near us, which was just as well for after we had fitted the engine and pushed off, we rounded a small headland along which was extensive low bush and out of which crawled numerous large crocodiles. They entered the water just in front of the boat and then submerged directly ahead of us. Our slightly nervy feelings at not knowing where they were or what they would do next were further heightened by the sight of several hippos suddenly emerging from the water all around us. The hippos, being inquisitive, would regularly surface, showing only their nostrils and eyes, and then sink below the surface again – all accompanied by a series of loud grunts. Occasionally, they would rise out of the water to reveal just how big and intimidating they were. We kept a discreet distance from them, and they constantly kept us under observation. However, the numerous tiger fish in the lake did not keep their distance at all. Disturbed by our propeller, they would frequently leap from the water, like small flashes of silver, before landing again in the water. One hit me on the back but still fell out of the boat, while another hit Mark a glancing blow on his hat.

For the first time, we saw many kinds of birds, including a flock or fascination of flamingos that constantly flew over the lake in elegant sweeping curves. Their pink feathers were clearly visible. Hassani said he had never seen them here before. Clearly, they should have been on some soda lake hundreds of miles away but we did appreciate their flying display. On the banks were various waders, apparently far too 'street-wise' to be bothered by crocodiles; on branches overhanging the water, we saw various kingfishers and a wonderfully majestic pair of fish eagles who kept calling to one another with their distinctive screech. The picnic on the boat itself was very enjoyable with the flamingos still flashing overhead and the hippos forming an imperfect half circle around us to keep an eye on what was happening. After safely stowing the boat and reloading the engine under the Land Rover, we returned to see the lions once more. They had shifted position a little but were still very much in 'laze around' mode. Further away, we came across a freshly dead zebra with its eyes plucked out and the rest of its body covered in vultures literally opening up routes to its flesh. We also saw a huge baobab tree that was thought to be thousands of years old.

In the morning, we arrived at a Maasai village - Mark and I armed with dozens of pens and even more sweets for the children who quickly surrounded our vehicle. This tribe of Maasai owned the land on which the village stood, which was given to them by the government. The tour was conducted by Hassani along with the village chief – a tall man who looked much younger than his real age. The chief carried a fearsome looking wooden stick with a pronounced bowl at one end, and a machete – symbols of his office apparently. Tucked into the folds of his traditional robes was a mobile phone; it went off and he sheepishly brought it out and answered it. It was his second wife. He had two wives, the second one of which was the local school teacher. It seemed that this educated woman did not mind being his second wife, but she had forbidden him from having any more. We saw various huts and were encouraged to look around inside. A school was being built on the site. That might be the single biggest factor in the future in ending a practice that westerners usually find abhorrent. At about fifteen years of age, Maasai boys spend a short time in the bush away from home and family and are then circumcised; but the young girls are subjected to the worse experience of genital mutilation. It may be increasingly difficult to carry on this tribal tradition when young girls are educated. The Maasai measure wealth in terms of how many cows a man owns. The chief told us he was not that wealthy since he only had 200 cows and a really rich man would have two thousand.

In the morning, we settled a rather expensive bill at the lodge and drove with Hassani to the airstrip near the rangers' camp by Matambwe Gate. At the camp we picked up an official who accompanied us the kilometre or so to the grass strip. He was there to make sure that the pilot actually paid the landing fee. There was a small thatched structure to protect passengers from any rain – a straw roofed circle built around an old tree with a few wooden seats and, a little way off behind bushes, a very dilapidated toilet almost now in ruins. Such were the departure arrangements. The twelve-seat, single engine plane arrived about an hour late, soon loaded everyone and everything on board and sped down the bumpy grass strip and off towards Zanzibar Island. Hassani stood by the Land Rover and waved energetically to us as we sped past. Pity poor

Hassani: his company wouldn't pay for a return trip by air so he had to take the bone-juddering train back to Dar. Still, he did get the big bird book he wanted a few weeks later from Mark and me via Amazon.

After manoeuvring ourselves through the chaos that was Zanzibar Airport, we met our new guide for the rest of the holiday, Nzori. We drove through the streets of Zanzibar City, bustling with people and activity, to the Dhow Palace Hotel in the narrow lanes of Stone Town. Our room was very large with a tall ceiling, three beds, a small stepped window overlooking the narrow lane outside, and old carved wooden furniture. The television had a dedicated cricket channel on it, 'Ten-Cricket,' and in the centre of the hotel on the ground floor surrounded on all sides by several balustraded floors, but no roof, was a swimming pool next to which was a restaurant.

After lunch, the group toured the town, stopping to see the meat, fish and spice markets, various places of worship and admiring some of the intricately carved doors. Later, Nzori took out just Mark and me on a separate quest to find a beach-side place where we could both eat and be served alcohol. The hotels and most restaurants were Muslim-owned and only served soft drinks. Having been taken to a suitable place and having found that we liked it very much, Mark and I decided to stay there and eat and not to join the others in their 'dry' restaurant. After an excellent meal, we moved to the bar and met a bizarre blonde woman originally from South Africa who came over to speak to us, mostly about a load of mystic rubbish. Eventually, after holding our hands, feeling our inner 'spirits' and offering all sorts of homespun nonsense, she went away and left us alone. After that, two delightful local prostitutes came over to introduce themselves – one very heavily pregnant - and they were very polite and even apologetic when we quietly asked them to go away.

Around six a.m. there was a torrential downpour with rain thundering into the corrugated metal roof and also falling right through the open inner part of the hotel into the swimming pool and its environs below. After breakfast by the decidedly wet pool area, we strolled down to the beach and saw a few boats leaving for Prison Island in the distance. Many looked overcrowded and bobbed about rather violently on the white tips of the waves. In the town, I was accosted by a local who wanted me to give him money in return for nothing, and who then turned even more insistent. As I walked into an air-conditioned shop with Maasai guards at the entrance to be rid of his incessant demands, I heard this old chap call after me "Yes that's right, march off into the hands of the capitalists and make the pigs even richer, while you leave a poor man like me outside to rot!" It was like something out of a Marxist comedy show, if such ever existed. He was in many ways right, but he had no idea how to approach westerners if you wanted something from them. We ate that night at the same restaurant, but this time there were no prostitutes or eccentric ex-pats, only a lot of cats begging for food and whose fleas did a good job of biting Mark's exposed feet.

It was tipping down again the next morning, in the way it only can in the tropics. Umbrellas were found for the group just to go the short distance to the minibus taking us to the north of the island to the Zanzibari Hotel near the village of Nungwi. The road to the north was tarred but narrow with police stations periodically along the way where everyone had to stop. For much of the journey, the road passed through many villages where there were always all kinds of different shops and stalls and everywhere buzzing with activity. There were many small vegetable patches close to village houses if the ground was fertile enough and not too rocky. The traffic moved much too fast for the road conditions and clearly it was up to pedestrians to get out of the way. On arriving at the Zanzibari Hotel, we found that the entrance, the grounds, and the small staircase from the beach to the grounds were all guarded by young Maasai warriors although there seemed no threat at all from anyone. Our room had a small wooden balcony surrounded by bougainvillea.

Today, we left for a morning's drive south to see a community-owned spice farm in a village called Kitunda. Juma, the farm's MD, did the tour with an almost theatrical flourish. He provided us with samples of the sight, taste and smell of many spices and fruits as we walked around the farm. At one point, it poured with rain, but that did not stop one young man who shinned up a very tall tree and hurled down some coconuts. Finally, we ended up in a thatched round house where we were presented with hats and ties woven from banana leaves, which made us look jolly but quite mad, and where we also tasted more fruits. Before we left, everyone in the group bought spices from a stall packed with many different varieties.

In the morning, just Mark and I left for a lengthy tour of the village with Nzori. We struck out along the beach at first and then inland to see the fish market, the small 'yards' where the dhows were built by hand, the place where the old dhow boats were turned into 'dhow furniture' for use in hotels, the local school, and much more. To get to the furniture place, we walked along the top of a narrow wall – Mark easily and me struggling a little - and this was considered a normal way of entering. We visited an old lady's house who wove baskets and purses for tourists, and Mark helped an old man to make breeze blocks from sand and cement using a wooden mould. At the local school, we met some teachers and then entered one of the classrooms where typically sixty pupils in their smart white uniforms took their lessons. I was introduced as a 'teacher,' and was welcomed by the whole class. Just as we left, it was lunchtime and hundreds of children rushed out of the classrooms and formed lines to buy things to eat from local women who were all sat in a row along one of the paths inside the school compound. Then we went to see Nzori's first home, which he now rents, before eventually visiting his current, larger house. To get to both we had to walk along uneven and often narrow pathways between a jumble of houses, all of which were at different stages of construction. There was no town planning at all here. At the family home were Nzori's wife, children, other relatives and various adult friends. Mark and I played a great board game, with Nzori as Mark's partner and me with one of the minibus drivers. It ended up one game all but was very competitive – at one point flour was sprinkled over the board to make it easier to hit the plastic disks into the holes at each corner. In all we were out for about five hours on this tour. We got caught in a rainstorm just as we arrived back at the hotel. It was a terrific tour of Nungwi, largely as locals see it and live it, and Nzori didn't even charge us; we made sure we gave him a good tip as a consequence. Mark and I had thoroughly enjoyed our time in Tanzania including its electrical plug arrangements. It has the modern UK three square-pin type but also the much older 1950s round-pin type in both large and small formats – sometimes all three in the same room. We had fond memories of Selous Mountain Lodge, not least because of an event in its bar whose roof was a high conical thatch. We heard a splat as a small green gecko fell from the apex right into the middle of the bar's floor. For a while, it lay there motionless, as if the fall had killed it. Then, just as suddenly as it had fallen, it took off at speed. A minute later, a snake also plummeted to the ground from which the gecko had been trying to escape.

In September 2015, Mark and I travelled to Zimbabwe. Our flight was with South African Airways to Johannesburg where we waited a short while to take a plane to Bulawayo. Although the latter city is quite large, the airport is tiny – just one luggage belt inside a very small arrivals hall. Two uniformed women working for the Immigration Service stamped our passports and took our US$55 visa fee and showed us the kind of smiling welcome that was to become commonplace wherever we went in Zimbabwe. Within an hour, the waiting driver had deposited us at Camp Amalinda in the Matobo Hills just outside the Matobo Hills National Park, a world heritage site. The hills are an array of kopjes, granite boulders of varying sizes and colours – some only as big as cars and houses but others like shimmering hills erupting from the earth. The chalets at Amalinda all incorporated kopjes into their design. In fact, Zeph, one of the staff at the lodge gave us a conducted tour of them, so we could appreciate their originality. Part of the tour involved squeezing through a narrow gap between adjoining kopjes. One entire wall of our own chalet was a granite block, and the washbasins and showers were forged out of the natural stone. Chalet No.10 was spread over two kopjes with a small chain bridge linking the living quarters with the sitting out area.

In the morning, we left for the Matobo Hills National Park to see Bushman paintings in an under-hang high on one of the kopjes. For the first part of the morning game drive, we huddled under thick covers to fend off the cold, and Mark and I were grateful that we had brought the fleeces we had been given at Zebra River Lodge some years before. Later, as the weather brightened and warmed up, we saw two magnificent black eagles flying overhead and calling to one another, and two male giraffes one of which was trying to mount the other as a show of dominance. In the afternoon, we visited the burial place of Cecil Rhodes sited on the top of an especially large and impressive kopje. On the way up to the grave, we passed several groups of local schoolchildren, a few of whom (without in any way being sarcastic) addressed us directly with a "good afternoon sir, how are you today?" In the late afternoon our guide, Kevin, drove to more remote parts of the park to find rhino. We saw very little game at all and no sign of even rhino spoor. Kevin parked the vehicle and ran off with his binoculars to climb a nearby kopje overlooking a shallow valley. When he returned, he indicated that he had not seen anything of note, but the way he drove off as if in a hurry to beat the approaching sunset told me something different. After a few kilometres, he stopped again and we climbed through a game fence and jogged along through the high yellow grass into the valley our guide had previously surveyed. Soon we dropped to a walk and then, at Kevin's instruction, to a bent-over crawl as a very imposing male white rhino came into view. We crept to within forty metres of what turned out to be 'Rhino 114' – they were all well-known and protected in this area – but who was otherwise known as 'Billy', after our camp's manager. Billy, the rhino, was impressive and stood his ground, occasionally half turning and snorting in our direction. Had he charged, there were only a couple of termite mounds nearby where we might have found protection. Kneeling and squatting, we kept our full silhouette from him and thus he remained calm; eventually after some ten minutes in full view, the rhino turned away and trotted off into the bush. As we made our way back to the vehicle through the bush and long grass, the sun was just starting to set. It caught the swaying sprays of grass, alternatively the colours of straw and gold as they moved in the wind – it was a moment in time that, for me, encapsulated the adventure and excitement of being on foot in the bushveld. We only just exited the park before closing time but at the barrier we met some of the rangers who told us about 'Billy.' One of them gave me a special kind of berry to eat, or rather to chew since the berry was nicknamed 'African man's chewing gum.' It was slightly sweet but soon became harder and harder to chew. It was very much an acquired taste and none of the rangers minded when eventually I spat it out. In fact, they seemed to like the fact that I'd had a go. Indeed, most of the people we met were very appreciative that we were visiting their country. When we met black Zimbabweans and greeted them with the traditional three-part African handshake, faces would at first register surprise and then delight since this was not expected from white westerners. Moreover, the delight was even greater when we spoke just a couple of words in the local Matabele language such as linjiani (how are you?) and siyabonga (thank you).

All too soon we had to leave this lovely lodge for a three-hour drive to Half Way House on a main road. There, the people from Camelthorn met us and took us to their camp, which involved a further long journey along fifty kilometres of very sandy and bumpy track and which took us to Hwange National Park where we would spend the next week. Much of the journey was through very dry terrain that had been blackened by fire. It was three o'clock before we got to Camelthorn but soon after we went out with Aubrey and Pete (the apprentice) for a sundowner drive. We saw a few animals but most of the fun came from finding out that Aubrey supported Liverpool and Pete was a Manchester City fan – we plotted to leave Pete all alone in the bush for daring to criticise my team, Spurs. The meal that night was excellent, which was typical of all the places we stayed in. The choice of wine was equally impressive and our chalet, one of only eight, had a minibar stocked with everything we could want – and regularly replenished. Our accommodation even had a hammock and a second-floor landing where Mark and I could sit outside on a settee and watch the stars. At night, however, we were always escorted to and from the chalet by someone with a gun, as the camp was completely open to wild animals. I reflected that on the occasion we encountered rhino 114 no one had a gun. On a night drive that evening after dinner, we were exceptionally lucky to catch a brief glimpse of an aardvark; there are professional guides who have never seen one.

Just before dawn, someone brought us hot water to make tea and, shortly afterwards, we left the camp to look for cats. We came across two female lions and a male but did not see the cubs that were hidden in the thick scrub. Much of the terrain around Camelthorn was marked by stunted trees, or upturned stumps that the elephants had destroyed – the park could accommodate up to 25,000 but there were many more than that. There were so many elephants and such a weight of their droppings that the pathways in the camp were made from compressed elephant dung – no nasty smells only a slightly springy surface. Other areas of Hwange National Park were more open savannah with thick straw-coloured dry grass simply gasping for rain at that time of year. It was in this type of terrain that later that day we saw several herds of elephant. The most striking aspect of Hwange were those parts populated by mature camelthorn trees, most of which were in bloom with myriads of intense yellow flowers. These trees had grown so large that the elephants could rarely push them over. Teak trees, which formed impressive stands in some places, also managed to grow and thrive in good measure, largely because elephant do not like the taste and so they tended to leave them alone. However, we did see small herds of elephant sheltering in the shade of these trees during the heat of the day – adult elephants could often be seen leaning against them, while youngsters would typically lie on the ground and fall asleep. Indeed, there was so much teak that it was the wood of choice for throwing on the fires that we sat around after dinner, drinking and chatting with staff or with the very few other guests in the camp. Sometimes, we would see the Southern Cross and the Milky Way in a crystal-clear night sky.

This morning, we left with chief guide, Sibs, for a walking safari. I was told to walk directly behind Sibs and his .458 rifle and soon we encountered a breeding herd of elephant but Sibs did not try to get any closer to them. He explained that during the height of the dry season breeding herds are very stressed and can therefore be unpredictable and dangerous to approach too close. It's easier to approach mature bulls who have more experience and tend not to over-react unless in musth. To get at better tasting and more luscious food to eat, the elephants will often dig up the root bowl of certain trees knowing that this is where the tree itself has concentrated its reserves to ride out the dry season. Sibs also showed us the kinds of plants that locals have used for many years as sources of 'bush medicine.' He explained how tracks leading to water get wider; how you can find water by following baboons who must drink regularly; how to measure the height of an elephant from the circumference of its foot print; how to tell an elephant's approximate age from the distinctiveness of the pattern on the sole of its foot; and how to tell if an elephant was increasing its speed and whether a calf was trying to keep up. Indeed, so distinctive are the patterns on the soles of elephants that, like fingerprints, they can be used to identify or track an individual animal.

After Sibs returned to the lodge, we were taken by vehicle to Ngomo Primary School where a group of about thirty boys and girls met us outside their classroom to sing and dance for us. Then these eight-to-ten-year-olds invited us inside to look at their work and to hear them read passages in English. When we had checked with the teacher that it was okay, Mark opened a bag of sweets and was instantly surrounded by a group of eager, smiling children all jostling to get a sweet. I repeated the process with a bag of sweets of my own and I was almost swept away in the tide of insistent children who seemed to gain so much pleasure from receiving such a small treat. There were no computers in the classroom, only a large wall-mounted blackboard, a big box of white and coloured chalk stubs, and lots of rather battered reading books all in English and most donated by charities in the UK, USA, and Australia. Around the walls, like a frieze, were A4-sized depictions of the alphabet – Aa, Bb, Cc, etc. But there was no mistaking how these children loved their learning. Many of them had to walk up to seven kilometres each way to school, sometimes encountering dangerous wild animals en route. After they returned home, they would have work to do; the boys looking after livestock and the girls fetching and carrying water. Their parents paid US$30 per term to keep them in primary school but even at this price not all parents could afford to educate their children.

Leaving the school, we visited the nearby dwelling of the headman of Ngomo village, a Mr Johnson and his wife, Dorothy. Mr Johnson was quite elderly and exceptionally well-spoken and had the charming and entirely unaffected habit of referring to himself in the third person, such as: "Mr Johnson is the headman of this village by birth and he takes his role very seriously." He also had some power to back up the performance of his duties. While serious issues were reported to the police, he (along with a council of elders) had the power to sentence villagers to a form of community service for minor misdemeanours. Mr Johnson struck me as very informed and he was not afraid to answer questions from tourists frankly. He did not disguise how bad the economy was in Zimbabwe, and it was clear he did not think a great deal of the current government regime. He contended that the growing Chinese involvement in Zimbabwe would eventually leave the country impoverished. The only praise he gave to Mugabe, then the president of the country, was on AIDS education and the partially successful attempt to change attitudes towards condom use. He spoke especially enthusiastically about the communal enterprise between the village and Camelthorn Lodge. The lodge was built using local labour; it employs local people who can learn various trades there, and eventually the lodge itself will become the property of the community. Mr Johnson told us that his people now recognised the value of preserving wild animals since they know that's what the tourists come to see. Indeed, he has banned his people from all forms of poaching. When he thanked us for coming to visit and impressed on us how important such visits were to his people, this was not some idle buttering up of outsiders intended to make them feel good about themselves – this was a genuine belief. Dorothy showed us her home and the chickens they kept to eat and to sell. There was a quiet intelligence about Mr

Johnson's wife; no doubt that had something to do with the fact that she was his only wife. In many places in Africa, a man may take more than one wife but in rural areas he will have to pay a dowry to the woman's family in the form of an agreed number of cattle. Wealth in rural sub-Saharan Africa is still often measured in cattle. In fact, Pete, our apprentice guide, was himself trying to save up so that he could buy enough cows and marry his fiancé. Before we left, we saw some of the handicrafts made by villagers and I bought a wonderfully fashioned teak bowl.

Our sundowner drive later that afternoon was rather quieter than all the commotion of the morning, but we still saw elephant – one herd broke into the nearest thing to a run that they can muster as they approached the waterhole. In their quest to ease their thirst they kicked up a lot of dust. We patrolled a large savannah area close to the railway line that runs to Victoria Falls in the hope of seeing hunting cheetah, but no luck.

This morning, we saw a few of the increasingly endangered ground hornbills, the biggest of this species but which can only breed every five or so years. Mid-morning we arrived at the underground hide positioned close to a fresh water outlet, and the vehicle was driven off some distance so as not to discourage game from approaching. There were several visits by elephant whose trunks were only a few metres from us as they siphoned up the water. One bull, which we were told was the oldest in the park and thought to be sixty-five years of age, was so close that we could hear the water being expelled down his throat. He had one very long and heavy tusk, the other having snapped off. Later, a small family of elephants came to drink and it was as if they were right on top of us.

To enjoy lunch on this all-day safari, we journeyed some distance from the underground hide into the wilds of Hwange. Suddenly, in the distance not far from a waterhole attended by a herd of elephants was the unmistakable profile of a lone human being. What was he doing in the middle of nowhere; how had he got here and why was he barefoot and without any gun? We stopped next to him and were introduced to the park's head of anti-poaching who was staying with some of his men in a small camp behind a screen of trees in the distance. (Weeks later and back in the UK, I read that a number of elephants had been poisoned with cyanide in Hwange, so clearly there was still much work to do to stop the poachers).

We said goodbye to our unexpected visitor, and our vehicle pulled over under a stand of mature acacias, driving away an annoyed band of baboons in the process and there we sat for the next hour and enjoyed our lunch. In front of us, about 100 metres away, was the waterhole and behind it a very large but dead tree. Just to the side of it was 'the heartbeat of Hwange' – the soft thump, thump of a diesel-powered pump drawing up water through a bore hole. During the extensive dry season, Hwange would have had no standing water anywhere were it not for these artificial waterholes, which depended on the pumps to draw water from the water-table below. This water was filtered through as much as seventy-five metres of Kalahari sand and, thus, it was possible for humans to drink it safely directly from the ground. Without it, Hwange would have very few animals in the dry season. As we ate an excellent lunch, several herds of elephant came to the hole, and a few even came around to our side of the water before going off to dust themselves. In the open savannah surrounding us, we could see the herds coming from a distance – often they quickened their pace, especially the young elephants, as they got closer and closer to the water. There was lots of drinking, mud-slinging, calves playing, juvenile males sparring and older females scolding and generally keeping order. Two hippos in the middle of the hole were trying to mind their own business and to stay away from over exuberant elephants. In the background, a lone sable cautiously walked around the hole, not daring to come any closer;

and behind him was an even more wary eland. They would have to wait until the elephants had left.

We retraced the long and bumpy ride back to Half Way House, the small hotel and restaurant midway between Bulawayo and Victoria Falls but it was only a relatively short transfer from there to Khulu Ivory in the north west of Hwange National Park. This is the sister lodge of Camp Amalinda but even smaller with only six chalets and a central dining area surrounded by a boma with a floodlit waterhole. Once again, we had an armed escort at night between our chalet and the boma (a low protective barrier made of tree stumps and boughs to protect against animal incursions). At one end of the boma and forming a part of it was a small plunge pool. As we ate our salads, six elephants came to the pool and reached over with their trunks to drink the water. Sharon, the camp's owner, told us that if a guest was already in the pool the elephants tended to ignore that person and would drink confidently, but they do not like it if anyone tries to get into the pool after they have started to drink. A few of the animals in each of the elephant herds have learned that the freshest water is in the plunge pool and not in the nearby waterhole. Camp staff clean the pool afterwards and refill it with clear, fresh water. Dudley, the chief guide with some thirty years of experience, took us out almost immediately after our lunch for a sundowner drive through the lodge's concession area. We enjoyed our drinks among a stand of acacia trees just before sunset in a low broad valley that many thousands of years ago had been a river, but which was now known as Rete Vlei.

The next morning, we entered Hwange National Park proper and did so again in the afternoon when we were exceptionally lucky to spot a lone cheetah almost hidden in the thick bush. We got quite close and the cheetah simply ignored us. We visited several waterholes in this part of the park whose life-giving water was all fed by diesel or solar pumps, and we always saw large numbers of elephant. At one hole, a small group of elephants walking around the water's edge suddenly reacted with a mixture of fear and anger and veered away from the edge very quickly. They had come unexpectedly on a lone crocodile and even elephants must be wary of them. We had already seen a mature female elephant missing the last eight inches or so of her trunk – lost to crocodile attack - but she looked healthy, was with her herd, and clearly had learned to adapt. There was a terrific sunset at the final waterhole where Mark and I saw the sun sinking down through the immense boughs of a camelthorn tree. After dinner, we sat out in the middle of the boma by the fire; it was our small salient into the world of the wild where the dangers to us were minimised but I couldn't help but notice that almost any creature could have stepped over many of the defences of this particular boma. A regular supply of chilled South African white wine caused me not to fixate on this fact.

Our next destination was the Painted Dog Protection Initiative near the main entrance to Hwange. This not-for-profit organisation has an educational and conservational function and often puts on residential camps for local children to explain why it is important to preserve wild dogs. They prefer the name painted dogs since that is more suggestive of the coloured spots on their coats that are different for each individual. Many are caught in snares set for animals hunted by local people for food. Indeed, its staff spend a lot of time trying to clear these snares and, at their headquarters, I bought a model of an oryx fashioned from wire recovered from such snares. We were able to see two painted dogs that were kept on site because they could not be rehabilitated and returned to the wild.

We returned to Khulu Ivory for lunch and to while away the hot mid-afternoon before our last sundowner drive. A breeding herd of elephants came to the waterhole and a small number detached themselves and approached the plunge pool. Soon there was a small scramble to drink, with one female in particular insisting on her dominance, and some of the others sneaking their trunks in from the side to siphon off the fresh water, while trying to avoid the dominant elephant barging them away. Mark and I were in full view no more than few metres away and the elephants ignored us. One even managed to spray a little water over me as she squirted the liquid anywhere but down her throat. One elephant tried to step over a low barrier to enter the lodge, while another walked over to a toilet facility and simply stopped outside it and stayed there for several minutes. What a shock that would have been for anyone leaving. The whole event was one of the best and nearest encounters with elephant and one I thought could not be beaten. I was wrong.

Khulu Ivory is built on and close to ancient elephant pathways which were well known to Dudley. Our guide's sundowner drive was on the lodge's concessionary area, in particular to a small track underneath which was buried a pipeline taking water to another lodge. The elephants can smell the water even though it is buried and Dudley took us to a spot where the elephants had been digging a small hole with their tusks to puncture the pipe. As we approached, we could see a small pool of bubbling water and about fifteen elephants with young drinking quietly from it. Dudley slowly took the Land Rover closer and closer until finally he was within touching distance of outstretched trunks. So calm were the elephants that a few of them even picked up their favourite acacia seed pods from right by the vehicle's wheel where Dudley had dropped them. Dudley explained that these elephants were part of the so-called Presidential Herd, which were very habituated to humans in vehicles. They were still wild however and a human outside the vehicle and so close would probably be attacked. Dudley recognised by sight some of the herd before us, including one female who had a habit when it was very cold of putting her trunk on the vehicle's bonnet in order to warm up. We were so close it was possible to see the colour variations in their eyes, to inhale their rather damp smell, and to hear all the internal rumblings that they make to communicate. The only moment of apparent anxiety was when Dudley restarted the motor but almost instantly they settled again to drinking and ignored us as we pulled away.

During our two-and-a-half-hour transfer to Ilala Lodge in Victoria Falls, we were only stopped twice by the police; it had been ten times on our way from Bulawayo to Half Way House. All these flimsy roadblocks were rather perfunctory and not at all threatening, though it was said that the police were usually on the lookout for some minor problem with the vehicle in order to solicit a bribe. Soon after checking in at the excellent and rather large hotel that is Ilala Lodge, we found ourselves at the falls about to walk the few kilometres along the gorge to the iconic bridge linking Zimbabwe and Zambia. When Mark and I were there, the water flow over the falls was at its lowest, but we could still hear the roar from the hotel and nearer the gorge there was often quite a lot of spray. However, we were not overwhelmed with spray, which meant that we could take decent photographs of the falls including the shear drop to the bottom, but there was just enough spray to cause a rainbow effect. At places there were no barriers at all just a sign to say: 'Take extreme care' – presumably before one toppled over the edge. The best views were from our side, but on the Zambian side we saw one man fishing close to the 100-metre drop and even some tourists in a natural infinity pool close to the edge. At the lovely little cafe within Victoria Falls National Park, Mark tried a crocodile wrap – well he would have done if a vervet monkey had not sprung from nowhere, pinched the food, and ran off. A waiter soon replaced what had been stolen and two others appeared with slingshots, which hastened the disappearance of the monkeys at least for a while. Outside the park, we met some young boys working as street sellers and bought billion-dollar examples of the old Zimbabwean currency. They were glad of a few US dollars from us as the rate of unemployment in Zimbabwe was eighty per cent - another reason why so many people were so desperate for more westerners to realize that the country was safe and to come there as tourists. The visit to the falls was well worth it since it is indeed a natural wonder but we were in a town for the first time and that was very different altogether to the rural and wilderness Africa that we had hitherto experienced. There was also a huge difference between Zimbabwe and South Africa, which superficially we had glimpsed. At Johannesburg Airport as we waited for our flight home, I read a local newspaper. Mark asked me what was in it – I replied that the first three pages were reports of murders, attempted murders, and rapes in the city, whereas page four covered the Cape Town shooting to death of two police officers. In Zimbabwe, the greatest threat to us had been sunburn and, possibly, 'Billy.'

The contrast between the popular tourist destination of South Africa and the largely ignored Zimbabwe could not have been more ironically obvious. Victoria Falls was a good place to end our visit to Zimbabwe, but it won't be the falls I remember best in years to come. I shall remember walking in the tall straw-coloured grass as the sun was setting with no cares in the world.

Chapter Fifteen: Last Journey in the Bushveld

Our flight to Johannesburg in September 2017 in business class went well, but our arrival in Windhoek the following morning was a most annoying and tedious affair. The authorities had very recently introduced a new immigration system where each visitor was photographed, fingerprinted and iris-scanned before being allowed in. Thus, it took over two and a half hours to clear immigration. Having to stand in an airless and cramped room for so long was a poor start to the holiday. In the event, when I got to the immigration desk, the official there took none of the electronic scans and simply stamped my passport and let me in. I was the only one to be treated in this fashion, and Mark accused me of being in the country illegally. I did wonder whether this apparent oversight might have repercussions when we would have to leave and re-enter Namibia later in the holiday. I needn't have worried for at those two immigration outposts everything was still strictly paper-based and entry and departure stamps were swiftly and considerately placed on the page. The delay did mean, however, that we could not reach Okonjima Plains Camp in time for a sundowner drive, but we arrived comfortably for dinner at the newly opened site. Mark and I were not at all impressed with our Renault Duster four-wheel drive, in which we covered about 2,400 kilometres on the trip; it was such a clunky and plastic lump to drive.

In the morning, our guide took us out to locate leopard. Very soon, we found a male leopard who was eager to be rid of us and made urgent progress through quite thick scrub to a steep rocky escarpment where he knew we could not follow. He quickly climbed the imposing slope with such grace and power and then was gone. A female was spotted a while later lying in the cleft of a worn-out termite mound as if she were enjoying an early siesta. They are such stunningly attractive animals, and this one was content simply to ignore us as we busied ourselves taking photographs. She looked so composed that the photographs might appear staged to anyone who had not been there. Eventually, she rose, jumped down from the mound, and was gone from view almost instantly. Already our experiences on safari had made up for the tedium of our arrival in the country.

Leaving Okonjima for Etosha, Mark and I drove along roads even quieter than normal until we arrived at Otjiwarongo where we found the supermarkets were open on Sundays but unwilling to sell us any of the fantastic bottles of South African wines on their shelves – something I only found out after I had filled a small cart with such gems. Our bush chalet in Okaukuejo in Etosha National Park was very close to the justly famed floodlit waterhole. Around the hole swarmed literally tens of thousands of red-billed quelea, constantly drawing dark shapes in the blue sky as they whirled and spiralled. Sometimes, a mere fraction of them would alight all at once on one of the trees nearby and completely alter its shape and texture. Returning to the hole after dinner, we saw ten white rhinos, some with calves, spread out around the perimeter and enjoying the freshly pumped water. We had never seen so many at once before. We spent two nights at the camp before spending another two at the fort-like Namutoni Camp, which was a first for us.

It was unusually hot during our time in Etosha, occasionally as high as forty Celsius, and it might have been for that reason that we encountered fewer animals than normal in the park. Even so, we were not exactly lacking in animals to see. We were delayed on a dirt road for some minutes as several hundred zebra crossed it on their way to a waterhole. As ever, there were many elephant, including at Kalkheuwel. The old fort at Namutoni was largely deserted, supposedly awaiting refurbishment. One lone gift shop was open but the central crenelated square was eerily quiet and all the former vitality of the working bars and cafés had gone.

Mark and I left Etosha and set off on the long drive north to Hakusembe River Lodge at the western edge of the Caprivi Strip where, unlike most of the rest of Namibia, there is permanent water to be found in the several river systems in that area. Even so, at Hakusembe, the Kavango River separating Namibia from Angola was unexpectedly low for that time of year; so much so that our boat trip had to pick its way slowly and carefully past exposed rocks and hidden sandbanks. However, the low water level did not detract from our enjoyment of the champagne as the sun set, nor our appreciation of the singing and dancing put on by the staff as we returned to the lodge. This lodge had been recently enlarged and upgraded and we thoroughly enjoyed the oryx main course as we dined outside on a spacious raised wooden terrace overlooking the river. In the day, we saw Angolan people from a local village on the far bank of the Kavango washing clothes, bathing children, and cleaning pots and pans. We knew that not far away were hippos and crocodiles, either of which could prove a deadly threat. Their experience of the river was vastly different from ours.

The next part of our journey was along the Caprivi Strip, which teemed with activity in contrast to the much drier and more sparsely populated south. There were many villages along the road with wooden stalls laden with fruits and vegetables, and the occasional butcher's 'shop' with carcasses of meat slung over the branches of a tree. There were brick-built schools and clinics, and more roughly hewn but garish shabeens selling liquor and beer. Mark and I wondered what these shabeens and bottle cellars were like. Was there any point in us entering one? During the day, the only time it was at all sensible to drive in Namibia, the shabeens were often open but mostly deserted. In the end, we never did visit one and had no need to with such a good selection of wine in the town supermarkets and at the lodges.

Along much of the Caprivi, neatly uniformed children walked by the side of the road to and from their classrooms, always careful to retreat onto the apron of the tarmac whenever a car drove by. The children were dressed in blue shirts and white short trousers or skirts until we came within the range of the next school where the uniform might change to red and white or blue and black. They all looked splendid in their uniforms. Often, even quite young children walked up to seven kilometres to school, avoiding dangerous animals at times, and after classes the boys had to look after livestock and the girls to fetch and carry water. Obtaining water can be a lengthy and exhausting affair. A few lucky ones had a mechanical pump in their village, of which we saw a few from the road. More commonly, water was available some distance away and was carried back to the home on one's head – always by the women and girls. If we saw any men transporting water in plastic containers, they were always strapped to the side of a bicycle or inside a wheelbarrow. Indeed, we saw no girls at all with bicycles not even to ride for fun; it was always the boys or grown men who seemed to enjoy such a privilege. Perhaps surprisingly, cars are more in evidence than bikes or barrows but there is minimal traffic. These cars ranged from expensive models owned by gone-up-in-the-world city dwellers who have returned briefly to their ancestral village home, to clapped out smoke-belching jalopies. Then there were the actual wrecks, often dotted around a village, inside a familial compound or by the side of the road, completely denuded of every last article and now just rusting hulks left on the spot where they finally came to a halt.

Piles of wood for cooking, neatly stacked and bound, would suddenly spring up at the margins of some of the villages, while other spots were reserved for batches of reeds precisely bound into bundles and intended as roof coverings or partition walls around homes to keep out some of the dust and to provide some privacy. Homes in the villages were typically made from wooden poles and mud or plaster in-fill supporting a thatched roof. Some were brick-built with a roof of corrugated metal sheeting that must have been unbearably hot. The most expensive homes were made from brick or breeze block with a tile covering. In most villages we could easily spot differences in status or wealth in the size and composition of the dwellings, yet in overall terms nearly all these people were poor by Western standards. Occasionally at the side of the road, we saw small carved wooden elephants and in the distance under the shade of a broad tree an old man waiting to make a sale to passing tourists. Indeed, Mark and I did stop and make a purchase at one site, and enjoyed a pleasant conversation with the seller. Less pleasant by far was the sight of an array of corrugated-sheet 'boxes' standing in rows and surrounded by plastic bags of personal possessions and clothes drying on lines hooked between the dwellings. These sites, which we encountered occasionally, looked both basic and 'brutal,' and served as sleeping berths for an army of labourers working on nearby projects. They had little more than a metal box for accommodation. God knows what their working conditions were like.

Rundu is one of the towns rather than villages along the Caprivi Strip. It crackled with industrious activity and was full of small cars with a distinctive livery that served as cheap taxis for the locals. We refuelled there at a completely chaotic petrol station and then set off eastwards to the edge of Bwabwata National Park where we turned south, eventually crossing into Botswana at the Mohembo border point. The road from the border to Nxamaseri Island Lodge was the worst road we encountered in southern Africa; only in Kenya in the early 1980s did I drive on anything worse. Some of the numerous potholes were so deep that hitting one would have probably meant a broken axle unless driving at a snail's pace. This road followed, in part, the route of the old 'Road of Death' so called not because of the potholes (it was not tarred then), but because of the persistence along its length of malaria, sleeping sickness and more. Today, it was definitely the potholes that would kill you. Eventually, in what seemed to us to be a remote location, we saw the lodge's pickup truck sent to meet us some distance from the side of the road. We left our car at a small village under a covered wooden and palm leaf 'garage' and drove the short distance to the small boat that would transfer us along the river to Nxamaseri, deep within the Okavango Panhandle.

The Panhandle has flowing water all year whereas the Delta below it only becomes a huge wetland in the winter. Here our safaris would all be by boat except for the long drive Mark made to visit the Bushman paintings in the Tsolido Hills. The various channels of the river were bordered by copious papyrus reeds and bulrushes, and the lodge itself sat strikingly on a small island within the Panhandle. It was a place once much frequented by the Nxamaseri Ladies Fishing Society whose impressive book of records as to who caught what, by what method, and how much it weighed was kept in the lodge's bar. However, without any doubt, the best at catching fish were the resident fish eagles, one of whom swept down effortlessly from a very high tree serving as a look-out point to snatch a meal right in front of us as Mark and I watched from our boat at the edge of the river.

While Mark set off to see the Bushman paintings, I went out in a small boat with 'Nine' – so called by his friends because as a child he always insisted on being the number nine centre forward when they played football. His tribe call themselves River Bushmen who have lived, farmed, and fished in the Okavango for centuries. They also raise cattle, many of which are exported to Europe as meat. We went downstream into the main channel of the river and encountered lots of different birds, as well as crocodiles and occasional hippo. We also met adult male friends of Nine out fishing in a narrow mokoro boat hewn from indigenous tree trunks, and one group of five boys where the two older ones were teaching the younger ones the art of rod fishing. Later, we tied up our metal-hulled boat and disembarked on to a small island full of very old and tall trees – local people are now banned from making mekoro (plural form of noun) from wood as the Botswana government wants to preserve these old trees. Now they must buy mekoro made from plastic and fibreglass but they still use a wooden paddle or a long pole to navigate – just like an Oxford punt. On the island, we saw where recently a group of fishermen had smoked some of their catch, and large depressions made by hippo wallowing in the mud during the wet season, and in so doing making 'escape chutes' for quick entry to the river.

Our chalet at the lodge was very private, set in deep forest overlooking the river and reached by traversing a long twisting path of raised wooden walkways. Birds rumbled in the thatched roof and, at dawn, vervet monkeys galloped noisily across it directly above our heads. The bar operated on an honesty system where you poured yourself whatever drink you desired and entered it in the bar book. With us in the bar and dining area at night was an elderly American couple – the husband was a keen fisherman and his wife tolerated his hobby because she obtained very good photographs of birds and animals from the fishing boat. His fishing equipment and her cameras and lenses would probably run a small country for a few days so expensive were they.

Another trip with Nine offered Mark and me the unexpected chance to eat parts of papyrus and bulrushes plucked directly by their roots from the river, where the water was filtered so thoroughly by these plants that it was safe even for outsiders like ourselves to drink it. However, the starchy and very chewy bits we were given are definitely an acquired taste; but as Nine pointed out such a food store meant that if all else failed one would not starve here. God knows what a small party of Germans we met later at the lodge would have made about our eating habits and the drinking (if only by default) of the river water. They fell into a fractious argument with the management as to what guarantees could be supplied that none of them would contract bilharzia by inhaling the spray from a mokoro boat – a boat that barely moves at walking pace. Mark did a mokoro trip later and survived.

Our final boat trip together was a fishing expedition in which we used silver-coloured lures dragged through the water to attract bites from cat fish and tiger fish – the larger denizens of this environment which preyed on a variety of smaller fish inhabiting the dense tangle of roots and stems formed by the papyrus and other reeds. Of course, grey, black and squacco herons, white and little egrets, and other birds hunted these same small fish and their way of rooting them out was to perch on the stems of papyrus just above the water line at the edge of the bank and to spear them with their long beaks. Black herons formed a deep cover of shade into which they hoped to lure fish by folding their wings across the water like an umbrella. Naturally, some of these small fish were intimidated by these actions and while most bolted deeper into the rushes, others escaped into the river proper where the cat and tiger fish were waiting. The birds tended to congregate along a 100-metre stretch of papyrus-lined bank for five minutes and then flew away to relocate at another stretch and repeat their feeding technique. This was called a run. The noise and disturbances in the water during a run were very obvious as the smaller fish desperately flapped about in the tangle of reeds and rushes. Added to this was the noisy commotion of birds flitting from reed to reed, with their wings and beaks darting here and there. Not only did the cat and tiger fish follow these runs, but so too did human fishermen who positioned their boats so that they could cast along the run as close to the reeds as possible in the hope of catching a prize fish. This was what Mark and I were doing under Nine's tutelage. Once, I cast my line and lure too close to the foot of the papyrus and it got caught. Nine had to drive the boat up to the reeds to untangle the line and lure. A short while later, Mark seriously over-cast his lure so that it got caught among the papyrus a good three metres above the waterline. Nine had to drive the boat deep into the reeds and then with him and Mark at the front, they had to stretch up on tip toe to try to untangle the line. Both became comically embedded in the papyrus while I almost wet myself with laughter at the other end of the boat. We enjoyed our trip but needless to say we caught bugger all!

The next morning, we retraced our steps north to re-enter Namibia and then travelled further east along the Caprivi to Lianshulu Lodge located alongside the Kwando River within the lush riverine forest of Mudumu National Park. On a boat safari from the lodge, as we drifted along the river, we witnessed a bad-tempered encounter between a pod of hippos and a breeding herd of elephants. The elephants prevailed and forced the hippos to move away as the herd crossed the river. A while later, as our boat nestled motionlessly by the bank, one of the larger female elephants ran towards us and threatened to charge into us before Alfred tactfully reversed a few metres away, Honour thus satisfied, she returned to her companions. We enjoyed some wine after dinner that evening as we sat by the fire, and were blessed by the arrival of a lone elephant that walked into the far side of the camp and engaged in some angry and loud trumpeting for some minutes before returning to the pitch-black bush beyond. The following morning, Mark and I had an excellent vehicle safari through dense tree and scrub but still managed to see lots of elephant, roan antelope, impala, baboons, buffalo, zebra, warthogs, and some giraffe. Impala and baboons are often seen close together, for some baboons will remain high up in the trees and thus provide visual warning of the approach of predators to those below. Impala, meanwhile, can hear or smell danger and thus provide warning to the ground-feeding baboons.

We returned to Botswana to the last place on our tour, Muchenje Safari Lodge, positioned on an escarpment overlooking the Chobe River flood plain. As we neared the end of our journey and the return of the car to the hire company in Kasane, I was pulled over by four police officers. The woman in charge showed me that I had been clocked doing 102 kph in an eighty zone. I apologised immediately and the officer kindly let me off with a warning. No hint of any attempt to obtain money from me corruptly. I was impressed with their professionalism and courtesy. We were picked up at the car hire site and taken to Muchenje. Shortly after arrival, we were enjoying an excellent game drive with our guide, Lips, who remembered Mark and me from a few years ago. He was one of the people who extricated our car stuck fast in the sand of the 'red zone' a few kilometres from the lodge.

We went out early for a whole day trip including a boat excursion on the Chobe River. There were many elephants along the banks of the river, some of them enjoying a delicious experience in a mud bath. Others were dusting themselves on the plain, while even closer to our boat was a herd of elephants swimming briskly across a narrow channel to fresh grazing. We had lunch on the boat moored to a tiny islet on which there basked a seemingly unconcerned crocodile for the complete duration of our stop. Back in the Toyota Land Cruiser, an excellent vehicle in which to explore the riverine forests and bush around the Chobe, we were lucky to see a leopard almost completely hidden in the scrub. He was stalking an impala which eventually spotted his potential attacker and made off. This prompted the leopard to break cover and we got a much better view of him. After a traditional sundowner drink, we drove off towards the lodge as the sun began to set, and then encountered three male lions lounging by the side of the river. One of them raised himself onto his front paws, lifted his head and stared at us and then slowly collapsed in a heap with no concern for us whatsoever. That night, Mark and I enjoyed a bottle of wine on the balcony of our chalet and hoped that the porcupine said to occupy a deep hole nearby would put in an appearance. It did not.

Our last full day on holiday in the wild started exceptionally well with a huge flock of great white egrets flying past our chalet and down the escarpment towards the flood plain. The afternoon game drive with a new guide, Paulus, turned out to be a most curious experience. He drove deep into the national park and while we saw a lot of game on the way, we had an exceptionally long journey to get back. We ended up about 130 kilometres from the lodge and faced a substantial trek along dirt roads before we hit the tarmac, much of which we covered in gathering gloom and then complete darkness. Just before we set out on this epic manoeuvre, we saw a pride of eighteen lions, all quite close to one another and doing what lions usually do when you see them ... nothing. After that, we made uncomfortable progress on a narrow sandy track through thick bush in increasing murkiness. This was not done at a leisurely pace but at high speed so that it felt like a ride on a bucking bronco, and we had to duck and swerve to miss the tips of branches lashing against the side of the open vehicle as well as hang on to our hats and belongings. Suddenly, as we turned or rather skidded around a corner, for an instant, I saw what looked like a life-sized cardboard cut-out of a lion in the middle of the track. Just as I was thinking what idiot put that there, it moved; and then three more immature male lions followed him across the track and disappeared from view. We tore off again at speed along a track that should only be used by the park authorities until we hit the tarmac road along which in pitch blackness we drove at ridiculous high speed with only very feeble headlamps to light our way. This was the very same road on which a few days earlier we had stopped to watch a herd of elephant as they crossed it. We would never have stopped in time that night had a herd walked in front of us. On our return to the lodge, there was barely time to shower or change before dinner, so late were we. Indeed, we were so shaken up (literally) by the journey, Mark and I simply had a drink in the bar.

Our journey home was another largely tedious affair with one transfer to Kasane Airport, then another to the border crossing with Zimbabwe, and yet one more from there to the airport at Victoria Falls and a connecting flight to the UK. At the border crossing, we encountered a good deal of friendly disorganisation at the Zimbabwe customs post. We learned that the drivers of the trucks that made their way between Zimbabwe, Zambia, Angola, Namibia, and Botswana - exporting the mineral wealth of a continent - could often be held for weeks in a form of incommunicado at the border waiting for customs clearance. The local sex workers enjoyed a good trade. The drive from the border to Victoria Falls can only be described as desolate. No inhabited villages, no people in evidence, no sign of work or human activity, only the occasional articulated lorry carrying sheets of copper out of a ravaged Zimbabwe to be sold to the Chinese. Britain may have been the supreme power in Africa years ago; now it was the Chinese.

Chapter Sixteen: The Final Safari

In February 2019, finally, I returned to Kenya – with my brother a willing accomplice in what was to be our last great adventure together. We stayed only nine nights, but we conspired nevertheless to make this our most expensive holiday by far, by virtue of the exclusivity of two of the camps we visited, and the number of flights around Kenya in light aircraft. Paying extra for business class seats on Kenya Airways may have been an additional unnecessary expense, but worth it for we arrived very early in Nairobi soundly rested and able to take full advantage of the hectic activities that followed later that day. However, our arrival at Nairobi's international airport was anything other than hectic. As business class passengers, our luggage was offloaded before all the other bags and, accordingly, Mark and I were quickly outside the main airport building waiting to meet our driver, who had not yet arrived. He had been told we were flying economy class and had not expected us to clear customs so early; hence, Mark and I sat on a low stone wall opposite arrivals with a few other drivers who assured us our guide would be along soon. In a short while, Darren, duly turned up and transported us through the thick city traffic to Wilson Airport – Nairobi's smaller domestic airfield. Like Dar in Tanzania, and Windhoek in Namibia, Nairobi was a busy, noisy, almost bewildering experience. So much of the city was modern and then, in a moment, it slipped into a montage of shacks and tin-roofed slums. It had an air of being unfinished, even untidy, and many of the tarred roads were full of potholes, which served only as obstacles for lorries and cars to swerve around.

At Wilson Airport, we had the unusual experience of being weighed separately from our luggage before we boarded a single-engine, twelve-seat light aircraft for our flight to Nanyuki Airport. It was a tight fit onboard and the plane acted more like a bus than an aircraft, landing here and there on dirt or grass airstrips to drop off and pick up passengers. One of these flights cost us about US$400 per person. The terrain was urban at first – full of roads and buildings in paroxysms of proximity - and then agricultural as the plane flew over rich, apparently well-watered, fields of colourful produce. Eventually, the land below became more and more rugged and we knew then that we were nearing those magical places where so many wild animals were to be found. From the small airport, it was a further two-hour drive north in a Land Rover to our small lodge, Laikipia Wilderness. The camp, recently opened, had only five spacious tents on site, and was part of the Ol Doinyo Lemboro Ranch. Set overlooking the Ewaso Narok River, the camp focused on game walks as well as safari drives. When you stay at a camp that accommodates no more than ten or twelve guests, you are always outnumbered by the staff and the levels of service are usually excellent, even outlandishly extravagant given their secluded locations. The food with which we were so elegantly presented was always marvellous but in Kenya the policy was to serve no bush meat, such as oryx and impala.

The plateau on which the Laikipia region sits was rugged terrain, as Mark and I discovered after lunch when we ventured out on a walking tour. Jasper, our guide, was armed with a rifle but made no fuss about it; it was a simple tool of his trade. In the UK, one rarely goes for a walk with someone dangling a powerful firearm over their shoulder but, in the bush, it was a sensible precaution. We walked through a mixture of dry savannah and ragged-edged gullies. The lodge had supplied us with aluminium water bottles with our names engraved on them rather than use a succession of plastic bottles and create unnecessary waste. Jasper pointed out many things of interest on the walk and eventually we arrived at an elevated wooden viewing platform with a roof of dried grass, overlooking a large waterhole. We enjoyed some refreshments there; it was not long before a breeding herd of elephants arrived at the hole and, as ever, held me spellbound. The next day, Mark and I boarded our Toyota Land Cruiser and made our way through thick, undulating bush; even so, we saw elephant, giraffe, a pride of lions, and a large tortoise – which here I am tempted to call Tony. As we drove back to the lodge in the dark, we glimpsed some hyenas lurking in the bushes. Animals do a lot of lurking: snakes lurk in the ground; leopards lurk in anticipation of an ambush attack; gazelles and antelopes lurk in the bushveld to avoid predators; and tourists lurk in hides to photograph animals. There's a whole lot of lurking going on.

There is a misconception about lions held by many people who have not visited Africa and even by some who have. Sadly, lions are in decline and are a threatened species because of habitat loss, poaching and conflict with indigenous tribes, especially pastoralists. But this should not allow us to disguise the truth. They are not 'Kings of the Jungle' for there is no jungle; they live mostly in bush and savannah areas. They are not lords of all they survey for they will quickly run off if challenged by adult elephants, rhinos, hippos, and a sufficiently large group of hyenas. Yes, they will from time to time brandish their teeth in a threatening manner, which will cause a thousand shots on fast repeat or continuous shooting to be taken on fancy cameras by hordes of tourists gathered around the pride. Often, the trick is to take a photograph of the lions *without* the tourist vehicles appearing in the shot. Yes, they will occasionally loll on the floor, changing positions to look like favoured domestic cats. Yes, the cubs can be adorably lovely when they gambol together and are groomed by their parents. But, often, they do bugger all: they just sleep and sleep and sleep, and occasionally go looking for something to eat –

mostly at night. Nine times out of ten, I have passed them by and with no regrets. The romantic in me likes to think that the practised, beguiling look of coy innocence on their collective faces is lion-speak for: "Yes, you tourists are safe in that contraption you call a vehicle, but get out of it and you will see how quickly I move from innocent slumber to killer." But it does not impress me; I am not getting out of the vehicle in front of you reprobates.

Leaving Laikipia, we had to return to Nanyuki Airport where we enjoyed possibly the best airport experience in Africa. It was still early morning and Mark and I had some time before our light aircraft arrived to transport us to Musiara Airstrip in the Maasai Mara. There was a small café at the airport where we went for breakfast. A uniformed employee approached us and enquired if the bags by our table were ours, in which case he wanted to take them away. The young man assured us they would be safe with him and that, in due course, he would load them on our plane. Mark and I were enjoying our food, but had not quite finished, when the same employee returned and informed us that our plane was waiting to take off. "Please finish your breakfast," he said, "the pilot will wait for you."

The safety briefing on the plane was even briefer on this occasion, amounting to nothing more than an instruction to give the safety leaflet the once-over. The flying bus was off, dropping passengers in isolated locations but, of course, the pilots had informed the respective lodges of their impending arrival, and vehicles would have been dispatched to collect the guests. Musiara Airstrip was charming in the sense that only a romantic optimist could possibly apprehend wanting to land a plane there. Either side of the grass strip was a clear homage to minimalist architecture, not one solid building in evidence, just a place to turn around at the end of the runway. Two cars waited to take a small number of us to Governors' Camp on the thickly forested meandering banks of the Mara River, which was situated in the northwest corner of the

Maasai Mara National Reserve. Governors had over thirty large and comfortable tents. Luckily, ours was only a few metres from the Mara River whose steep banks it directly overlooked. Hot water inside the tent was supplied from a mishmash of pipes and a wood-burning stove outside at the rear, regularly topped up by the staff. It all looked as if it were tottering on the brink of self-destruction but, nevertheless, worked perfectly. The dining area was a very large and well-equipped mess tent; it felt as if entitled colonial officials swaggering through the camp were but an historical flicker of memory away.

In fact, Mark and I were fortunate to meet someone better than a colonial governor or some such: after dinner, we had a chat with the zoologist, Jonathan Scott, who was in the Mara with a film crew making a television series. He had special permission to drive off-road whereas other drivers would be subject to an instant fine of several hundred US dollars if caught driving outside the permitted boundaries. We never actually met Jonathan again, but we often passed each other in our respective vehicles. Unfortunately for the renowned photographer and television presenter, he went through a short period in which Mark and I had witnessed leopards or lions only for Jonathan to arrive after they had departed. Animals are like that – such fickle bastards! Misu, our guide from Governors' Camp, was a resource of great knowledge and experience. On several drives with him, he guided us through an immense expanse of grassland to view several herds of elephant, two different lion prides, eland, sable (often stood on small mounds as if in a pose for the cameras), hippo sheltering in shallow pools from the sun, leopards hiding in a tangle of bush and one sprawled across a thick tree branch with an air of supreme insouciance. At one point, it rained heavily and we had to scuttle back to the mess tent in camp for shelter, passing en route the forlorn Jonathan whose filming had been ruined by the weather. On another occasion, Misu found five male cheetahs walking across the savannah in their elegant fashion on the lookout for prey. Within a short time, the animals were surrounded by a dozen Land Rovers and Land Cruisers, which completely scuppered any intention they had then of hunting. Jonathan did not seem to be among the vehicles; no doubt he was on his way.

A few paces from the front flaps of our tent was the Mara River. The water level was not very high so the drop down the steep bank to the river was pronounced. The other side of the river was quite well forested but it was the hippos and crocodiles that caught our attention. A slip down that bank would indeed have been unfortunate since there was little chance of climbing back up it, and less chance of successfully swimming to the other side. We frequently heard the deep grunts of the hippos as they went about their business during the day. Our final destination in the Mara was Kicheche Bush Camp where, by virtue of the camp having only six tents spread through the nearby bush, we returned to sybaritic self-indulgent luxury. This marvel of opulence was situated in a quieter part of the Maasai Mara in the Olare Motorogi Conservancy. Our transfer was coordinated by Governors' Camp and Kicheche. After some while on what passed for a road, our vehicle from Governors was met by another from Kicheche at what I imagined was the halfway point between the two.

On our first safari drive from Kicheche, our driver, Charles, swiftly located a small pride of lions, lazing at the top of a grassy slope. From our position in the vehicle, we saw one adult female rise and walk slowly down the slope past us. About 150 metres or so ahead of her was a family of warthogs – one adult and three piglets marching with erect tails towards a small covert of bushes and trees behind which they soon disappeared. As they vanished from view, the lioness immediately increased her pace and crashed into the thicket. We heard one very loud, high-pitched scream that seemed to have been cut off in mid cry, and seconds later we saw one adult warthog and two piglets emerge, running quickly, on the ride-hand side of the trees. Charles gunned the Land Rover towards the other side of the covert where we expected to see a dead piglet and a triumphant lion. What we actually saw was one terrified leopard cowering high up in a tree. It had been the leopard that had ambushed the unsuspecting warthog family, and then in turn had been surprised by the sudden arrival of one of its deadly enemies. That enemy now held the piglet in its jaws and was beginning to enjoy its snack. A while later, the leopard saw its chance to escape, rapidly descended the tree, and ran off at speed. The following day, Charles led us to a marvellous encounter with a relaxed leopard spread nonchalantly across the branches of a tall tree. Outside our tent was a hammock on which guests might relax; they would have been hard pressed to be as tranquil as the leopard.

Misu wanted to show Mark and me more lions. On the way to where he thought he would find a pride, we stopped to view a small herd of elephants. A large female emerged powerfully from a dry gulley, saw us, and got very annoyed – the full repertoire of extended flapping ears, swinging trunk, and loud trumpeting. One mock charge later, we left the herd to it. It was not long after this altercation that we came upon the lions who were settled around a recent kill. Suddenly, appearing over a small mound of grass was a male lion holding in its mouth an adult zebra's severed head and neck. I took seven shots of this remarkable and (for me) unprecedented event, but only one where I captured the lion looking straight at the camera and with the severed head at right angles to its body. That photograph became the front cover of the book you are reading now.

Misu seemed to have an unfathomable ability to locate game: next, he found two mating leopards whose serial mating was remarkable. Towards dusk, we saw two giraffe on a ridge behind which the sun was about to set. Misu managed to position the vehicle so that I could get shots of them silhouetted against the last rays of the day. On our last full day in camp, we drove in near isolation rarely seeing any other vehicles but plenty of cats. We saw three more leopards, a second pride of lions with several cubs playing together energetically, or else jumping on the adults and demanding attention. It was one of the very few occasions when I found them truly interesting. The best of the day, however, was a serval. Normally, these long-legged cats are rarely seen in daylight. The serval prefers to stalk the long grass at night for its prey, but here we caught it in broad daylight. It was content to ignore us entirely as it swivelled its mobile ears to locate potential prey, such as rodents. Its golden-yellow coat with black stripes and spots shone in the clear light. When it was not investigating potential prey hiding in the tall grass, we could see its long legs and slender body. It was the prefect killing machine for this kind of habitat. It was a wrench to leave Kicheche; we had seen so much game in such beautiful terrain that we virtually had to ourselves. Mark and I were driven to Olare Orok Airstrip for our flight to Wilson Airport in Nairobi. There, we met our driver, Edward, and had the whole day to see whatever we wished.

We left the airport and headed directly for Nairobi National Park, a game reserve on the outskirts of the capital. Many of the animals Mark and I had seen in the remote parts of Africa were here on the metaphorical doorstep of millions of city dwellers. Within a few minutes of entering the park, we saw the elevated railway line that the Chinese had built for the Kenyan government right through the heart of the reserve. There was something surreal to photograph rhinos and giraffe in the bush and to have in the background the clear profile of Nairobi's skyline, but there was no redeeming aspect to this extrusive white concrete monster stretching its wretched stilted legs across the land. Mark wondered whether, in the future, the government would afford to maintain the line or would it fall into the pitiful state of the one on which we travelled in Tanzania.

Edward was able to position his car very close to many of the animals, especially white rhinos and zebra that remained very calm despite our proximity. We also saw a few wildebeest and a pair of lions partially in view behind thick bush. As we were leaving the park on our way to have a late afternoon lunch, we had to stop for an ostrich lying down in the middle of the road. If you had asked me when I first arrived in Africa in 1983 what would be the last animal I would like to see on safari, I would not have said ostrich. I'd have said elephant, but it was not to be.

Our lunch was in a swish restaurant in an upmarket area of the city. Its customers were a pleasant mix of tourists from around the world and local, mainly young, entrepreneurs. I could see no problem in people making money in places like Nairobi. But how do you make a profit from wild Africa? How can you generate enough money to keep the wild spaces secure, healthy, and free from exploitation and poaching? How do you involve the people who live among or close to the wild animals so that they see the wildlife as assets to be treasured and preserved? I, like many others, had no proven solutions to such questions but I was convinced by the arguments for local involvement and by the need to interconnect as many reserves, parks and conservancies as possible, and to provide safe wildlife corridors. Despite all the problems facing wildlife preservation, I was hopeful for the future. I felt that I had done my little bit just by visiting those blessed countries fortunate to hold in their care the creatures of the desert, savannah, bushveld, and forest.

The final night in Kenya we spent at the Crown Plaza Nairobi Airport hotel, which was located inside the international airport's secure perimeter. The security was so tight to get into the building that it started to remind me of my experiences in Madison when I visited high security mental hospitals and prisons. It was such a palaver to get in, Mark and I decided not to leave for a meal in the city and, instead, we dined in the hotel. The next morning, it was a short distance to departures and then home.

Chapter Seventeen: Endings

I did not know when I left Kenya in February 2019 that I would never return to Africa. The plans that Mark and I had to visit Japan and South America – and doubtless more trips to our beloved Namibia – never came to fruition. In fact, I never took another holiday. Like a leopard silently creeping towards its prey, ill health unexpectedly overcame me. Several operations followed and towards the end of the year, I had to spend two months in rehabilitation homes learning to walk again. I got out just before covid swept though care homes with such devastation but, in my own home, I still could not climb the stairs after a major leg operation that left me with far more metal than bone. When I did eventually achieve that personal Everest, I was reduced permanently to walking slowly using two elbow crutches. I doubted I could even get into a Land Cruiser any longer, although the desire to do so was still there.

Since late 2019, it has been very difficult for me physically to do anything even slightly impetuous. I have come to terms with the physical limits of my life and, indeed, I maintain an optimistic outlook, but I miss that infusion of impetuosity of former years – especially where travel was involved. As you will have read, my holidays abroad would often diverge in different directions from what was planned on arrival. Leaving Yugoslavia to cross the Adriatic Sea and visit Venice was an early example of taking off somewhere on a whim. In Thailand, supposedly wedded to a beach-side holiday, Linda and I flew north to the jungles of Chang Mai. In Kenya, we took an overnight train and a light aircraft flight to the Maasai

Mara to escape the Indian Ocean and coral reefs. The delights of Goa could hold us only for so long before Linda and I flew south to Mysore and a completely different experience. That sense of impetuosity, of doing something impulsively, has always been a factor in my life for better or worse. As a ten-year-old, I felt very strongly that I was being unfairly treated by the selectorial panel for Newport under-eleven football team – they picked the son of the chairman of selectors, who could not shoot straight for toffee, and not me – so when I met them, I told them they could fuck off. As an eighteen-year-old working as a bus conductor in Newport, my vehicle was crossing the old bridge near the bus station in the centre of town when I saw a pretty girl I knew from school. The bus was a rear-loading double-decker; I was standing on the rear platform in anticipation that my shift was finishing in just one minute when I saw her. Without any hesitation, I jumped off the moving bus, landed somewhere close to her with coins spilling out of my money bag, and asked her out.

My impetuosity, however, has been respectively less resentful and frivolous than the previous two examples, such as when I travelled to Chicago in January 2009. Jake, the son of my good friend, Susan, was having his bar mitzvah ceremony in Evanston, close to Chicago. Susan had sent me an invitation card on which she had written: "Mike, just thought you'd like to see this – in a perfect world you'd be there! S." The day I received the card, I booked my flight to Chicago and accommodation in Evanston, but told Susan nothing. My surprise appearance at the ceremony was one of the few occasions when she was lost for words.

The following day, Sunday 1st February, was the date of Super Bowl XL111 between the Pittsburgh Steelers and the Arizona Cardinals. You may find it incredible but there was a Mike's Bar in Evanston for I had stayed there previously on earlier visits to Chicago. I duly arrived at the bar only to be refused entry. Entrance was by pre-paid ticket only to watch the Super Bowl on the bar's numerous television screens and to enjoy a meal at half-time. With bare-faced whimsy, I complained that I had flown all the way from London to enjoy the match in convivial surroundings only to be denied. Perhaps it was the British accent, or the doormen felt sorry for me, but they let me in for nothing.

The likes of that would not come my way again. Do I have regrets? I miss the travel, the companionship, the adventures, and the delight at finding what lies around the corner. But that is not a proper regret because I had already travelled so far: it was like a rich man with a million pounds saying that he regretted the lack of one more. My regrets are few but of the important kind. There were many questions I asked my father but there were so many I never got to put to him because he died so young. There were things I should have discussed in more detail with my mother before her death. The regrets that remain are concerned with the living not the dead. It was very hard for both of us when Linda and I parted. I regret that outcome but value immensely the happy years we did have together and the fact that we remained friends. And then there is Zizi. I could write a requiem of regrets about our relationship, but it would do no good. Just before my wonderful friend David Russell died, he argued passionately that: "Loving and being loved are all that matters in this world. All the rest is bullshit." I wanted Zizi to love me as I loved her, but that never happened. She told me once that life was all about timing: it seemed the times were never right for us.

The elephants I first saw in 1983 in Kenya are not just memories; it is entirely probable that some of them are still alive. But when I die, so many things about my life will be memories and nothing else. Inevitably, when my loved ones come to clear away the physical manifestations of my life, they will uncover any number of items that have meaning for them and which they will hold dear. Just as inevitably, there will be artefacts that are of no use and, for them, hold no memories at all. They will find a cricket ball – highly polished on one side – with which I once took six wickets against a rival team. It will be just an old cricket ball to them. I have a black and white photograph of a teenage girl taken at Christmas time during a party in my house in Newport. In the background are some sprigs of mistletoe and a few decorations on the wall. The girl is fifteen or sixteen and she is facing several of her friends present at the party. Her lovely face and engaging smile are caught between juvenile moments – the moment that made her laugh out loud and the next one when she would giggle and confide something to her girlfriend. I do not know her name and it was an event that happened almost sixty years ago, but it saddens me to think that her image, that photograph, will become a piece of detritus.

This book will, to an extent, not only record many of my memories but also preserve them for a while longer in the lives of others but, essentially, my memories die with me. I can bear that. What I miss is the emotional resonance of a beautiful woman reaching out to hold my hand – just as Zizi did. Occasionally.

Also by Mike Stephens

Staying Down
A Life in Travel

About the Author

Mike Stephens was born in 1951 into a mining family in Tredegar but grew up in Newport, south Wales. At various times, he has worked as a bus conductor, airport worker, power station operative, and as a dolomite in a steel factory. Mostly, however, he has long been employed as a university academic, specialising in the fields of policing and criminal justice. When not working, he has travelled extensively in the far east and Africa, especially Namibia and Botswana. He supports Welsh rugby and Tottenham, and spends a great deal of his time watching cricket.

www.ingramcontent.com/pod-product-compliance
Ingram Content Group UK Ltd.
Pitfield, Milton Keynes, MK11 3LW, UK
UKHW030940030325
455781UK00001B/72

9 798230 901549